"This book is a must read for those who want to explore why water for food and nutrition security should be a basic human right and what it takes to deal with water shortages for agriculture under climate change. This book successfully establishes the rationale of putting people at the center and addressing ecosystems health as entry points to achieve a paradigm change in the way we think of and use water for food security and nutrition."

– *Patrick Caron, Chair, High Level Panel of Experts (HLPE) on Food Security and Nutrition and CIRAD, France*

"This interdisciplinary book boldly studies the connectivity of the crucial "cluster" issues of water for food security and nutrition. In making the quantum leap towards securing this as a human right, it demonstrates that our moral obligation to protect human dignity through basic needs can no longer be ignored."

– *HRH Prince El Hassan bin Talal of Jordan, Chairman of The Higher Council for Science and Technology*

"This ground-breaking book analyses vital but hitherto ignored intersections between the human right to food and the right to water. Citing recent trends, the authors comprehensively disentangle the multiple linkages between the management and distribution of water resources for domestic and productive uses, malnutrition and food insecurity from local to global levels. These novel perspectives provide pertinent policy guidance to further advance human rights and social justice."

– *Barbara van Koppen, Principal Researcher, International Water Management Institute*

"This highly readable book breaks new ground by framing food and nutrition security in terms of both the right to food and the right to water. It clearly highlights the importance of agroecological practices in renewing the availability and quality of water for food systems and the environment. The gendered analysis of water governance is generative of critical proposals for equitable policies and inclusive practices. In sum, this scholarly work fills a major gap in the literature. It is a "must read" for many academics, policy makers and development professionals."

– *Michel Pimbert, Director of the Centre for Agroecology, Water and Resilience, Coventry University, UK*

"Farmers, indigenous peoples and fishers are well aware that land, water and food are interconnected and crucial for human wellbeing. However, policies, programmes and right-based approaches on water and food have developed often without their participation and thus with little understanding of the livelihoods and wellbeing of rural communities, including customary communities, and in isolation from each other. Local people's rights to water and food are routinely violated. This book boldly highlights the faultlines in policy debates and practices and provides a very welcome and much needed social justice perspective to water, food security and nutrition."

– *Jennifer Franco, Transnational Institute*

WATER FOR FOOD SECURITY, NUTRITION AND SOCIAL JUSTICE

This book is the first comprehensive effort to bring together Water, Food Security and Nutrition (FSN) in a way that goes beyond the traditional focus on irrigated agriculture. Apart from looking at the role of water and sanitation for human well-being, it proposes alternative and more locally appropriate ways to address complex water management and governance challenges from the local to global levels against a backdrop of growing uncertainties.

The authors challenge mainstream supply-oriented and neo-Malthusian visions that argue for the need to increase the land area under irrigation in order to feed the world's growing population. Instead, they argue for a reframing of the debate concerning production processes, waste, food consumption and dietary patterns whilst proposing alternative strategies to improve water and land productivity, putting the interests of marginalized and disenfranchized groups upfront.

The book highlights how accessing water for FSN can be challenging for small-holders, vulnerable and marginalized women and men, and how water allocation systems and reform processes can negatively affect local people's informal rights. The book argues for the need to improve policy coherence across water, land and food and is original in making a case for strengthening the relationship between the human rights to water and food, especially for marginalized women and men. It will be of great interest to practitioners, students and researchers working on water and food issues.

Lyla Mehta is Professorial Fellow at the Institute of Development Studies, UK, and a Visiting Professor at the Norwegian University of Life Sciences.

Theib Oweis is Director of the Water, Land and Ecosystems research program at the International Center for Agricultural Research in the Dry Areas (ICARDA) and a Distinguished Guest Professor of water management at the

International Platform for Dryland Research and Education (IPDRE) of Tottori University, Japan.

Claudia Ringler leads the Natural Resource Management Theme at the International Food Policy Research Institute and is also a flagship co-lead with the CGIAR Research Program on Water, Land and Ecosystems.

Barbara Schreiner is a water resources policy expert and Executive Director of the Water Integrity Network.

Shiney Varghese is Senior Policy Analyst with the Institute for Agriculture and Trade Policy, USA, and a member of the High Level Panel of Experts to the UN Committee on World Food Security.

Pathways to Sustainability Series

This book series addresses core challenges around linking science and technology and environmental sustainability with poverty reduction and social justice. It is based on the work of the Social, Technological and Environmental Pathways to Sustainability (STEPS) Centre, a major investment of the UK Economic and Social Research Council (ESRC). The STEPS Centre brings together researchers at the Institute of Development Studies (IDS) and Science Policy Research Unit (SPRU) at the University of Sussex with a set of partner institutions in Africa, Asia and Latin America.

Series Editors:
Ian Scoones and Andy Stirling
STEPS Centre at the University of Sussex

Editorial Advisory Board:
Steve Bass, Wiebe E. Bijker, Victor Galaz, Wenzel Geissler, Katherine Homewood, Sheila Jasanoff, Melissa Leach, Colin McInnes, Suman Sahai, Andrew Scott

Titles in this series include:

Grassroots Innovation Movements
Adrian Smith, Mariano Fressoli, Dinesh Abrol, Elisa Around and Adrian Ely

Agronomy for Development
The Politics of Knowledge in Agricultural Research
James Sumberg

The Water-Food-Energy Nexus
Power, Politics and Justice
Jeremy Allouche, Carl Middleton and Dipak Gyawali

The Circular Economy and the Global South
Sustainable Lifestyles and Green Industrial Development
Edited by Patrick Schröder, Manisha Anantharaman, Kartika Anggraeni and Tim Foxon

Water for Food Security, Nutrition and Social Justice
Lyla Mehta, Theib Oweis, Claudia Ringler, Barbara Schreiner and Shiney Varghese

WATER FOR FOOD SECURITY, NUTRITION AND SOCIAL JUSTICE

Lyla Mehta, Theib Oweis, Claudia Ringler, Barbara Schreiner and Shiney Varghese

First published 2020
by Routledge
2 Park Square, Milton Park, Abingdon, Oxon OX14 4RN

and by Routledge
52 Vanderbilt Avenue, New York, NY 10017

Routledge is an imprint of the Taylor & Francis Group, an informa business

© 2020 Lyla Mehta, Theib Oweis, Claudia Ringler, Barbara Schreiner and Shiney Varghese

The right of Lyla Mehta, Theib Oweis, Claudia Ringler, Barbara Schreiner and Shiney Varghese to be identified as authors of this work has been asserted by them in accordance with sections 77 and 78 of the Copyright, Designs and Patents Act 1988.

All rights reserved. No part of this book may be reprinted or reproduced or utilised in any form or by any electronic, mechanical, or other means, now known or hereafter invented, including photocopying and recording, or in any information storage or retrieval system, without permission in writing from the publishers.

Trademark notice: Product or corporate names may be trademarks or registered trademarks, and are used only for identification and explanation without intent to infringe.

British Library Cataloguing-in-Publication Data
A catalogue record for this book is available from the British Library

Library of Congress Cataloging-in-Publication Data
Names: Mehta, Lyla, author. | Oweis, Theib Yousef, author. | Ringler, Claudia, author. | Schreiner, Barbara, author. | Varghese, Shiney, author.
Title: Water for food security, nutrition and social justice / Lyla Mehta, Theib Oweis, Claudia Ringler, Barbara Schreiner, Shiney Varghese.
Other titles: Pathways to sustainability series
Description: New York : Routledge, 2019. |
Series: Pathways to sustainability | Includes bibliographical references and index. |
Identifiers: LCCN 2019024119 (print) | LCCN 2019024120 (ebook) | ISBN 9781138729162 (hardback) | ISBN 9781138729186 (paperback) | ISBN 9781351747622 (ebook)
Subjects: LCSH: Water resources development–Research. | Food security–Research.
Classification: LCC HD1691 .M438 2019 (print) | LCC HD1691 (ebook) | DDC 333.91–dc23
LC record available at https://lccn.loc.gov/2019024119
LC ebook record available at https://lccn.loc.gov/2019024120

ISBN: 978-1-138-72916-2 (hbk)
ISBN: 978-1-138-72918-6 (pbk)
ISBN: 978-1-351-74762-2 (ebk)

Typeset in Bembo
by Swales & Willis, Exeter, Devon, UK

CONTENTS

List of figures   *x*
List of boxes   *xii*
List of tables   *xiii*
List of acronyms   *xiv*
Preface and acknowledgements   *xvii*

1 Introduction   1

2 Linking water and food security and nutrition (FSN)   16

3 Agricultural water management   65

4 Water governance for FSN   123

5 Water, FSN and social justice   165

Index   *202*

FIGURES

2.1	The multiple interfaces between water and food security and nutrition (FSN)	17
2.2	The four dimensions of food security and the scale at which they operate	19
2.3	Internal renewable water resources per capita in m^3	22
2.4	Country-wise classification of different countries along hydrological complexity	23
2.5	The four pillars of water security and of food and nutrition security	26
2.6	Distribution of Water Productivity (= Ya ETa-1) from rainfed production within food categories in diets in Burkina Faso, Ethiopia and Tanzania	36
2.7	Dietary Water Productivity (WP$_{diet}$) for socio-economic diets in Ethiopia	37
2.8	Estimates for regional drinking water coverage, 2015	39
2.9	Estimated regional sanitation coverage, 2015	39
2.10	Rainfall variation, growth in agricultural GDP and growth in GDP, 1982–2000	42
2.11	The water storage continuum	45
3.1	The ten elements of agroecology	73
3.2	Relationship between water productivity and land productivity for durum wheat in a Mediterranean environment	95
3.3	Total national wheat production in Syria from years 1980 to 2016	98
3.4	Syria imports and exports of wheat from 1980 to 2016	98
3.5	Contribution of agricultural inputs and management to wheat yield increase in Syria	99

3.6 Mechanized MICWH: (a) laser guided vallerani bunds maker, (b) mechanized intermittent contour bunds, (c) Bunds planted with shrubs after a rain storm, (d) Sheep grazing shrubs and vegetation from restored landscape   111

BOXES

2.1	Challenges to gender and social inclusion in small-scale irrigation	30
2.2	Drought – the new normal?	43
2.3	Hydropower: support or challenge to regional cooperation and energy security?	48
3.1	India's agri-trade implications for its water security	69
3.2	FAO's scaling up agroecology initiative: ten elements to guide the transition to sustainable food and agricultural systems	72
3.3	The gendered nature of irrigation and water management	76
3.4	Supplemental irrigation package may triple rainfed systems productivity	97
3.5	Restoring degraded pastoral 'badia' system in Jordan	111
4.1	Water allocation and regulation in Maharashtra	127
4.2	Water and conflict: Palestinian water insecurities	128
4.3	Race, class and water contamination in Flint, USA	129
4.4	Gender discrimination in African water management	131
4.5	Australian water governance regime	135
4.6	Contradictory positions and actions taken by Coca-Cola globally	146
5.1	Transboundary cooperation for FSN	169
5.2	Trade and investment agreements: implications for water quality and water availability for food security	172
5.3	Relevant international human rights instruments, agreements and texts applicable to water policies and other measures to enhance food security	174
5.4	Multiple water use services	180
5.5	The right to water in South Africa	182

TABLES

3.1 Comparison of metric tools for water management and use (adapted from HLPE, 2015)   86
3.2 Global survey of groundwater irrigation   105

ACRONYMS

AAAS	American Association for the Advancement of Science
CA	CGIAR Comprehensive Assessment of Water Management in Agriculture
CAFOs	Concentrated Animal Feeding Operations
CBD	Convention on Biological Diversity
CEDAW	Convention on the Elimination of All Forms of Discrimination against Women
CETA	Comprehensive Economic and Trade Agreement
CFS	Committee on World Food Security
CGIAR	Consultative Group for International Agricultural Research
CMPs	Catchment Management Platforms
COHRE	Centre on Housing Rights and Evictions
CPR	Common Property Resources
DFID	UK Department for International Development
DWM	Developmental Water Management
EAC	Environment Audit Committee
EPA	USA Environmental Protection Agency
ESC-Rights	Economic, Social and Cultural Rights
ETO	States' Extraterritorial Obligations
EU	European Union
FAD	Food Availability Decline
FAO	United Nations Food and Agriculture Organization
FIES	Food Insecurity Experience Scale
FSN	Food Security and Nutrition
G-20	Group of Twenty
GCC	Gulf Cooperation Council
GIZ	Gesellschaft für Internationale Zusammenarbeit

GWP	Global Water Partnership
HIV/AIDS	Human Immunodeficiency Virus Infection/Acquired Immune Deficiency Syndrome
HLPE	United Nations High Level Panel of Experts on Food Security and Nutrition
HRSDWS	Human Right to Safe Drinking Water and Sanitation
IATP	Institute for Agriculture and Trade Policy
ICARDA	International Center for Agricultural Research in the Dry Areas
ICSID	The International Centre for Settlement of Investment Disputes
ICESCR	International Covenant Economic, Social, and Cultural Rights
ICESR	International Conference on Environmental Systems Research
ICWE	International Conference on Water and the Environment
IFAD	United Nations International Fund for Agricultural development
IFI	International Financial Institution
ILA	International Law Association
IPCC	Intergovernmental Panel on Climate Change
IUCN	International Union for the Conservation of Nature
IWA	International Water Association
IWMI	International Water Management Institute
IWRM	Integrated Water Resources Management
JMP	WHO/UNICEF Joint Monitoring Programme (for progress on drinking water and sanitation)
JWC	Israeli–Palestinian Joint Water Committee
LTI	Land Transparency Initiative
MDG	Millennium Development Goal
MENA	Middle East and North Africa
MUS	Multiple Use Water Services
NGO	Non-Governmental Organization
OECD	Organization for Economic Cooperation and Development
PHL	Post-Harvest Losses
RBOs	River Basin Organizations
RSA	Republic of South Africa
RTF	Right to Food
RTW	Right to Water
SDC	Swiss Agency for Development and Cooperation
SDG	Sustainable Development Goal
STEPS	Social, Technological and Environmental Pathways to Sustainability
TERI	The Energy and Resources Institute
TPP	Trans Pacific Partnership
TTIP	Transatlantic Trade and Investment Partnership
UDHR	Universal Declaration of Human Rights
UK	United Kingdom
UN	United Nations
UNCCD	United Nations Convention to Combat Desertification

UNCED	United Nations Conference on Environment and Development
UNCESCR	United Nations Committee on Economic Social and Cultural Rights
UNCPR	United Nations Committee of Permanent Representatives
UNCRPD	United Nations Convention on the Rights of Persons with a Disability
UNDESA	United Nations Department of Economic and Social Affairs
UNDP	United Nations Development Program
UNDRIP	United Nations Declarations on the Rights of Indigenous Peoples
UNECE	United Nations Economic Commission for Europe
UNEP	United Nations Environment Programme
UNESCO	United Nations Educational, Scientific and Cultural Organization
UNFCCC	United Nations Framework Convention on Climate Change
UNGA	United Nations General Assembly
UNHRC	United Nations Human Rights Council
UNICEF	United Nations International Children's Emergency Fund
US	United States
USAID	United States Agency for International Development
VGGT	Voluntary Guidelines on the Responsible Governance of Tenure of Land, Fisheries and Forests in the Context of National Food Security
WANA	West Asia and North Africa region
WASH	Water Supply, Sanitation and Hygiene
WCD	World Commission on Dams
WEF	World Economic Forum
WEF	Water-Energy-Food (Nexus)
WFF	World Forum of Fish Harvesters and Fish Workers
WFFP	World Forum of Fisher Peoples
WFP	United Nations World Food Programme
WHO	World Health Organization
WSSD	World Summit on Sustainable Development
WTO	World Trade Organization
WUA	Water Users Association
WWAP	World Water Assessment Programme

PREFACE AND ACKNOWLEDGEMENTS

The authors of this book were part of the project team for the High Level Panel of Experts on Food Security and Nutrition's (HLPE) 2015 report on water for food security and nutrition. The HLPE provides the United Nations' Committee on World Food Security (CFS) with evidence-based and policy-oriented analysis on several food security related topics as identified by the CFS.

For over a year, we worked intensely on several drafts and versions of the report, taking into account the comments from an open consultation as well as those of the HLPE Steering Committee, independent reviewers and various UN agencies. It was an intense, and at times difficult, but also rewarding process, and we thank HLPE Steering Committee members, in particular Michel Pimbert. We also thank the HLPE Secretariat for their support, especially Vincent Gitz and Fabio Ricci.

As is common in such UN processes, many issues that we raised did not make it into the final version. We thus decided to write this book to bring together a broader body of thought. We also felt that this publication would be accessible to a broader audience. While this book builds on material and drafts developed for the HLPE, it also presents entirely updated materials and data as well as new thinking on water, food security and nutrition. We thank the HLPE for enabling and supporting the earlier work and its broad dissemination. This book does not reflect the views of the HLPE.

This volume is part of the ESRC STEPS Centre series on Pathways to Sustainability. We thank the STEPS Centre, in particular Ian Scoones. At Routledge, we thank Leila Walker and Rebecca Brennan for being fantastic editors and for their patience despite the many slippages on our part. It was quite challenging to write this book with each of us juggling multiple commitments, often across different continents and time zones, and there have been many delays along the way. We are deeply grateful to Leila Walker, in particular, for motivating us to finish and also for her crucial support at every stage in this project.

For our background research, we acknowledge the crucial assistance provided by Martha Kimmel, Maria Caceres, Shilpi Srivastava and the support from colleagues and friends who shared their data, knowledge and insights and provided valuable comments. We thank Jennifer Franco, Sophia Monsalve, Sylvia Kay, Barbara van Koppen, Synne Movik, Alan Nicol, Tom Slaymaker, Jeremy Allouche, Frank van Steenbergen, Kifle Woldearegay, Daniel Langmeier, Hua Xie, Tingju Zhu, Gauthier Pitois and Quentin Grafton.

Claudia Ringler acknowledges the CGIAR Research Program on Water, Land and Ecosystems for support. Lyla Mehta acknowledges the crucial support received from the Institute of Development Studies (IDS) UK and thanks, in particular, IDS director Melissa Leach.

Water is crucial to sustain life, food, ecosystems, human health and wellbeing. Still, millions of poor and marginalized women and men around the world face challenges in accessing water due to a range of ecological, sociopolitical, institutional and economic reasons. These undermine their ability to lead healthy and productive lives. Millions of poor, powerless and vulnerable women and men also face daily violations to their basic rights to water and food. For far too long have the management, institutional and governance aspects of water and food been separated in both policy and practice. This makes little sense for local users who experience these issues as deeply connected in their daily lives. It is thus important to improve coherence between water and food security and nutrition related policies, strategies and plans, achieve equal access to water for all (especially for the most vulnerable and marginalized), improve water management and water governance for food security and nutrition as well as to join up action regarding protecting and realizing the human rights to water and food. We hope this volume will be an inspiration and encouragement for future work and struggles addressing the various challenges related to water's contribution to food security and nutrition for all, for now and in the future.

Lyla Mehta, Theib Oweis, Claudia Ringler,
Barbara Schreiner and Shiney Varghese

1
INTRODUCTION

In Tanzania's Uluguru mountains villagers operate complex networks of locally managed springs, canals and wells for productive irrigated horticulture, cropping and domestic use. Yes, most of these small-scale users remain invisible to the government which often vests permits to use land and water to male-dominated user groups that risk alienating the vast majority of informal users of land and water, especially women.[1]

In many slums and informal settlements in the global South, the quality of water accessed by poor people is so bad that it adversely affects health and nutrition, especially of children and babies. Moreover, many of these settlements lack adequate sanitation, which contributes to disease, such as diarrhoea, which further contributes to poor nutritional outcomes. Nutrition, ill-health and cognitive and other important human development outcomes are mutually reinforcing. But these populations tend to be ignored by both the state and large-scale private operators.

The 2009 Bolivian constitution recognizes both the human rights to water and food; and potable water, sanitation, irrigation and small-scale agriculture are all deemed important. In reality, tensions between water for agriculture, urban use, mining and industry abound and often get in the way of ensuring the water and food security of indigenous and poorer populations.

Since rainfed farming is a risky business in sub-Saharan Africa, it is important to establish and scale up practices that can enhance the effective management and use of water for smallholder agriculture. This includes improving storage and capturing run off, using groundwater sustainably, applying supplementary irrigation and improving soil water retention.

As these vignettes show, there are compelling linkages between water, food security and nutrition.[2] As stated in the Koran 21: 3, 'By means of water, we give life to everything'. Indeed, water is a fundamental element on which human beings depend for their lives and livelihoods. Water is also an essential input to agricultural production and is required for the preparation and processing of food (CA, 2007; FAO, 2012; Rosegrant et al., 2002). According to WWAP (2014), 70% of human water withdrawals are for agriculture, 20% for industrial uses and 10% for domestic uses. However, even this 70% of water only produces 40% of agricultural crops, the rest comes from rain or 'green' water (Ringler, 2017). As water applied for irrigation evaporates, it is largely removed from further direct human use, as compared to other sectors where most of the water tends to return to water bodies for reuse. The importance of the agriculture sector as the world's largest water user and the associated responsibilities to use water sustainably was affirmed during the 2017 Global Forum for Food and Agriculture[3] and the G-20 meeting of ministers of agriculture.[4] Despite rapid increases in non-irrigation uses of water, water for food production will remain the largest user of human freshwater withdrawals, making farmers in many ways the main stewards of the world's water resources.

Water is also the lifeblood of many ecosystems, such as forests, lakes or wetlands that are essential for people and the environment. These ecosystems are particularly important for poor people, providing them with nutrition and livelihoods. Water is also fundamental for all other productive sectors, including energy, manufacturing. Finally, water has important cultural and aesthetic values.

Safe drinking water and sanitation are fundamental to the nutrition, health and dignity of all (UNDP, 2006). Despite the progress made in achieving global targets around water and sanitation in the past decades, about 3 in 10 people, or 2.1 billion lack access to safe, readily available water at home, and 6 in 10, or 4.5 billion, lack safely managed sanitation (WHO and UNICEF, 2017). Accessing water can be particularly challenging for smallholders, vulnerable and marginalized populations and women. Even though the human right to drinking safe water and sanitation was globally endorsed by the UN in 2010, it is violated every day across the globe. This situation undermines health, nutrition, human well-being and dignity and is a global and moral outrage.

This book is probably the first comprehensive effort to bring together water, food security and nutrition (FSN) in a way that goes beyond the traditional focus on irrigated agriculture.[5] Apart from looking at the role of water and sanitation in human well-being, it proposes alternative and locally appropriate ways to address complex water management and governance challenges from local to global against a backdrop of growing uncertainties. It argues for the need to improve policy coherence across the water and food domains and is original in making a case for strengthening the relationship between the rights to water and food, especially for marginalized women and men. The volume is thus in line with the Sustainable Development Goals (SDGs) which call for progress on all dimensions of human development while ensuring that our planet supports both humans and nature.

Our starting point is that global inequality in access to water and sanitation is unacceptable and one of the largest inequities of the 21st century. According to the 2006 Human Development Report (UNDP, 2006), no act of terrorism generates devastation on a daily basis on the scale of the crisis in water and sanitation. However, this crisis occurs largely in silence. Unlike wars and natural disasters, it remains invisible and has been quasi naturalized – that is, accepted as part of life – by both those who enjoy access to safe water and the millions who do not. The water crisis is largely caused and legitimized by different forms of unequal gender and social relations, as well as structural violence vis-à-vis poor and marginalized people, that prevent universal access (Mehta, 2016). In the case of millions of women and girls who spend hours collecting water, this naturalized gendered nature of water collection has undermined their health, education and chances in life. Poor water quality affects human health and the functioning of ecosystems, with adverse impacts for poor and vulnerable groups that directly depend on this resource base for their livelihoods. Climate change, including growing climate variability, affects everyone on the globe and adds irregularity and uncertainty to the availability of and demand for water with known effects on the vulnerability of the poorest and their food security (see Bates *et al.*, 2008). Complex governance challenges shape the access to and allocation and distribution of water for FSN and the land, water and food domains are disconnected in policies and programmes. Poor people's rights to water, sanitation and food are not realized effectively and there are few efforts to interlink these rights effectively.

The complex challenges of water and FSN

There are at least five distinct dimensions of the challenge of water and FSN:

- Changing demographics, lifestyles and diets, and increasing demands from water-using sectors including agriculture, energy generation, mining, and manufacturing, are putting stress on limited freshwater resources.
- Increasing pollution in many parts of the world from both agriculture and industry is rendering water unfit for use and impacting on human and ecosystem health.
- Unsustainable resource management is reducing the ecosystem functions and services of land, fisheries, forests and wetlands, including their ability to provide food and nutrition to rural and urban poor communities in particular.
- Inadequate or lack of access to safe drinking water and adequate sanitation facilities and hygiene practices is reducing the nutritional status of people through water-borne diseases and chronic intestinal infections.
- Complex governance challenges shape the access to and allocation and distribution of water for FSN as well as increasing commodification of land, water and food resources. There is also a marked lack of policy coherence across land, water and food domains from national to global. This also includes a lack of political will to realize the human rights to water, sanitation and food of poor and marginalized people and to join them up effectively (see also HLPE, 2015).

In general, these core problems, exacerbated by climate change, tend to disproportionately affect poor and marginalized women, men and small children across the globe due to existing power imbalances and unequal gender relations. How to solve these problems is not obvious, partly due to the nature of water itself. Water, more than most resources, is highly variable across time and space (Mehta, 2014). Its availability is characterized by the complex interactions of a number of elements which include rainfall, temperature, wind, runoff, evapotranspiration, storage, distribution systems and water quality. Unlike energy, or food, freshwater is a limited resource, and creating additional water supplies through, for example, increased storage or desalination, has limited opportunities. It is thus necessary to manage within the natural limitations of available freshwater.

While accessible water resources are adequate at global levels to meet the water needs of the world, these resources are unevenly distributed across the globe with per capita resources particularly low in the Middle East, North African and Southern Asia regions (see Chapter 2). Within regions and countries there are significant variations in water availability. Availability also varies considerably over time, with significant intra- and inter-annual water variations, concentrated in poorer regions (Grey and Sadoff, 2007). Inequality within and between countries, communities and households means that many people continue to have inadequate access to water embedded in food, as reflected in unacceptably high under-nutrition rates (see, for example, FAO, 2013), as well as limited or no access to clean drinking water and sanitation, with significant adverse food and nutrition outcomes. In parts of the globe, historical rainfall patterns are changing, adding significant uncertainty to the reliable availability of water in many regions in the future.

The human population is expected to grow to 9.8 billion people by 2050 (UN DESA, 2017), with the result that per capita water availability will continue to decline over the next few decades, particularly in the global South where almost all the additional population will be added. Per capita water availability is also declining due to growing water pollution, which makes water unusable for many human purposes (Palaniappan et al., 2010), and variability of supply is growing to different degrees as a result of climate change (Bates et al., 2008). While future water demand estimates vary, there is agreement that domestic, municipal and industrial demands are growing faster than irrigation demands; that municipal and domestic demand increases are closely aligned with urbanization trends; that there is particularly high uncertainty regarding industrial water demand trends; and that irrigation demands will continue to account for the largest share of total water demands. Taken together, these various trends point to a serious dilemma of dramatically increasing, competing demands on what is after all a limited natural resource, and one that is crucial to all life and particularly the food security and nutrition of all humanity.

Growing water scarcity and variability will increase the competition for water resources across sectors, with water often being taken away from the agricultural sector to drive greater economic value per unit of water in other sectors.

Increasing competition also often results in smaller, and poorer, water users losing their access to water. Conflicts are likely to grow between urban and rural users, upstream and downstream users, between in-stream (aquatic resources) and off-stream (mostly human) users (CA, 2007) and between countries dependent on shared or transboundary water resources. All this makes questions of water governance and decision making with regard to water an urgent imperative. The underlying issue is: who should get what access to which waters when, for how long and for what purposes? Answering this question is complicated and often controversial enough within a single country. Yet this is clearly not enough. While it is often observed that 'water flows uphill to money and power', it is also clear that water is a resource that 'ignores' national boundaries, thus complicating the challenge of governing our limited water resources even further.

In general, water scarcity, flooding and pollution are most acutely experienced locally, and generally affect those with least resources and those depending on water as an input to their livelihoods the most. Still, the fluidity of the resource ensures linkages within hydrological basins, which are often different from national boundaries. Most countries in the world have at least some of their water resources coming from a transboundary basin where water must be shared between riparian states. In addition to the transboundary nature of much of the world's water, several processes link water with global processes, through, for example, trade in agricultural (and other) commodities; global climate policy, as reflected in the United Nations Framework Convention on Climate Change (UNFCCC); national and global energy policies, which are, in part, driven by global climate policies as well as by financial policies; foreign direct investment levels and surrounding policies; global water reports such as the World Commission on Dams (WCD, 2000) and other international processes, such as the Millennium Development Goals and the 2030 Sustainable Development Goals, the Convention on Wetlands of International Importance (Ramsar), the United Nations Convention to Combat Desertification, and the Convention on Biological Diversity (Ringler *et al.*, 2010; WWAP, 2012).

Conflicting pathways and perspectives

There are competing pathways and discourses regarding water and food security. According to the European Commission (2012), pressures on water availability will continue to grow – not only through the need to feed and hydrate a growing global population, but also from changes in consumption patterns. In the context of the OECD's 2050 projections, global water demand is projected to increase by 55%, due to increases in manufacturing, electricity and domestic use, leaving little scope for increasing water use for irrigation (OECD, 2012). A report by the Global Harvest Initiative (2014) argued that with growing population, the world may not be able to feed itself by 2050 unless food production increases drastically. This supply side vision is based in part on neo-Malthusian visions of scarcity and crises. We follow the UNDP (2006) in rejecting this 'gloomy arithmetic' vision and acknowledge the massive water injustices that poor women and men around the world encounter daily in accessing water for food security. Our starting point is that there is enough food and water to go around, now and in the future.

Another perspective put forward by some members of the CGIAR system argues that world food demand can be satisfied with available water and land resources by a) increasing water and land productivities through upgrading rain fed and irrigated systems, b) optimizing virtual water (trade) between countries based on comparative advantages and c) reducing food demand by adjusting diets and improving the efficiency of food processing and distribution (CA, 2007). These issues are largely addressed in Chapters 2 and 3 of this book.

And finally, there are discourses that argue that there is enough water to ensure food security and nutrition for all sustainably, if water governance and water management are informed by social, gender and environmental justice concerns. Chapters 4 and 5 thus focus on how water for FSN is accessed, governed, managed and distributed at different levels from local to national and global. The book thus argues that it is important to focus on how problems are framed and their various solutions; the multiple ways in which poor women and men access water and how their rights to water and food can be strengthened; the interactions between various actors from local to global and their implications for local rights to water and land; and finally how decision making and power structures affect water for FSN and how these interact with issues concerning poverty, gender and social difference.

In his seminal study of starvation and famines, Amartya Sen argued that the fixation with the per capita food availability decline (FAD) is a misleading way to look at hunger and famine, since hunger is more about people not having access to food due to wider social and political arrangements as opposed to there not being enough food to eat. (Sen, 1981, 1983). Looking at per capita availability of a resource lacks relevant discrimination and is even more gross when applied to the population of the world as a whole (Sen, 1981). Water scarcity is also often misleadingly perceived as per capita water availability rather than inequality in access to water supply. But usually, water access is determined by social and political institutions, cultural and gender norms and property rights. Some groups may suffer from lack of water even when there is no decline in water availability in the region. Thus, water shortages (like famines) are best understood as entitlement failures requiring effective and democratic governance solutions that can be accepted as legitimate by all (see also Anand, 2007; Mehta, 2014).

In keeping with other volumes in this series, we follow the STEPS pathways approach (see Leach *et al.*, 2010) to take a critical approach to water and food that is concerned with social justice, human rights and the politics of framing. The first lens is the human rights framework, particularly the rights to food and water, how these two rights intersect, support each other and how they can be further advanced. The second is a lens that looks at alternative trajectories and the possibility of reframing the challenge in order to reframe the solution –

looking at issues of redistribution, social and gender equity, reduction of consumption and waste, and change of dietary practices in order to ensure water for FSN as well as ecologically and socially sustainable agricultural practices. We also make a case for doing away with silo driven discourses (i.e. between water, food and land and between water supply and water for production) that are highly problematic from the perspective of local users for whom there is little sense in separating out these dimensions so crucial for survival.

Problems with metrics and knowledge

There are methodological problems concerning the lack of timely and adequate data to understand and manage water for FSN. For example, data are rarely sex disaggregated and do not say very much about intrahousehold challenges, water access, control and food production or indeed about informal water and food systems. Data on water pollution and on water use across sectors are equally inadequate, and aggregate figures as well as the use of certain data in mainstream water discourses obscure challenges related to rights, access and tenure, especially of vulnerable people.

Why is this important? In every sector, indicators serve to monitor progress in a way that is measurable, sustainable and time bound and are also key to establishing accountability. However, as we highlight in this book, many global indices and debates in the water domain are highly generalized and often too aggregate to take on board local nuances and differences. These have implications for how problems and solutions around water for FSN are framed and how these affect decision-making processes. We also demonstrate how the framings – or understandings and representations – that dominate policy debates at the international and national levels may be frequently at odds with the perceptions, knowledge and experiences of local water and food users (see Mehta and Movik, 2014). These include how water data are collected to ways to understand water consumption and water security. These highlight the importance of paying attention to the politics of knowledge and data in the water domain and how current and future 'crises' around land and water are portrayed. For example, water management often focuses on hydrologic units such as a basin or watershed (Edwards et al., 2015).[6] Drainage or hydrologic basins are considered to be the ideal units for measuring and reporting on water data, because the majority of water that discharges from the basin outlet originated as precipitation falling on the basin. However, these hydrologic units are often different from administrative units or country boundaries and thinking in hydrological, as opposed to administrative units, can be quite challenging for policy makers and water officials (see Moss, 2003 for Europe). Many approaches such as Integrated Water Resources Management (IWRM) ask for a sophisticated knowledge base and assessments of existing water withdrawals/use by different sectors (e.g. agriculture, industry etc.). This can be quite challenging in data-poor environments, especially in sub-Saharan Africa and a lot of financial and donor resources are used to improve the database, instead of actually enhancing access to water or improving water infrastructure.

The FAO AQUASTAT database (www.fao.org/nr/water/aquastat/main/index.stm) is currently the key source on agricultural water data. It lists about 180 possible data items but generally contains data on around 70 variables at the country level. The key data categories include water resources, water use, irrigation and drainage, conservation agriculture and water harvesting, and environment and health. Data are either collected, modelled or internally estimated by the FAO. A sample of two countries (Albania in Europe and Angola representing a country in the global South) shows that for Albania, out of a total of 180 possible water and related[7] variables for the period of 2008–2012, Aquastat data were available for 60 variables, and for Angola for 57 variables. Both countries had no information on water withdrawals or irrigation for that period. For both countries, for an earlier period, modelled withdrawal estimates are available as well as internally estimated irrigated harvested area. Key water data challenges that have been raised include lack of accounting for small-scale irrigation, and thus underestimation of actually irrigated area; poor understanding of groundwater use; and poor data quality on sectoral water withdrawals.

Water accounting is a sub-component of environmental accounting, which aims to incorporate environmental information into typically economic accounting and can be done either at the corporate level or for national economies. It is a way to help societies understand how they use their water resources and also help towards creating new policies that aim to create sustainable use of water resources (see FAO, 2012). But accounting can be complicated in many ways. One, it is difficult to capture the dynamic nature of water uncertainties and variabilities in water accounting. Two, there are also questions that concern the politics of water use and governance (ibid.). Take the case of water footprint. As discussed in Chapter 3, the water footprint concept measures the impact of specific firms or products on water resources and many studies now measure the water footprint of specific countries or products (see Chapagain and Tickner, 2012; Hoekstra, 2013). This concept has the potential to shape consumer behaviour – particularly though not exclusively in western countries – where consumer consciousness of consumption impacts is rising. The implications are not yet known, but they may not always be of use to poor producers and smallholders. For example, consumer boycotts in affluent societies could lead to an erosion of livelihoods in poorer countries. Furthermore, water footprint tools have not included the political nature of water distribution, especially at the local level (see Chapagain and Tickner, 2012). For instance, water footprint accounting does show that through the import of Peruvian asparagus, large amounts of virtual water is imported (Hoekstra, 2013), but it does not differentiate between asparagus produced under industrial agriculture with devastating effects on the local economy and depletion of a non-renewable aquifer on the one hand and asparagus produced under robust family farming with renewable (rain/green) water (see Progressio, CEPES and Water Witness, 2010). Finally, water footprinting does not take into account wider environmental impacts and issues concerning world trade and food dumping etc. The FAO (2012) has also identified that there are some methodological deficiencies, such as differentiating between consumptive and non consumptive use; the source of water (rainfall or fresh water from rivers and aquifers) when not exclusively rainfed, and the problem of tracing and adequately accounting for various issues such as the spillover effects upstream and downstream.

What do aggregate indices obscure?

Given these deficiencies in data and metrics, it is worth asking what they obscure. Usually, assessments done at the global level, for example of 'hotspots' of water scarcity, floods and droughts are often very aggregate and focus on the volumetric aspects of water. There are currently few reliable statistics at more disaggregated scales. A challenge here is much of the available data are either modelled or estimated for hydrological units or national levels, and then disaggregated using algorithms or statistical tools. They also tend not to disaggregate users and their entitlements or look at the politics of distribution (Mehta and Movik, 2014). Nor do they focus upfront on the social relations underlying how technological choices are made that have a bearing on water and food insecurity (ibid.). In the era of the Millennium Development Goals (MDGs), MDG progress ignored peri urban and slum areas which are some of the fastest growing areas in the world (see JMP, 2012). Issues concerning equity, sustainability and discrimination were also often overlooked as a result of focusing on the quasi 'low hanging fruit' and the areas in which it is easy to extend coverage.

The Sustainable Development Goal (SDG) on water and sanitation is a huge improvement. It seeks to by 2030 achieve universal and equitable access to safe and affordable drinking water for all, as well as achieve access to adequate and equitable sanitation and hygiene for all and end open defecation, paying special attention to the needs of women and girls and those in vulnerable situations. For the SDGs, addressing inequality is key. This is done in terms of the focus on universality (i.e. achieving universal access to water and sanitation), monitoring and eliminating inequalities by improving service levels and by going beyond the household to focus on access in schools, health centres etc.) (see Cumming and Slaymaker, 2018). In addition, water quality concerns that were missing from the MDGs are addressed, including a commitment to reduce the number of people suffering from water scarcity and support and strengthen the participation of local communities in improving water and sanitation management (WHO, 2016). These trends are to be welcomed, alongside a commitment to improving data collection, monitoring and use at the country level. Still, like the other SDGs, there is a risk that there are too many indicators and hence problems with monitoring and tracking and the risk of an SDG industry in every country. Like with the MDGs, there is also a lack of clear mechanisms of accountability and similarly what each goal and target will mean in every country, district etc. will always be different and will need to be locally defined. Also generalized, globalized arguments that underpin policy debates tend to remain disconnected from the everyday experiences of local people. For example, while SDG 6 is far more nuanced than the MDG in stating what constitutes an 'improved' water source by creating a 'service ladder' from 'safely managed' to 'basic', 'unimproved' and surface water sources (WHO, 2016), as Katharina Welle's (2013) research in Ethiopia has demonstrated, there is a big gap between the ways global agencies, national agencies as well as local people understand, define and measure water access and inequality (see also Cumming and Slaymaker, 2018).

While there is greater awareness to gender inequalities, there has also been little comparable international data on gender indicators and most of the agencies lack proper sex-disaggregated data, making it impossible to monitor progress or devise gender sensitive policies. It is alarming that a source which can be accessed within 30 minutes (round-trip collection time) is considered an 'improved water source' as per the SDG indicators tracking progress in drinking water, sanitation and hygiene. No doubt, poor women in many parts of the global South may need to make multiple trips of 30 minutes or more with heavy water pots. That such a situation is considered acceptable reflects the critical need to ensure that more women are part of the decision-making processes when such standards and targets are being set. As argued by Mitra and Rao (2019), in the enthusiasm to meet the global targets, governments tend to ignore the interconnectedness between water services and food production and their wider embeddedness in ecology (i.e. land use and water flows), gendered labour patterns and how these are determined by power relations.

The water domain has been traditionally divided by two sectors: water supply/services and water resources management, or as the 2006 Human Development Report puts it, 'water for life' and 'water for production' (UNDP, 2006). Water for life refers to water for drinking and domestic purposes and is considered key for human survival. Water for production refers to water in irrigation, industry and small-scale entrepreneurial activities as well as using water to produce food for subsistence. This distinction, however, is highly problematic from the perspective of local users whose daily activities encompass both the domestic and productive elements of water and for whom there is little sense in separating water for drinking and washing and water for small-scale productive activities so crucial for survival. It is particularly limiting when advancing water for FSN and also gives rise to some limitations in the conceptualization of the right to water as opposed to the right to food (see Chapter 5). Added to this complication is sanitation which was only added to the MDG discussion in 2002. Even though sanitation and water issues are highly interlinked, they have different logics, politics and disciplinary underpinnings and usually when water and sanitation are mentioned in the same breath, sanitation issues are often ignored. Traditionally, wastewater and issues concerning water quality were also treated separately and not in an integrated manner.

Chapter 4 will highlight how knowledge in the water sector tends to be framed by a few powerful players that largely focus on the economic and engineering aspects of water that often ignore the deep cultural and symbolic values that local people assign to water in their daily lives. These can lead to contestations around the meaning of water and around issues of assigning value which makes water pricing and water market systems difficult to implement. Water policy debates are often abuzz with concepts and ideas such as water footprinting, security, the nexus etc. that we also focus on critically in our book. While examining these global issues in our book we highlight the importance of seeking out local knowledges and perspectives as well as alternative knowledge systems, including citizen knowledge and the use of digital media. This is why our book focuses on diverse framings and ways to view and cope with water and food scarcity and ways in which local women and men can develop resilient systems and knowledges. This should be done in a way that avoids romanticism about local knowledge and local communities but still points to alternatives to dominant metrics and framings.

Structure and argument of the book

This book addresses a key global challenge: namely, how the world can ensure food and nutrition security given competing demands, competition and growing scarcities of water, especially in some regions against a backdrop of growing uncertainties, not least due to climate change. This book explores the relationships and linkages between water and FSN across multiple scales. This is done against a backdrop of future uncertainties and drivers of change. The book takes a comprehensive approach in its focus on the technical, institutional, socio-economic, cultural and political dimensions of water for FSN. It challenges conventional pathways concerning how to provide the world population with FSN. It approaches the solutions in a different way by putting human rights for food and water at the forefront of the solutions and by strongly advocating issues concerning equity, redistribution, poverty reduction, gender and social justice. The book addresses how water for FSN is accessed, governed, managed and distributed. It focuses on how problems are framed and their various solutions, and how land and water productivities can be improved and strengthened. Agroecosystem sustainability around water for FSN is addressed, not only physically, but in the context of people's lives and rights to use the resources across generations. The book highlights the multiple relationships and linkages between water and FSN across multiple scales, including the interactions between various actors and policies from local to global and how decision making and power structures affect water for FSN and how these interact with issues concerning poverty, gender and social differentiation. It looks at the multiple ways in which poor women and men access water and how their rights to water and food can be strengthened and joined up.

Chapter 2 highlights the multiple linkages between water and FSN and focuses on challenges concerning accessing water for FSN, in particular for marginalized women and men. It focuses on four dimensions of water security that mirror the four dimensions of food security, namely availability, access, utilization and stability. The chapter also engages with emerging trends and challenges such as changing diets, climate change uncertainties and the corporatization of land and water resources.

Chapter 3 spells out the challenges pertaining to water management at a range of scales and explores various approaches and alternative pathways to improve water management and productivity in order to reduce risk and improve food security amidst growing uncertainties. The major focus is on how to improve rainfed and irrigation systems.

Chapter 4 looks at the different processes affecting water governance, allocation, access and use from local to global. It shows how land and water are linked and how water reform processes and large-scale land acquisitions have tended to overlook and threaten the customary and informal rights of poor and marginalized women and men, with impacts on FSN. It makes a case for inclusive water governance to allow for sustainable, equitable and gender-just decision making and allocation around FSN as well as policy coherence at the national and global levels around agriculture, environment, water, food and land issues in order to improve food security outcomes. It also looks critically at the political implications of the nexus debate.

Chapter 5 focuses on how to advance a social justice perspective on the water for FSN debate through its focus on how to strengthen human rights and global frameworks around water and food security. It calls for an exploration of how the rights to water and food can be joined up in a meaningful way in order to promote a human rights approach to water governance and water management for FSN in order to ensure water for FSN for all, now and in the future.

Notes

1 See van Koppen *et al.*'s (2013) unpublished field study of the Uluguru mountains.
2 The World Food Summit in 1996 adopted the following definition of food security: 'Food security exists when all people at all times have physical and economic access to sufficient, safe and nutritious food to meet their dietary needs and food preferences for an active and healthy life' (FAO, 1996). This definition is based on four dimensions of food security: 'Food availability: the availability of sufficient quantities of food of appropriate quality, supplied through domestic production or imports. Food access: access by individuals to adequate resources (entitlements) for acquiring appropriate foods for a nutritious diet. Utilization: utilization of food through adequate diet, clean water, sanitation and health care to reach a state of nutritional well-being where all physiological needs are met. Stability: to be food secure, a population, household or individual must have access to adequate food at all times' (HLPE 2013: 19, see also FAO, 1996). See Chapter 2 for a more thorough discussion of food security.
3 For the Declaration and Action Plan of the GFFA please see www.g20.utoronto.ca /2017/170122-agriculture-en.html (accessed March 2019).

4 The G-20 Declaration and Action Plan can be found here: www.bmel.de/Share dDocs/Downloads/EN/Agriculture/GlobalFoodSituation/G20_Action_Plan2017_EN .pdf?__blob=publicationFile (accessed February 2019).
5 While the Comprehensive Assessment of Water Management in Agriculture (CA, 2000) provides a large amount of useful data and analyses on water management in agriculture and we draw on some of the material, this book goes beyond the agricultural focus to also look at nutrition and the human rights aspects of water and food governance and how to join up these rights. For anthropological insights on how to link water and food insecurity see Wutich and Brewis (2014).
6 This refers to the area of land where surface water from rain and melting snow or ice converges to a single point at a lower elevation, usually the exit of the basin, where the waters join another water body or flow into the ocean. Approximately 260 international rivers cover close to half of the Earth's land surface (excluding Antarctica) (Cooley and Gleick, 2011).
7 Related variables include population, land area etc.

References

Anand, P.B. 2007. *Scarcity, Entitlements and the Economics of Water in Developing Countries*. Cheltenham, UK: Edward Elgar.
Bates, B.C., Kundzewicz, Z.W., Wu, S. and Palutikof, J.P. (eds). 2008. *Climate Change and Water*. Intergovernmental Panel on Climate Change Technical Paper VI. Geneva: IPCC Secretariat.
Chapagain, A.K. and Tickner, D. 2012. Water footprint: Help or hindrance? *Water Alternatives*, 5(3): 563–581.
Comprehensive Assessment of Water Management in Agriculture (CA). 2007. *Water for Food, Water for Life: A Comprehensive Assessment of Water Management for Agriculture*. London: Earthscan; Colombo, Sri Lanka: International Water Management Institute (IWMI).
Cooley, H. and Gleick, P.H. 2011. Climate-proofing transboundary water agreements. *Hydrological Sciences Journal*, 56(4): 711–718.
Cumming, O. and Slaymaker, T. (eds). 2018. *Equality in Water and Sanitation Services*. London: Routledge.
Edwards, P.J., Williard, K.W.J. and Schoonover, J.E. 2015. Fundamentals of watershed hydrology. *Journal of Contemporary Water Research & Education*, 154(1): 3–20.
European Commission. 2012. *The European Report on Development 2011/2012: Confronting Scarcity: Managing Water, Energy and Land for Inclusive and Sustainable Growth*. Available at: https://ecdpm.org/publications/european-report-development-2011-2012-confronting-scarcity-water-energy-land-inclusive-and-sustainable-growth/. Accessed April 2019.
FAO. 1996. *World Food Summit: Rome Declaration on World Food Security*. FAO [online]. Available at: www.fao.org/docrep/003/w3613e/w3613e00.htm.Accessed February 2019.
FAO. 2012. *Coping with Water Scarcity: An Action Framework for Agriculture and Food Security*. FAO Water Reports 38. Rome: FAO.
FAO. 2013. *The State of Food and Agriculture. Food Systems for Better Nutrition*. Rome: FAO.
Global Harvest Initiative. 2014. *Global Agricultural Productivity Report*. Washington, DC: GHI.
Grey, D. and Sadoff, C.W. 2007. Sink or swim? Water security for growth and development. *Water Policy*, 9: 545–571.
High Level Panel of Experts on Food Security and Nutrition (HLPE). 2013. *Investing in Smallholder Agriculture for Food Security*. Report by the High Level Panel of Experts on Food Security and Nutrition of the Committee on World Food Security. Rome: FAO.

HLPE. 2015. *Water for Food Security and Nutrition*. Report by the High Level Panel of Experts on Food Security and Nutrition of the Committee on World Food Security. Report No. 9. Rome: FAO.

Hoekstra, A.Y. 2013. *Water Footprint of Modern Consumer Society*. Abingdon, UK: Taylor & Francis Group.

Joint Monitoring Programme (JMP). 2012. *Drinking Water. Equity, Safety and Sustainability*. JMP Thematic report on drinking water. New York and Geneva: UNICEF and WHO.

Leach, M., Scoones, I. and Stirling, A. 2010. *Dynamic Sustainabilities: Technology, Environment, Social Justice*. London: Earthscan.

Mehta, L. 2014. Water and human development. *World Development*, 59: 59–69.

Mehta, L. 2016. Why invisible power and structural violence persist in the water domain. *IDS Bulletin*, 47(5): 31–42.

Mehta, L. and Movik, S. 2014. Liquid dynamics: Challenges for sustainability in the water domain. *Wiley Interdisciplinary Reviews: Water*, 1(4): 369–384.

Mitra, A. and Rao, N. 2019. Gender, water and nutrition in India: An intersectional analysis. *Water Alternatives*, 12(1): 169–191.

Moss, T. 2003. Solving problems of 'fit' at the expense of problems of 'interplay'? The spatial reorganisation of water management following the EU Water Framework Directive. In H. Breit, A. Engels, T. Moss and M. Troja, eds. *How Institutions Change: Perspectives on Social Learning in Global and Local Environmental Contexts*, pp. 85–122. Leske and Budrick, Opladen: VS Verlag für Sozialwissenschaften.

OECD. 2012. *OECD Environmental Outlook 2050: The Consequences of Inaction*. OECD Publishing. Available at: http://dx.doi.org/10.1787/9789264122246-en. Accessed April 2019.

Palaniappan, M., Gleick, P., Allen, L., Cohen, M., Christian-Smith, J. and Smith, C. 2010. *Clearing the Waters: A Focus on Water Quality Solutions*. Editor: Nancy Ross. Nairobi: UNEP. Available at: www.unep.org/PDF/Clearing_the_Waters.pdf.

Progressio, CEPES and Water Witness. 2010. Drop by drop: Understanding the impacts of the UK's water footprint through a case study of Peruvian asparagus. London: Progressio.the impacts of the

Ringler, C., Biswas, A. and Cline, S.A. (eds.). 2010. *Global Change: Impacts on Water and Food Security*. Berlin: Springer.

Ringler, C. 2017. *Investments in Irrigation for Global Food Security*. Washington, DC: International Food Policy Research Institute (IFPRI). Available at: https://doi.org/10.2499/9780896292543.

Rosegrant, M.W., Cai, X., Cline, S. and Nakagawa, N. 2002. *The Role of Rainfed Agriculture in the Future of Global Food Production*. EPTD Discussion Paper 90. Washington, DC: IFPRI.

Sen, A. 1981. *Poverty and Famines: An Essay on Entitlement and Deprivation*. Oxford, UK: Clarendon Press.

Sen, A. 1983. Development: Which way now? *The Economic Journal*, 93(372): 745–762.

UN World Water Assessment Programme (UN WWAP). 2012. *The United Nations World Water Development Report 4: Managing Water under Uncertainty and Risk*. Paris: UNESCO.

UN WWAP. 2014. *UN World Water Development Report 2014: Water and Energy*. Paris: UNESCO.

United Nations Development Programme (UNDP). 2006. *Beyond Scarcity: Power, Poverty and the Global Crises*. Human Development Report 2006. New York: UNDP.

United Nations, Department of Economic and Social Affairs (UN DESA), Population Division. 2017. *World Population Prospects: The 2017 Revision*. DVD Edition.

Van Koppen, B., Tarimo, A., Sumuni, P. and Shimiyu, K. 2013. *Uluguru Mountains Field Study*. Unpublished report. Pretoria: International Management Institute.

WCD (World Commission on Dams). 2000. *Dams and Development: A New Framework for Decision-Making*. London: Earthscan.

Welle, K. 2013. *Monitoring Performance or Performing Monitoring. The Case of Rural Water Access in Ethiopia*. Unpublished PhD Dissertation. Brighton, UK: University of Sussex.

WHO. 2016. *WASH Post-2015: Proposed Indicators for Drinking Water, Sanitation and Hygiene*. Available at: www.who.int/water_sanitation_health/monitoring/coverage/wash-post-2015-brochure/en/. Accessed 29 July 2016.

World Health Organisation (WHO) and the United Nations Children's Fund (UNICEF). 2017. *Progress on Drinking Water, Sanitation and Hygiene: 2017 Update and SDG Baselines*. Geneva and New York: WHO and UNICEF.

Wutich, A. and Brewis, A. 2014. Food, water, and scarcity: Toward a broader anthropology of resource insecurity. *Current Anthropology*, 55(4): 444–468.

2
LINKING WATER AND FOOD SECURITY AND NUTRITION (FSN)

Water is fundamental to the achievement of food security and nutrition and there are complex and critical links between the two. Water is not only a food in itself, essential for human life, but is also a key factor in food production and transformation, food consumption and nutrient absorption. Food security and nutrition are thus strongly influenced by issues of access to water, water availability, water quality, and stability of these factors across time.

This chapter details the key linkages between FSN and water and unpacks the issues of access to water for FSN for women, men and children living in poverty and marginalized groups in particular. The key linkages between water and FSN are depicted in Figure 2.1. Four dimensions of water: availability, access, quality and their stability over time and space are depicted on the left.

These four dimensions of water security (referring only to fresh and brackish water, not sea water) mirror the four dimensions of food security: availability, access, utilization and stability (see also a similar approach by Webb and Iskandarani, 1998 and Figure 2.5), with interactions taking place at a range of levels and scales.[1] The translation of available water resources into food security and nutrition is dependent on a number of factors, including competition between different water use sectors; relevant policies and strategies including those relating to water, trade, and environmental management; and investment in water infrastructure, including maintenance investment, and investment in agricultural development. Other factors that affect access to nutritious food are sociopolitical, such as class, race, gender and other forms of social exclusion. Each of these is discussed briefly below.

Freshwater enters the Earth's surface as rainfall or snow that runs off or melts to form rivers, lakes and groundwater sources that can be used by humans, or

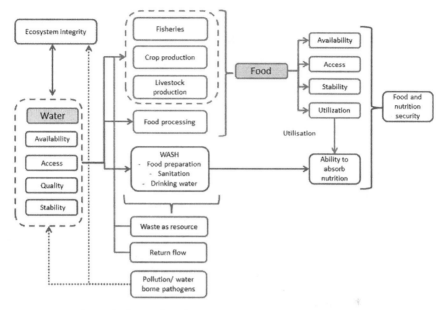

FIGURE 2.1 The multiple interfaces between water and food security and nutrition (FSN)
Source: © B Schreiner 2013

returns to the atmosphere through evapotranspiration within the hydrological cycle. Water availability relates to the physical and economic availability of water in a particular area – globally, regionally and locally through, for example, rainfall, rivers, aquifers, wetlands, dams and lakes. Availability is shaped by climate, land use and local geology, among others.

While more than 100,000 km^3 of water reaches the Earth in the form of precipitation, only around 40,000 km^3 are available for human use. Moreover, only a share of these resources can actually be accessed by humans; access is subject to the co-location of water resources and human settlements, appropriate infrastructure, such as pumps, pipelines, taps and canals, as well as existing rules and laws that govern actual water extraction and use. For many human water uses, specific water quality standards need to be considered, which further restricts water access.

While there may be sufficient water in dams, rivers, lakes and aquifers globally, on average, distribution across the year and among geographies is highly varied with some areas, countries and regions being blessed with abundance and others subject to seasonal or chronic scarcity. Moreover, the allocation of water and the authorization to use water, as well as the infrastructure to get water to where it is needed, and at the quality needed, varies dramatically across the globe, and this allocation may either support FSN or hamper it (see Chapter 4). The issue of access to water for FSN is particularly important for people living in poverty, and marginalized groups. Access is profoundly shaped by socio-cultural, economic and political factors.

Water quality has different implications for FSN depending on its use in the food value chain, whether it is being used for irrigation, food processing, food preparation, drinking or hygiene. Quality requirements are particularly high for drinking water and some industrial processes, such as food processing and food preparation, with somewhat lower quality needs for irrigation of some horticultural crops and yet lower levels for cereal crops. Polluted water applied to plants not only affects human health and the environment, but also the crops themselves. As an example, while some crops tolerate relatively high concentrations of salt in applied irrigation water, such as barley or date palms, others, such as strawberries and beans, tolerate little or no salinity.

While agricultural production relies on water of a certain quality, it also pollutes water resources – through the runoff of fertilizers and pesticides, but also soil erosion – as well as livestock waste and runoff from aquaculture systems. Water pollution is also caused by food processing and preparation. Management of water pollution generally differentiates between addressing point source pollution, which emanates from point sources, such as polluting industries or cities, and nonpoint source pollution, such as runoff from agricultural fields. In most countries that have effective policies in place to control water pollution, some success in pollution control has been achieved for point source pollution, while managing nonpoint source pollution remains a major challenge.

The stability of water refers to the adequate availability, access and quality of water over time. The hydrological cycle and climate manifest themselves through dry and wet, and cold and hot seasons within years and through dry and wet years or periods across years. Stability of water security is also affected by human interferences into the water cycle, such as climate change, which disturb the availability, access and quality of water.

Aquatic ecosystem integrity not only supports these four dimensions of water security, but the effective management of water enables the maintenance of ecosystem integrity. Water is an input into fisheries, crop and livestock production, and water supply, sanitation and hygiene (WASH). Arising from these processes are return flows and wastewater and pollution. These can be harnessed positively to support further production of food, but can also have negative feedback effects if not appropriately managed. As shown in the diagram, WASH is particularly important in relation to the preparation of nutritious food and is also possibly linked to the ability to absorb nutrients. Finally, water bodies, if not well managed, are also breeding sites for vector- and water-borne diseases. The interlinkages between water and these four dimensions of food security are discussed in greater detail below.

Food security and nutrition

Food security has four dimensions – availability, access, utilization and stability. Availability refers to the physical existence of sufficient, diverse, nutritious food that is culturally appropriate (see HLPE, 2012). Access refers to the ability of people to gain access to an appropriate food supply to provide a nutritionally diverse diet. Utilization refers to the ability of an individual to ingest and absorb the necessary nutrients from food in order to live a healthy life. And stability refers to the stability of these three elements over time.

These elements operate at different scales, as indicated in Figure 2.2. Access to and use of sufficient water of adequate quality is essential for the production of food. Food security can be measured at a global, regional, national and household level. Different policies, investments and institutions are used by actors at these varying levels to address identified levels of food insecurity. Access to food can be examined at the community, household or individual level. Utilization, on the other hand, only operates at the individual level. Stability, finally, transcends all of these scales.

The number of undernourished people in the world has increased to nearly 821 million in 2017, from around 804 million in 2016 as a result of civil conflict and strife, dispossessions from natural resources and agrarian crises combined with climate-related uncertainties, according to various UN agencies. Food insecurity has thus returned to levels last seen almost a decade ago – with increases in Africa but also South America and slowing declines in Asia. In sub-Saharan Africa, close to a quarter of the population may have suffered from chronic food deprivation in 2017. Clearly, the trends are opposite from the goals laid out in SDG2 and water is a key factor in worsening food security. Without increased efforts, the world will fall far short of achieving the SDG target of eradicating hunger by 2030 (FAO, IFAD, UNICEF, WFP and WHO, 2018).

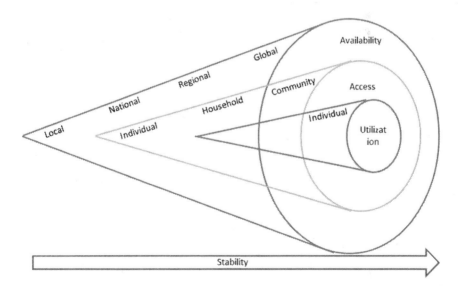

FIGURE 2.2 The four dimensions of food security and the scale at which they operate

Nutrition is an important indicator of food security and food insecurity increases the risks of malnutrition. The triple burden of malnutrition relates to undernutrition, micronutrient malnutrition and overweight and obesity. Trends in all three areas are linked to the four pillars of water (availability, access, quality and stability). In 2017, 22% of children (or 151 million children) below the age of five were stunted, while 51 million suffered from wasting. A further 6% of children were overweight. At the same time, adult obesity continues to rise and now affects about 13% of the global population. On the other hand, in terms of micronutrient deficiencies, globally, one in three women of reproductive age is still affected by anaemia, with significant health and development consequences for both women and their children (FAO, IFAD, UNICEF, WFP and WHO, 2018). In the United States, with its longer-term prevalence of an affordably priced, heavily processed, densely caloric, low-nutritional food system, obesity among adults is about 39.8%, with those over 40 years of age having a higher rate of obesity (Hales *et al.*, 2017).

While globally and in the group of developing countries more than half of the population resides in urban areas, the majority of the poor and hungry continue to live in rural areas, where family farming and smallholder agriculture is a prevailing – albeit not universal – mode of farm organization. Although the ability of family farming and smallholder agriculture to spur growth through productivity increases varies considerably, its role in reducing poverty and hunger is key. Labour and land productivity increases can have significant, positive effects on the livelihoods of the poor through increases in food availability and incomes (FAO *et al.*, 2015).

At the same time, food insecurity and poverty are closely linked. This is because the poorest have limited or no access to physical and financial resources, little or no education, and often suffer from ill health. Poor agricultural households lack access to sufficient, high-quality land and other natural resources or to remunerative sources of income (self-employment, wage labour). At the same time, hunger creates a trap from which people cannot easily escape. Hunger and undernutrition mean less-productive individuals, who are more prone to disease and thus often unable to earn more and improve their livelihoods. Poorer food producers are also less likely to invest in higher-return, higher-risk assets than better-off households. All of this, in turn, hinders progress in alleviating extreme poverty and fighting hunger – particularly as labour is the principal asset held by the poor (Barrett *et al.*, 2016; FAO *et al.*, 2015).

Women play important roles as food producers managing productive resources, and also as income earners; and they are key providers of unpaid care work in rural households and communtunities. However, despite decades of efforts to address gender inequalities, many rural women continue to face gender-based constraints that limit their capacity to contribute to growth and take advantage of new opportunities arising from the changes shaping national economies. This has serious consequences for well-being – not only for the women themselves, but also for their families and societies at large. Moreover, gender inequalities contribute to economic underperformance of agriculture as women's full potential in productive activities remains underutilized. Inequities are also prevalent in the food security and nutrition area. Analysis of Food Insecurity Experience Scale (FIES) data collected by the FAO suggests that the prevalence of severe food insecurity is slightly higher among women (FAO, IFAD, UNICEF, WFP and WHO, 2018).

The linkages between food security and international trade are complex and context-specific. The expansion of agricultural trade has helped provide a greater quantity, wider variety and better quality of food to a growing number of people at lower prices. Trade in agricultural commodities has gradually increased globally and imports of agricultural commodities (livestock and crops) now constitutes around 35% of the total agricultural production value for the same commodity groups, up from 28% in the mid-1990s. Due to the food security role of agricultural trade, policies supporting food trade are frequently influenced by national interests, which has led to widespread distortions in world agricultural markets. One of the most damaging distortions, the practice of export dumping – that is of selling products in the export market at a price lower than their cost of production – can adversely impact food security of competing farming communities in importing nations as it undermines their economic viability (Murphy and Hansen-Kuhn, 2017).

As a result of growing urbanization, the farm economy is shrinking almost everywhere in the world (with the exception of Africa where the rural population continues to grow). Another challenge is lack of interest among youth to enter farming, and this is due to a number of factors, including agrarian crises, unfavourable farming conditions and low prices for agricultural produce, as well as a lack of support for newer and younger farmers. Policies that affect exports and imports of food contribute to determining relative prices, wages and incomes in domestic agricultural markets, and hence shape the ability of poor people to access food, and smallholder farmers to make a viable living. Trade is, in itself, neither a threat nor a panacea for food security. While the possibility to import food is essential for countries that suffer from chronic water scarcity and those subject to climatic shocks, the opportunities and risks to food security associated with trade openness should be carefully assessed and addressed through an expanded set of policy instruments (FAO, 2015), such as grain-reserves and supply management to help ensure stable food prices for food producers and food security for consumers.

Water security

Less than half of the approximately 110,000 km^3 of rainfall that falls every year on the globe, around 40,000 km^3, is available for use in dams, lakes, rivers, wetlands, streams and aquifers (CA, 2007). Aquifers receive around 13,000 km^3 of the annual rainfall (Döll, 2009) while over half of the annual precipitation evapotranspires. Rainfall runoff into rivers, lakes, wetlands and groundwater is known as 'blue water', while rainfall that is stored in soils is known as 'green water'.

Freshwater resources show significant variation in distribution across different regions of the world, as well as between and within years. With similarly large variations in the distribution of the global population across the world, there are significant variations in per capita water availability between countries (UN WWAP, 2012) (see Figure 2.3). Thus, while there are sufficient freshwater resources at global level to meet human needs, their uneven distribution across regions means that in some areas there are significant water constraints, including for food production and other human needs, while other areas are characterized by abundance and sometimes over-abundance, such as parts of Bangladesh during the monsoon season. Annual per capita freshwater resources are particularly constrained in the Middle Eastern, North African and South Asian regions.

As the global population, urbanization rates and living standards increase, demand for water is rising across all water-using sectors. Over recent decades, the rate of water demand has been around twice the rate of population growth (Shiklomanov, 1999). The global population is estimated to reach 9.8 billion people by 2050. Of these, 2.2 billion people will be living in sub-Saharan Africa which is the region with the greatest differentials in per capita water availability (see Figure 2.3) (UNDESA, 2017).

As the largest user of freshwater withdrawals, the agricultural sector is key to addressing global water challenges. While agricultural water use is expected to continue to grow, demand is increasing much faster in the non-agricultural sectors, putting pressure on water availability for food production (Rosegrant et al., 2002). However, the issue of water scarcity and shortages of water for food production is not a purely physical or hydrological issue. It is also, at its heart, a political and economic issue (see below). Lack of infrastructure and management capacity may impact at the national, sub-national or even at the community level, and in all cases, people living in poverty experience the largest challenges to access and use water resources (Mehta, 2005; UNDP, 2006).

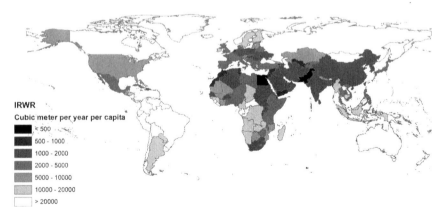

FIGURE 2.3 Internal renewable water resources per capita in 2005 in m^3
Source: IFPRI IMPACT Simulations. 2019

Sadoff et al. (2015) differentiate between 'simple hydrologies' – those that provide relatively reliable and plentiful water resources, generally located in more temperate regions – and 'difficult hydrologies' – characterized by unpredictable climate extremes and high inter-annual and/or intra-annual variability of rainfall and runoff. They proceed to identify an inverse relationship between hydrological complexity and per capita wealth. As such, poorer countries have the double burden of needing to find resources to manage water security within highly constrained budgets and to manage more complex water resource availability, stability and associated access and quality situations. Figure 2.4 links hydrological complexity with relative investment needs. Many poorer countries are in quadrant IV with high hydrological complexity and low capacity to meet the high costs of the information, infrastructure and institutions required to increase water security. Latin America and the Middle East and North Africa region cover parts of all four quadrants (Grey et al., 2013). Thus, issues of water availability, stability, access and quality do not equally apply to all individuals, households, countries and regions and in each situation access will always be socially mediated.

Those households and countries facing higher hydrological complexity and larger needs for investments are generally more vulnerable to both water and food insecurity, whereas those countries and households in areas of low hydrological complexity and with high levels of investments in infrastructure and institutions face reduced water and food insecurity. Water demands generally continue to grow in the global South whereas demands have stabilized in industrial countries and in those with declining populations and limited irrigated agriculture.

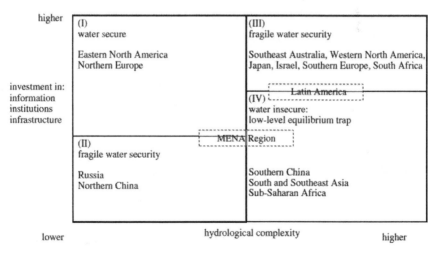

FIGURE 2.4 Country-wise classification of different countries along hydrological complexity

Source: Grey et al., 2013

The dynamics of water scarcity

A key element of the issue of water and FSN is the concept of increasing water scarcity (see Falkenmark and Lannerstad, 2005; FAO, 2012a). Water resources have particular characteristics that make them distinct from other natural resources. Water is fluid in nature and mostly a renewable resource. This means that the availability of water fluctuates in space and time, which is relevant when assessing water allocation and distribution. Water scarcity is a complex phenomenon and can be analysed differently from social, political, meteorological, hydrological and agricultural perspectives. There has been the tendency to direct attention to the lack of supply of water due to natural and economic forces rather than to look at human-induced land and water use practices and at socio-political considerations (see Mehta, 2005; UNDP, 2006).

Scarcity of water is typically examined through two lenses – the first looks at the amount of water available per capita in a particular area, taking into account the average volume of water available in rivers, lakes, dams and groundwater aquifers per person. This is considered physical scarcity of water. For example, Figure 2.3 shows differences in per capita freshwater availability across the world. The Swedish hydrologist Malin Falkenmark and colleagues (see Falkenmark and Widstrand, 1992) have classified countries according to a 'water stress index' on the basis of their annual water resources and population. This widely adopted definition proposes a threshold of 1700 m^3 per person per annum below which countries are said to be water-stressed and water scarcity is less than 1000 m^3 per person per annum.

However, this does not indicate whether that water is available for use or accessed. For example, according to UNEP (2011), an estimated 51 million people in the Democratic Republic of the Congo (DRC), around three quarters of the population, had no access to safe drinking water in 2011, even though the country is considered water rich and has more than half of Africa's water reserves. Thus, in some areas there may be a sufficient volume of water available per person, but lack of infrastructure means that the water is not available where it is needed, or of an appropriate quality for use. This is deemed economic water scarcity (CA, 2007). There are a number of countries, such as the DRC, where the challenge lies in economic water scarcity, rather than physical water scarcity and where with appropriate infrastructure and management, there is sufficient water to provide for the needs of the population and for equitable and sustainable economic development, including improved agricultural yields. In these countries, access to water is determined by lack of investment rather than lack of water.

But both these lenses obscure other key dimensions of water scarcity. They tend to direct attention to natural and economic forces rather than look at human-induced land and water use practices and at socio-political considerations and how scarcity can be socially mediated or constructed (Mehta, 2005; UNDP, 2006). They also tend to take an aggregate view of populations lacking access to water, rather than breaking down groups due to gender, caste, race and so forth. Thus, it is important to also focus on the socio-political dimensions of scarcity and how access to water is often determined by social difference as well as political will and levels of national economic development. Thus, people's lack of access to water may have little to do with physical scarcity per se but may instead be due to exclusions arising from social positioning, gender or because of the way water is managed, priced and regulated (see Mehta, 2014 and UNDP, 2006). Mehta (2005) distinguishes between 'lived/experienced' scarcity (something that local people experience cyclically due to the biophysical shortage of food, water, fodder etc.) and 'constructed' scarcity (something that is manufactured through socio-political processes to suit the interests of powerful players). Her focus was water scarcity in western India and the role of the dam-building lobby and rich irrigators and agro-industrialists in promoting large dams over more decentralized approaches to deal with water scarcity in the drylands. A similar approach to water is provided by the 2006 Human Development Report entitled 'Beyond Scarcity: Power, Poverty and the Global Water Crisis' (see UNDP, 2006) which has explicitly focused on the role of power relations and unequal access in determining water scarcity.

Finally, scarcity can also be induced through policies and planning. Subsidies for electricity have led to increased pumping for irrigation in India and inefficient use/overexploitation of water resources (Narula and Lall, 2009) and also in Mexico (Scott, 2011). In western India, the over-extraction of groundwater and the planting of water-hungry sugarcane in drought-prone areas by large irrigators is juxtaposed with dryland farmers who struggle during droughts to meet their basic food requirements (Mehta, 2005). Finally, decisions outside the water domain such as those concerning energy, trade, agricultural subsidies and so on, often impact on water supply and demand, and hence on water scarcity (FAO, 2012a: 60; Ringler et al., 2010).

Water and food security and nutrition

Water is a critical factor in achieving each of the four dimensions of food security (FAO, 2000; see Figure 2.5).

Water is in itself a food and source of important micronutrients, particularly for fluoride, calcium and magnesium, but there is also a risk of undesirable nutrients, such as arsenic, or excess nutrients, such as too much fluoride, in some regions (Olivares and Uauy, 2005; Wenhold and Faber, 2009). Water is also essential for food production (fisheries, crops and livestock), food processing (industrial to household level) and food preparation (at household level as well as by formal and informal food vendors). Drinking water polluted with human or livestock waste is a major contributor to diarrhoea; water is also the breeding habitat for a series of vector-borne diseases, such as malaria; and runoff from agricultural fields can pollute water with nitrates or pesticide compounds that can cause cancer and other diseases in humans and animals. Water is also a key

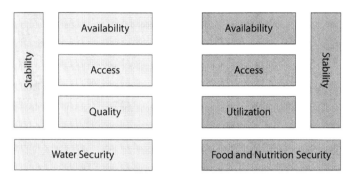

FIGURE 2.5 The four pillars of water security and of food and nutrition security
Source: Authors

input for industry and to support economic growth. Finally, it is the lifeblood of ecosystems on which all humans depend, including forests, lakes and wetlands, and which are central specifically to the food security of those communities that engage in small-scale production systems.

Water and the availability of FSN

Availability of food refers to the physical existence of enough food to support the FSN needs of all people. This food can be derived from domestic production and stocks, food imports, or food aid. The growing and processing of food, whether livestock, aquaculture, rainfed or irrigated crops, requires sufficient water of an appropriate quality. Processing of food is an important way of extending its shelf-life which contributes to the availability of food over time. The availability of food, particularly at the regional level, is vulnerable to changes in water availability, particularly arising from droughts, but also from floods where too much water can directly affect livestock and crop survival and indirectly destroy rural infrastructure that supports transportation, storage and retail of these agricultural commodities. Water quality is also an important element of food production and processing. Poor water quality can affect human well-being and health (see also Chapter 4). It can also impact negatively on crop growth, on livestock, and on food processing as well as on the humans who labour in the fields.

While less than a third of the world's harvested land is irrigated, irrigated crop areas generate 40% of global food production. Almost 40% of total irrigated farmland is concentrated in the East Asia and Pacific region, and more than 30% in South Asia. The largest irrigated areas can be found in India, China and the United States, which are also major contributors to the world's food supplies. At the same time, only 5% of harvested crop area in sub-Saharan Africa is irrigated (Ringler, 2017).

Over the last five decades, extraction of groundwater has increased dramatically to support agricultural development in many parts of the world, including China, India, the United States and parts of the Middle East (Siebert *et al.*,

2010). Today, more than one third of global irrigated cropland relies on groundwater. Resulting groundwater depletion and degradation impacts farmers, rural communities and the environment through drying up of springs and wetlands, and salinization and pollution of water resources. Availability of free or cheap electricity for pumping (more recently through solar) contributes to the overuse of groundwater. Addressing groundwater depletion is particularly challenging because it cannot be easily observed and the many users of groundwater are often dispersed.

While groundwater development continues to expand, particularly with the increased availability of cheap solar pumps, overall possibilities for expanding irrigation for food are increasingly under threat, as non-agricultural demands for water and biofuel production rapidly rise, and soil degradation, groundwater depletion and water pollution from poor irrigation management continue to worsen. Climate variability and climate change only exacerbate these challenges. Moreover, if not properly managed, irrigation can cause increased exposure to waterborne diseases, such as malaria, as well as toxic compounds in pesticides and, therefore, to possible health risks. While irrigation has reached physical and economic barriers in many places, an assessment by IFPRI suggests that between 2010 and 2030, total irrigated crop area will increase by 12% to 394 million hectares, with the largest increase in sub-Saharan Africa (44% of the total), followed by South Asia and Latin America and the Caribbean (Ringler, 2017).

Despite these irrigation developments around the world, rainfed agriculture continues to support most food production globally, that is, around 60% of total production in 2010; and irrigated production too, in most locations, depends to some extent on precipitation supplies. The largest rainfed areas are located in sub-Saharan Africa, but these areas are subject to large inter-annual variability in precipitation levels, which hinders investment in agricultural intensification.

While there have been various scenarios and projections in terms of water requirements by different sectors over various timescales, there remains considerable uncertainty with regards to the development of real demand due to poor baseline data in many countries on national and sub-national sectoral withdrawals, rapid changes in use patterns informed by different drivers, and high uncertainty regarding technological change (UN WWAP, 2012). There is also insufficient understanding of future demands for water for food production. According to the IPCC, climatic changes (including changes in precipitation, temperature and radiation) are likely to result in an increase in agricultural water demand in irrigated and rainfed systems (Jiménez Cisneros et al., 2014). Irrigation demand is projected to increase by more than 40% in some areas, with significant regional variance (ibid.). This is over and above the increasing water demand for the expansion of agriculture in order to meet the FSN needs of a growing population. However, there are other experts who suggest that agricultural water demand will decline substantially over the next several decades (Konzmann et al., 2013; OECD, 2012) due to the beneficial CO_2 effects on plants, shorter growing periods, regional precipitation increases under climate change and presumed stagnation of irrigation development.

One key factor that affects future water-for-food demands is changing diets (see Emerging Trends, this chapter). Income growth and urbanization are linked to changing consumption patterns toward more livestock, sugar, fruit and vegetable products, many of which are either more water-intensive or more water-polluting agricultural commodities (Ringler and Zhu, 2015). Poultry, pork and beef require much larger quantities of water per unit of nutritional energy compared to foods of plant origin (Gerbens-Leenes *et al.*, 2013). As a result, animal-sourced food is currently associated with one third of freshwater withdrawals (Mekonnen and Hoekstra, 2012). Willett *et al.* (2019) propose scientific targets for achieving healthy diets from sustainable food systems, with a focus on vegetables, fruits, whole grains, legumes, nuts and unsaturated oils, as well as a low to moderate amount of seafood and poultry, and no to limited consumption of red meat, processed meat, added sugar, refined grains, and starchy vegetables.

Generally, few economic instruments are used to manage the demand for water for food production while many complementary policies, such as agricultural input and output price policies, lead to injudicious or wasteful use of agricultural water for food production as well as water pollution. As discussed earlier in this chapter, examples include subsidized electricity and, more recently, subsidies for solar pumps, which contribute to increased pumping for irrigation and overexploitation of groundwater resources in India (Narula and Lall, 2009); and elsewhere (Closas and Rap, 2017). Finally, decisions outside the water domain such as those concerning energy, trade, mining and extractive industries and agricultural input subsidies often impact on water supply and demand, and hence on relative water scarcity for other economic or social sectors (Ringler *et al.*, 2010).

Water and access to FSN

According to the FAO, food security is achieved, 'if adequate food (quantity, quality, safety, socio-cultural acceptability) is available and accessible for and satisfactorily utilized by all individuals at all times to live a healthy and happy life' (FAO, 2000: 4). Food can be grown, bought, or obtained through gifts and donations, including food aid. In low-income tropical and water-scarce countries, access to food is generally higher during the rainy season when water is available or sufficient for food production and lower during the dry or lean season when food access is limited to existing storage, imports and areas with sufficient irrigation.

The development of irrigated agriculture has boosted agricultural yields and increased the number of cropping seasons to two or more in many parts of the world, thereby conserving important forest resources, contributing to price stability under climate variability, and helping to feed the world's growing population. Growing food at the household or community level is a critical element of ensuring access to FSN. This is strongly affected by the quality and availability of water for the production of household crops and livestock. Access to water for productive purposes and for domestic purposes tends to differ by socio-economic status, gender, age and position within the household. Gender, social and other dimensions in access to irrigation vary in both small-scale and large-scale irrigation systems and challenges can be larger in private or so-called farmer-led irrigation as, in those cases, individual farmers are responsible for accessing the water source as well as for acquiring the irrigation technology.

Irrigation can bring many benefits to a community, including greater diversity in available foods; income from market sales and employment generation, particularly in the lean season; and water supply, sanitation, and hygiene through multiple-use irrigation systems that can help reduce environmental enteric dysfunction (an acquired disorder of the small intestine). In addition, irrigation can increase women's opportunities for asset ownership, their control over resources, and their time, because they are often responsible for collecting water. As such, irrigation can make important contributions to women's empowerment as well as to nutrition and health outcomes. Domènech (2015) describes several potential pathways through which irrigation can positively influence food security, nutrition and health outcomes, including 1) a production pathway, 2) an income pathway, 3) a water supply pathway and 4) a women's empowerment pathway. A fifth pathway links irrigation with water pollution and disease via the application of fertilizers, pesticides and via vector-borne diseases, such as malaria or schistosomiasis. The production pathway relates to how irrigation can support increased agricultural productivity, shift crops grown to more nutrient-rich crops, such as fruits and vegetables, and extend the production calendar into the lean season, all of which could contribute to improved food security, dietary diversity, and nutritional status. The income pathway describes how irrigation can grow income from market sales of crops grown with irrigation as well as irrigation-related employment. Irrigation can also improve the WASH environment by providing multiple water uses, but this requires systems that are designed to meet the needs of both agricultural production and domestic uses. Irrigation is also a potential entry point for women's empowerment through increased asset ownership, due to the transfer of time spent on water collection to other income-generating activities, due to reduced time use in agriculture (particularly for motorized irrigation technologies) and control over resources from selling crops produced on their own plots. To achieve any of these potential positive nutrition benefits, irrigation will also need to be designed, developed and managed to reduce potentially adverse impacts on nutrition and health, through judicious fertilizer and pesticide applications and control of vector- and water-borne diseases (Passarelli et al., 2018).

Empowering women through access to irrigation is particularly challenging (Theis et al., 2018a, Box 2.1). According to Lefore et al. (2019), in sub-Saharan Africa most smallholder farmers face large barriers to access water management technologies or the complementary inputs and markets required to benefit from irrigated production. The women who do irrigate are more likely to use highly labour-intensive manual methods of lifting and applying water, such as buckets and watering cans, while men are more likely to use more expensive, labour-saving mechanized technologies such as solar or diesel pumps.

Moreover, among smallholders with access, better-off male farmers are more likely to manage irrigation enterprises (Colenbrander and van Koppen, 2013) while women are constrained by limited access to credit, weak land rights, competing demands on their time, poor market integration and inadequate information services (Theis et al., 2018b). Underdeveloped technology supply chains and limited financing options also limit the increase of irrigation technologies on the supply side (Merrey and Lefore, 2018). Without direct support, farmer-led irrigation could increase rural inequities and further marginalize disadvantaged groups (Lefore et al., 2019; see also Chapter 4 for a further discussion on gender, social difference and access to water and food). Mitra and Rao have built on HLPE (2015) to analyse links between gender, water and nutrition in India. They conclude that water availability, access, quality and stability are interlinked with local ecologies, farming systems, gender, caste and social relations, and argue for the need to shift away from the binaries of production and reproduction to include holistic and intersectional perspectives.

> **BOX 2.1 CHALLENGES TO GENDER AND SOCIAL INCLUSION IN SMALL-SCALE IRRIGATION**
>
> 1. **Design.** Women often prefer different irrigation technologies than men and will not adopt technology that does not meet their needs. This includes the location or portability of the technology, its suitability for multiple uses (drinking water, irrigation, livestock watering), associated labour requirements, the social acceptability of use, and upfront and operational costs.
> 2. **Dissemination.** For women to participate in the irrigation technology space, information about irrigation technology needs to reach them. Traditional channels, such as farmer field days and trainings or working through extension agents, producer groups, or equipment dealers, may leave women out. Instead, dissemination through women community leaders, savings groups, frontline health workers, or women-led farmers and producer groups needs to be considered.
> 3. **Adoption.** Limited access to credit remains a key challenge for women to purchase small-scale irrigation technologies. In addition, irrigators need access to irrigable land, water, labour and markets to buy inputs and sell irrigated produce. Women are disadvantaged in each of these areas. Furthermore, within the household, a woman often needs her husband's consent to purchase technologies, including irrigation technologies.

4. **Use.** Once the irrigation technology is adopted, men and women, even within the same household, may experience different impacts, such as on workload, power to decide on whose plots of land the technology is used, and control over the income generated. More powerful actors in the family or outside can appropriate land after women farmers make investments in irrigation.

Adapted from Theis *et al.* (2018a); see also Chapter 3, Box 3.3.

As water is, in itself, a food, access to water of an appropriate quality for consumption is a critical part of achieving universal access to food. In 2010, the United Nations General Assembly and the UN Human Rights Council recognized access to safe drinking-water and sanitation as a human right. Access to safe water is associated with reduced occurrence of enteric infection and reduced incidence of disease in pregnant women. Access is also important for reducing maternal and neonatal mortality rates. This in turn can reduce stunting and improve nutrition outcomes during the first 1,000 days (Cumming and Cairncross, 2016).

Those still lacking access to safe drinking water and sanitation tend to be poorer and more marginalized groups. WHO (2012) estimated economic losses associated with inadequate water supply and sanitation at US$260 billion annually, or 1.5% of Gross Domestic Product of the countries studied. They also estimated a global economic return on investment in sanitation and drinking water of US$5.5 and US$2.0 per US dollar invested using 2010 data. The key benefits from improved access to these services would be for health and time savings. Several important benefits from improved access, such as the potential of nutrient reuse, an overall cleaner environment, dignity and security have not been valued in this analysis. More than one third of total investment needs are in the sub-Saharan Africa region.

In addition to important water–nutrition linkages, if not managed and governed within the context of the wider landscape and other water users' needs, accelerated investments in irrigation can deplete water resources and reduce availability for other uses, including domestic and environmental uses of water, can degrade water and soil quality, and can increase conflict and civil strife, as well as create conflicts over shared natural resources (de Fraiture and Giordano, 2014; Theis *et al.*, 2018b).

Access to water as a socio-political construct

As discussed earlier in this chapter, aggregate views of water scarcity can be problematic because they can hide real inequalities in water access determined by property rights, social and political institutions, and cultural and gender norms. In Chapter 1, we highlighted that Amartya Sen has argued that the per capita food availability decline (FAD) is a misleading way to assess hunger and famine, since hunger is more about people not having access to food due to wider social and political arrangements as opposed to there not being enough food to eat (Sen, 1981). Similarly, people's lack of access to water may have little to do with physical scarcity per se but may instead be due to exclusions arising from social positioning, gender or because of the way water is managed, priced and regulated (Mehta, 2014). For example, deeply rooted traditional or historical inequalities can limit women's and other vulnerable groups' access to land and thereby to water for agricultural uses, which hampers livelihood strategies and negatively impacts food security (FAO, 2012a).

Gender and other markers of identities continue to mold water allocation and access among users. Cultural norms in much of the global South dictate that women and girls are responsible for water collection, and they may spend several hours per day collecting water. Unequal power relations within the household, and women's minimal control over household finances or spending, can force women into a daily trudge (taking precious time) for fetching cheaper or free untreated water, which may result in health problems and increased poverty and destitution. This time could instead be used to focus on livelihood and agricultural activities, to attend school and to improve maternal and infant health. This situation is worsened by the fact that women are often excluded from decision-making processes regarding water management projects or natural resource allocation (FAO, 2012a).

Lack of access to water is, however, unacceptable in the 21st century. This is particularly so because scarcity is not 'natural' but generated through sociopolitical processes, through exclusion, biases and discrimination (see also Mehta, 2005; UNDP, 2006). For example, in India, so called lower caste women are still denied access to certain wells. Similar shortages were created in apartheid South Africa, where around 80% of the poor in rural areas had no access to water or sanitation in 1994, at the birth of the new South Africa (see Movik, 2012). These were largely black populations, indicating how race and class lead to systematic exclusions from access to water.

According to the 2006 *Human Development Report*, which focuses in depth on water scarcity from a human development perspective, the global water crisis is overwhelmingly a crisis of the poor. The distribution of water access in many countries mirrors the distribution of wealth, and vast inequalities exist in both. The UNDP reports that those who lack access to clean water and adequate sanitation tend to live on less than two dollars per day. Furthermore, not only do the poorest people get less access to water, and even less to clean and safe water, but they also pay some of the world's highest prices for water (UNDP, 2006, p. 7, see Chapter 4 for a fuller discussion on water privatization). Overall, the public sector retains, at least in principle, the reach and the mandate to clarify rights, set prices, resolve trade-offs and ensure safe water and sanitation access for the poor and excluded, whether as a service provider or supporter, or through contracts with private firms, but in many water-scarce regions, the largest local water footprints are due to industrial and extractive activities (Chatham House, 2012; European Commission, 2012).

The persistence of water inequalities globally can be attributed in part to various power imbalances that prevent universal access. Mehta (2016) has argued that invisible power goes hand in hand with structural violence that allows certain political, social and cultural arrangements to persist that disadvantage and cause harm to marginalized social groups. This structural violence in particular disadvantages powerless and marginalized groups such as migrants, poor women, ethnic minorities, indigenous people and lower castes. Elite biases, democratic deficits (and distortions) and market-based mechanisms compound the structural violence that leads to such groups largely bearing the brunt of water-related injustices. This is why a human rights approach to water for FSN is necessary and could integrate the norms, standards and principles of the international human rights system into the plans, policies and developmental process related to resource security at the international, national and sub-national levels. The norms and principles include accountability, transparency, empowerment, participation, non-discrimination (equality and equity), and attention to vulnerable groups (see HLPE, 2015). Human rights approaches can assist in building social consensus and in mobilizing commitments to facilitate a fairer use of resources and to empower poor people. Policies and programmes that are designed from a human rights point of view are more likely to be equitable, sustainable and have the potential to eliminate extreme poverty. Clearly there are indisputable causal links between the violation of human rights, and the economic, social, cultural and political deprivations that characterize poverty and water injustices. Thus, the realization of all human rights and efforts to eliminate extreme poverty are mutually reinforcing. Chapter 5 focuses in detail on the human rights to water and food and the need to create more synergies and linkages between them.

Water quality and FSN

Water pollution affects all four pillars of FSN: the availability of food as a result of reduced availability of clean water for irrigation, the resulting reduced access to food as well as compromised utilization due to poor quality and reduced diversity of available food stuffs over space and time. Moreover, water pollution can affect all stages in the food value chain, from growing food, to processing harvested food, during the sale of food, the preparation of food and the actual consumption of food.

Agricultural water pollution is the largest nonpoint source pollution and as such much harder to control than point sources of pollution, such as those from cities or industries. Controlling nonpoint source pollution generally requires a different approach from that of addressing point source pollution, as it requires cooperation from a large number of actors spread over a watershed. The key sources of agricultural pollution are fertilizer use on crop land and livestock animal excreta. Excessive nitrogen (N) and phosphorous (P) in water bodies results in eutrophication, which can harm aquatic life by depleting oxygen. The presence of nitrogen-based compounds in drinking water can also be directly harmful to human health. Xie and Ringler (2017) estimate rapid increases in agricultural water pollution, particularly in the group of developing countries where monitoring and enforcement of water quality standards remains weak. Even less well understood and addressed are the impacts of water pollution from pesticides on ecosystems and human health. Moreover, both livestock and aquaculture production, when done on an industrial scale, are associated with significant wastewater discharge along their value chains with potential adverse impacts on human and animal health and the environment (Delgado et al., 1999).

At the same time, irrigation is also sensitive to water quality. For example, while some crops, such as barley and sugar beet are relatively tolerant to high salt levels, most fruit and nut trees and several vegetables, such as beans and carrots, are highly sensitive to salinity (Ayers and Westcot, 1985). However, regulations on the types of crops that can be irrigated with various levels of polluted wastewater are seldom enforced in the global South. As a result of growing water pollution, around 36 million hectares of irrigated areas, often in peri-urban areas, are now irrigated with untreated urban wastewater (Thebo et al., 2017). This does not include areas irrigated with arsenic-contaminated waters or waters polluted by industrial waste or other agro-pollutants.

In addition to the traditional large sources of pollutants from agriculture and affecting agriculture, a series of emergent pollutants are rapidly garnering increased attention. These include both contaminants affecting agricultural and other ecosystems, such as pharmaceuticals, antibiotics, hormones, personal care products, cyanotoxins, engineered nanomaterials, anti-microbial cleaning agents and their transformation products as well as emergent contaminants directly from agriculture, such as veterinary medicines, in particular, hormones and antibiotics, used in livestock and fish farming or aquaculture operations. Due to the global size of the livestock population and excessive use in agriculture, antimicrobial use in agriculture surpasses human use in many countries in the global North. However, impacts on human health are not yet fully understood (Evans et al., 2019).

Jawahar and Ringler (2009) note that while dietary diversification has improved the nutritional and health status in the global South, it has also added a new range of food safety risks along the value chain, principally caused by poor water management and quality which affects particularly the consumption of fresh fruits, vegetables, dairy and other animal products.

Many, if not most, food-borne illnesses can be related back to polluted water used in food production and/or postharvest processing and/or food preparation. Water can in fact be the vehicle for both pathogens and chemical contaminants that are transferred from the environment into the food chain, thus impacting on food safety and public health. WHO (2015) estimated the global burden of food-borne disease in 2010 at 33 million years lost due to ill-health, disability or early death; close to half of this burden, 40%, was among children under five years of age. Moreover, food-borne diarrhoeal disease caused an estimated 230,000 deaths in 2010.

Maintaining food safe is a complex challenge especially in the informal food production sector where street vendors and others engaged in food production face challenges to meet food safety and health standards due to lack of appropriate support policies and water services. According to FAO (2007), an estimated 2.5 billion people depended on at least one meal provided by street food vendors every day.

Many solutions exist to address agricultural water pollution and reduce exposure of pollution from food, nutrition and human health in the food value chain. Pollution from agriculture can be reduced through enhanced nutrient use efficiency, through technological interventions (either as a trait in plants or through improved fertilizer management or through biofertilization); economic interventions (chiefly the phasing out of subsidies for fertilizers); ecological interventions (including through conservation agriculture measures that reduce erosion and crop rotations with nitrogen-fixing cover crops); and through closing the nutrient cycle, based on a combination of these approaches, for example, through recovery from effluents and sewage, followed by reuse in agriculture. Appropriate reuse of wastewater can also reduce the cost of fertilizer applications, particularly phosphorus and nitrogen (Drechsel et al., 2010; Xie and Ringler, 2017). Measures to address the use of irrigation with domestic and industrial wastewater include increased investment in wastewater treatment, as well as development and enforcement of regulations for domestic and industrial waste production. The wide variety of pesticides and emergent pollutants need to be treated with pollutant-specific measures, as well as enhanced awareness raising and extension and outreach for the farming community and the general public. For some existing and emerging pollutants, international or national regulations that ensure their elimination in the manufacturing process might be preferable, particularly for those that cannot be removed through existing wastewater treatment processes and those that are highly toxic to humans, animals and plants.

Water and the utilization of food

In terms of FSN, utilization refers to the ability to ingest, digest and metabolize food. This is influenced by a number of factors which include the health status of individuals, as well as appropriate knowledge on what makes up a nutritionally appropriate diet (FAO, 2000). It also requires safe food preparation and storage processes and a clean environment in and around the house as well as acceptable access to drinking water and sanitation, as all these factors can affect household nutritional status.

The issue of utilization is an important addition to the concept of food security, recognizing, as it does, that people must be able to derive sufficient nutrition from the food to which they have access. Utilization of food is mediated by many factors, but unsafe water and sanitation have been identified as one factor that can adversely affect utilization in the form of metabolization of food.

Given the growing attention on healthy and sustainable diets (for example Willett *et al.*, 2019), combined with growing water scarcity, a substantial body of literature developed that focuses on the water content of various types of diets. Examples include Renault and Wallender (2000) who suggest that a 25% reduction in the consumption of animal products in developed countries could generate 22% of the additional water needed by 2025. Harris *et al.* (2017) find that diets in the northern part of India were more dependent on irrigation water than those in southern India and that diets of urban consumers relied more on irrigation water than diets of rural consumers.

While most global analyses assume average levels of water productivity, in reality, water productivity for different food groups and diets vary dramatically across countries, within countries, but also over time with key factors affecting final results including local climate, the quality of soils, seed and associated crop growth properties, the source of water and water management practices, among others. An example for this is presented by Malmquist (2018) who calculates the range of water productivity levels for rainfed production for different food groups in Burkina Faso, Ethiopia and Tanzania (Figure 2.6). Malmquist finds

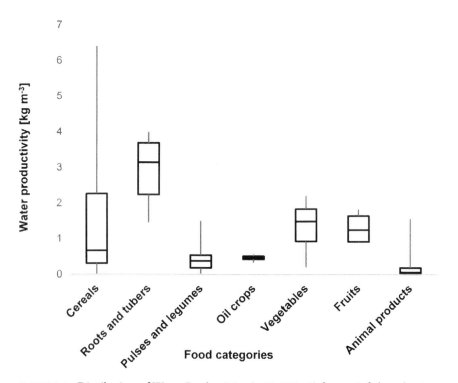

FIGURE 2.6 Distribution of Water Productivity (= Ya ETa-1) from rainfed production within food categories in diets in Burkina Faso, Ethiopia and Tanzania
Source: Malmquist, 2018

little variation in water use for oil crops and for forages and other plants and crops consumed in the animal food group. The latter is surprising, given the variation in types of meat products produced and consumed in the three countries. This narrow range contrasts with a much larger spread for cereals (which includes crops as varied as rice and teff) and roots and tubers, which also comprises a variety of crops across these countries.

Based on this assessment and insights on recommended intake levels and related income levels she then calculates the daily water use for a low, medium and high-income diet in Ethiopia as well as the calorie intake per cubic meter of crop water use (Figure 2.7). Water use of a low-income diet in Ethiopia is estimated at 0.83 m^3/capita and day, whereas water use of a high-income diet averages 6.4 m^3/capita and day. As a result, the dietary water productivity is considerably higher for the less well-off. This figure is a stark indicator of the growing agricultural water needs of wealthier populations, even in low-income countries. A second message is that while it is clear that different diets and different levels of income are linked with differential water usage, generalizations of water–nutrition relationships should be avoided.

Easy access to safe and convenient water supplies is also crucial to enhance women's and girls' well-being. Lack of appropriate sanitation facilities at schools reduces girl child attendance during menstruation, adversely impacting their

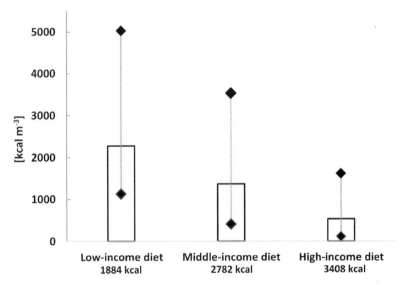

FIGURE 2.7 Dietary Water Productivity (WP$_{diet}$) for socio-economic diets in Ethiopia. Values represents lower-, median- and upper values of WP$_{diet}$ calculated with different levels of Water Productivity (WP) for ingoing food categories in the three diets. The bars present WP$_{diet}$ calculated with median WP for each food category. The lowest value for each diet is calculated with low WP per food category and the highest value is calculated with high WP per food category

education with potentially adverse impacts on the health, nutrition and well-being of their offspring.

In the transition from the MDGs to the SDGs, the Joint Monitoring Program (JMP) for drinking water and sanitation updated the definition of the indicator on the population using improved drinking water and sanitation (i.e. from JMP 2015 to JMP 2017). While the new SDG indicators for basic drinking water (improved source within 30 mins) and basic sanitation (improved facility not shared with other households) are similar to the earlier MDG indicators, the SDG indicators for safely managed drinking water (improved source located on premises, available when needed and free from contamination) and safely managed sanitation (improved facility that is not shared with other households and where excreta are either safely disposed of in situ or transported and treated offsite) are more ambitious. The global service ladders seek to disaggregate the population using improved sources located on premises, from those located within a 30-minute round trip ('basic' service) and those requiring a round trip of more than 30 minutes ('limited' service) and thereby focus attention on inequalities in accessibility and water collection times which were not addressed in MDG reporting. As such, the new, SDG-related, indicators have seemingly cut achievements of many countries under the MDGs, but for a good cause – that is, a stronger focus on the quality of the drinking water supplied.

National data on WASH are typically collected at the household level so it is not possible to routinely disaggregate by sex or other characteristics of individual household members. However, JMP has developed new questions for household surveys which identify the age and sex of the individual household member responsible for water collection, the frequency of water collection and whether the household is able to access sufficient quantities of water when needed. These, together with a new module on water quality testing and questions on Menstrual Hygiene Management among women, are now included as standard in UNICEF supported Multiple Indicator Cluster Surveys and are increasingly being adopted by other household survey programmes.

Figure 2.8 presents regional values for the updated access to drinking water indicators and Figure 2.9 presents the same for sanitation.

According to WHO/UNICEF (2017), in 2015, 7 out of 10 people across the globe used safely managed drinking water services, that is used an access point located on premises, available when needed and free from contamination. At the same time, 844 million people still lacked even a basic drinking water service and 263 million people spent over 30 minutes per round trip to collect water from an improved source (constituting a limited drinking water service). Finally, 159 million people still collected drinking water directly from surface water sources, mostly in sub-Saharan Africa. Both sub-Saharan Africa and Oceania continue to show high levels of usage of surface water and unimproved services (Figure 2.8).

Moreover, coverage remains particularly low in rural areas, where the poorest of the poor have been by-passed in the achievement of reaching the MDG target on drinking water (Mehta, 2013). The report also indicates continued lack of data coverage, disaggregation and data quality for a series of countries and regions. For

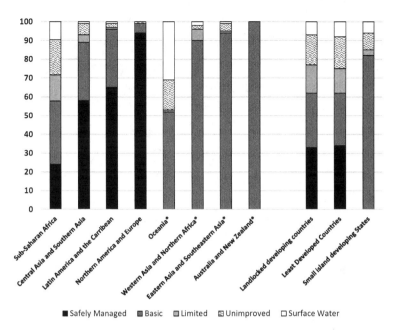

FIGURE 2.8 Estimates for regional drinking water coverage, 2015.
Note: Countries with * indicate those with insufficient data to estimate safely managed services
Source: WHO/UNICEF, 2017

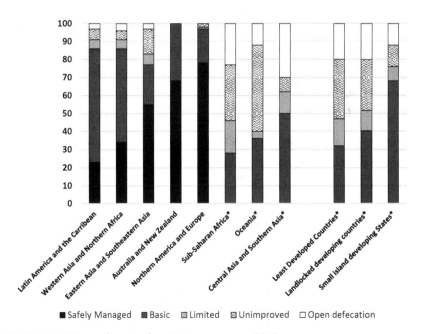

FIGURE 2.9 Estimated regional sanitation coverage, 2015.
Note: Countries with * indicate those with insufficient data to estimate safely managed services
Source: WHO/UNICEF, 2017

example, estimates for safely managed drinking water were only available for 96 countries (representing 35% of the global population). As a further example, figures provided by the South African government on the delivery of safe drinking water and sanitation are based on a national collation of figures provided by municipalities in terms of infrastructure provided, and do not always reflect the functionality of the infrastructure or the reliability of the service provided, according to the knowledge of one of the co-authors.

One of the challenges of high urbanization rates in countries of the global South is that the delivery of services does not necessarily keep pace with the rapid expansion of urban populations. Urbanization increases both water demand and pollution, putting pressure on water supplies. Denser populations and inadequate infrastructure can lead to poor wastewater management and changing urban landscapes can cause higher runoff of pollutants into local water supplies. This is a particular concern because of the expected increase in the variability of water, which already manifests itself through growing incidence of droughts and flooding in densely populated areas.

People living in informal urban settlements often do not have access to safe drinking water or adequate sanitation, with associated impacts on their food security and nutritional status. Public water provision services often do not reach informal settlements, leaving small-scale independent providers to fill the gap. There is some evidence that poorer households in informal settlements pay more for water supplies than wealthier households pay for public provision of water and, since private provision to informal settlements is not monitored, the poorer households have little power to ensure quality water or service provision (Kacker and Joshi, 2012).

In terms of sanitation, in 2015, 39% of the global population had access to safely managed sanitation services, which is defined as safe excreta disposal in situ or treated off-site (Figure 2.9). At the same time, an estimated 2.3 billion people still lacked even a basic sanitation service. Finally, an estimated 892 million people worldwide still practised open defecation (WHO/UNICEF, 2017), which has been linked with environmental enteric dysfunction. The shares of people practising open defecation are particularly high in Central and Southern Asia and in sub-Saharan Africa. Together with Oceania, these are the three regions with overall lowest access to improved sanitation services.

While poor sanitation is listed as the second leading risk factor for child stunting worldwide (Danaei et al., 2016), the causal links between improvements in WASH, environment and nutrition are still under investigation. Modest benefits from improved water quality, sanitation and handwashing interventions have been reported for height-for-age of children under five years of age, independent of the effects on diarrhoea (Dangour et al., 2013; Freeman et al., 2017). Moreover, environmental enteric dysfunction may be a major causal pathway between poor WASH environments and child stunting (Humphrey, 2009). But recent studies have had mixed results, with combined WASH and nutrition interventions not showing consistent improvements in the prevention of diarrhoea and for child linear growth (Luby et al., 2018; Null et al., 2018). Headey and Palloni (2019) summarize the limitations of the experimental and observational literature on WASH interventions and analyse the health linkages of WASH constructing sub-national panels using the Demographic Health Surveys. They find that among the various water supply options, only water piped into the home predicts reductions in child stunting. Improvements in sanitation are not associated with stunting or wasting, but are essential for reductions in diarrhoea prevalence and child mortality. Importantly, WASH interventions cannot only improve direct household water and FSN but can also reduce morbidity in the surrounding community through reduced contaminant loads (Miguel and Kremer, 2004; Ringler et al., 2018).

Water and FSN stability

FSN stability refers to the continuous, adequate access, availability and utilization of FSN over time. This implies stability of household food supply in the short and long term, either through food production, or through having sufficient income and economic resources to buy food. FSN stability is adversely impacted by natural disasters, climate variability and change, price volatility, conflicts and epidemics as well as socio-demographic change. Many of these factors are closely related with water, which itself varies increasingly due to a multitude of factors, with a growing importance of climate change.

As the instability of water contributes to the instability of food security, measures need to be adopted to improve the stability of water supplies as well as to provide ancillary measures for times when stability of water supply is violated due to extreme climatic events and other disasters, such as unplanned, large-scale migration or civil strife. To make up for shortfalls in water availability over time, historically, governments and other investors have resorted to supply augmentation, rather than managing human water demands, for example, through pricing or other economic incentives.

Availability of water varies considerably over time, with significant intra- and inter-annual variations concentrated in poorer regions (Grey and Sadoff, 2007). Very high variability can translate into floods and droughts, which, in some regions, may extend over several years (see Box 2.2). Floods and droughts have significant impacts on the production of food and on FSN in affected areas. Stability of water availability and access is a particular challenge in areas vulnerable to high levels of climate variability, and in places with limited infrastructure investment, operation and maintenance for both agricultural and domestic supply systems. Droughts have significant impacts on rainfed agriculture and livestock, which are the main livelihoods in most rural areas in the global South.

Droughts can result in crop failure and the death of livestock, particularly in rainfed agricultural systems in semi-arid and arid areas. Crop failures during periods of drought not only increase the incidence of hunger among poor and rural people but also reduce the purchasing power (and FSN) of the general population and affect the overall economy as failed crops have to be replaced with imports, often funded by budgetary transfer from education and other social services or food aid. Grey and Sadoff (2007) graphically represent the linkage between climate variability and agricultural and overall GDP for the case of Ethiopia. The example is representative for rainfed-dependent countries in Africa that have large shares of people employed and GDP derived in the agricultural sector (Figure 2.10).

Climate change affects precipitation, runoff, water quality, water temperature and groundwater recharge. It also significantly impacts sea levels. In regions with high food insecurity and inequality, these changes will particularly affect poorer households and may disproportionately affect women, given their vulnerability and restricted access to resources (IPCC, 2014). Climate change will particularly put indigenous peoples at high risk – specifically those in mountain regions, the Pacific Islands, coastal and other low-lying areas, and in the Arctic – as they often depend on the environment and its biodiversity for their FSN and as these regions are at heightened risk of significant climate change impacts (IPCC, 2014). A recent IPCC report (2018) describes greater Earth System Sensitivity to global warming with higher risks for agriculture and agro- and other ecosystems, putting further stress on water–FSN linkages out into the future. Many previous IPCC reports already identified the intensification of droughts in some seasons and areas, in particular in southern Europe and the Mediterranean region, central North America, Mexico and Central America, northeast Brazil and southern Africa (IPCC, 2012).

Even in irrigated agriculture, droughts can impact on the availability of water over time and therefore on FSN stability, with impacts particularly felt for small-scale irrigators, whose water source is often derived from shallow groundwater or harvesting of rainwater.

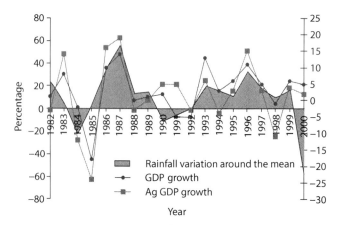

FIGURE 2.10 Rainfall variation, growth in agricultural GDP and growth in GDP, 1982–2000

Source: Grey and Sadoff, 2007

At the other extreme, floods can sweep away villages, roads, crops, fish nurseries, livestock and people, wreaking havoc and leaving affected communities without houses, services and food. Floods can result in the contamination of water supplies, resulting in outbreaks of disease and lowered nutritional security of affected populations (see also HLPE, 2012). Furthermore, uncertainty and risk in agricultural production hinder farmers and other actors from investing in agriculture, leading to sub-optimal outcomes for food security and farm incomes.

Predicting the actual impacts of climate change on water availability is difficult for several reasons. For many regions in the world, different general circulation models predict significantly different changes in precipitation, especially at finer geographical scales. Moreover, changes in rainfall do not linearly translate into changes in water availability; instead, factors such as rainfall duration and intensity, surface temperature, and vegetation, all play a role in determining what percentage of rainfall is converted into surface water runoff into rivers, dams and wetlands, or into groundwater. Current models only imperfectly capture these mechanisms. Similarly, impacts of climate change on groundwater storage and on water pollution remain areas that have been insufficiently researched. Also under-studied are linkages of climate change with nutrition, for example, changes in aflatoxin hotspots as a result of climate change, leaching of nutrients as a result of higher CO_2 concentrations, as well as changes in pest and disease patterns in response to predicted, but uncertain, changes in temperature and precipitation patterns.

BOX 2.2 DROUGHT – THE NEW NORMAL?

São Paulo, the largest city in South America, has year-round rainfall (with higher precipitation in October–March) with no dry season. Its water supply system was designed for a smaller population and assured and abundant water availability. The region benefits from the complex hydrological processes that generate rain-clouds from the Amazon rainforests, providing water for urban water supply, for power generation, for industry and irrigation. While the challenges of global warming and population growth are present in all megacities, the weather patterns in Brazil are clearly exacerbated by the loss of Amazon rainforests (Nobre et al., 2016).

In 2014, São Paulo witnessed one of its most severe droughts in decades, a situation that continued to worsen through mid-2015. The impacts were so severe that water supply had to be rationed, which affected access of the marginalized urban population (Davies, 2014). Reduced electricity generation and water supply had adverse spillover effects into neighbouring regions. Other impacts included losses in fisheries, agriculture and industry, amidst a series of water conflicts (Watts, 2014).

> A 22-year assessment of deforestation and restoration in riparian forests in the eastern Brazilian Amazon found increases in deforestation until 2004, followed by a subsequent decrease from 2004 to 2010 (Nunes et al., 2015). This coincides with the first coherent and consequential efforts to effectively reduce deforestation in the Brazilian Amazon that gained momentum starting in 2004, under the administration of President Luiz Inácio Lula da Silva. However, the severe cumulative extent of deforestation in the Brazilian Amazon, reaching 763,000 km^2 (the combined area of two Germanys or two Japans) by 2013, has led to a situation where the 'vegetation–climate equilibrium is teetering on the brink of the abyss' (Nobre, 2014). The global rise of Brazil's meat and feed grain industry in the last decade is further contributing to the massive transformation of the entire Brazilian landscape – from severe intensification and expansion of feed grain production in the Southeast and the Cerrado, to the displacement of cattle grazing into and then spreading out of the Amazon Rainforest (Sharma and Schlesinger, 2017). These processes are also negatively affecting the lives and livelihoods of indigenous people living in the Amazon.
>
> Without addressing large-scale deforestation, the region might well experience more frequent high-intensity droughts, making Sao Paolo's 2014–2015 experience the new normal.

Key measures to address the variability of water and food supplies include risk sharing and risk mitigation measures, such as insurance products to reduce negative production and consumption shocks, a more holistic understanding of water storage options, ranging from natural water storage underground, in the soil and in water bodies to grey infrastructure, ranging from small to large reservoirs (Figure 2.11). Direct water-based options to address variability in water availability also include the development of more efficient irrigation infrastructure, such as improved irrigation scheduling tools that can reduce excess water application. These tools, including soil moisture and yield sensors, are increasingly linked to large databases that support the development of yet more precise agricultural water management devices. Improved climate forecasting tools, drought monitoring bulletins and apps that provide real-time and near-future information on precipitation, temperatures, droughts and crop prices are further tools that help farmers manage climate, water and associated food production risks.

Water markets, on the other hand, are generally not proposed as a mechanism for addressing variability in water and food supply. Despite this, growing water scarcity and variability due to climate change might well support the development of new water markets, given the potential of water markets to alleviate growing water stress both in the long run and in response to short-term water variability (Rosegrant et al., 2014). In times of

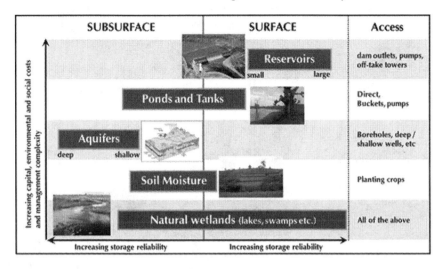

FIGURE 2.11 The water storage continuum
Source: McCartney and Smakhtin, 2010

scarcity, the expectation is that water markets will increase the economic productivity of water as they trigger a gradual shift in production from activities that generate little value added per unit of water to ones that generate more or low- to high-value activities (Debaere et al., 2017). Such market-induced reprioritization, however, needs to be carefully monitored to ensure that it does not undermine food and nutrition security of socio-economically vulnerable communities (see also Chapter 4).

Adaptation to climate change will need to carefully consider competing water uses and their various implications for FSN. Measures that can mitigate one type of adverse impact could also exacerbate another. For example, increased storage infrastructure to meet the water needs of irrigated agriculture arising from increased crop water demands, higher evapotranspiration, and longer or more intense dry spells, might negatively impact downstream fisheries.

Measures to directly address variability in food supply vary from the household to the national and global levels and include social safety nets, such as the direct provision of food aid (in cash or food), food-for-work programs for undernourished and vulnerable populations, food storage (real and virtual) options, as well as trade policies and measures.

Emerging trends and issues

This section deals with a number of emerging trends and issues in the water and food security area, leading to increasing inequalities in land and water distribution as well as causing uncertainties for local people and their rights to water and food.

Food and energy competition over water

Water use for energy is a key competitor to water availability for food. At the same time, food production is becoming increasingly energy intensive. Water and energy linkages impact food security and nutrition in terms of the amount of water available to the food and agriculture sector, and in terms of water quality.

Many energy generation systems require water as part of the generation process, including hydropower, thermal energy generation, and nuclear plants. Hydropower is currently the most common renewable form of energy and fully depends on the availability of water resources. According to the International Energy Agency (IEA, 2016), hydroelectricity accounted for more than 85% of global renewable electricity generation in 2015. There is growing pressure around the world to increase the use of renewables in energy generation processes to reduce carbon emissions from power generation and also as a solution to deal with the lack of water storage infrastructure. There is also longstanding evidence that micro-hydro power plants, in particular, help local communities increase agricultural production and meet the basic needs of their people (Khennas et al., 2000). However, hydropower can also create conflicts between water for energy and water for agriculture.

Water releases for hydro-electricity production favour the needs of hydropower over those of downstream farmers or ecosystems. This can have adverse impacts on irrigation and on inland fisheries and their contribution to FSN. Zeng et al. (2017) found that 54% of global installed hydropower capacity – an amount totalling 507 Gigawatts (GW) – directly competes with irrigation, meaning that increased hydro-electricity production might reduce food security (see also Box 2.3).

Some newer forms of energy generation compete for both water and land resources, and sometimes also for labour, with agriculture. Among these are biofuels (HLPE, 2013) and hydrofracking. The drilling practice of hydraulic fracturing, or 'fracking,' as it is more commonly known, is the process of injecting a mixture of water, sand and chemicals into wells at high pressure to crack dense rock formations and release oil or gas. Fracking has raised concerns about its potential impact on water pollution (Myers, 2012). A national study in the United States, on the impacts of fracking on national water resources concluded that because of data gaps and uncertainties, it was not possible to fully characterize the severity of impacts (US EPA, 2016). On the other hand, a recent study reviewing major shale-producing regions in the United States, assessing the water footprint of the full life cycle of the fracking process in six basins, found that there have been substantial increases in both water-use and wastewater (flowback and produced water). From 2011 to 2016 the water-use per well rose by up to 770% while wastewater volumes increased by up to 1,440% within the first year of production. The large increase in water-use across these areas as a result of hydro-fracking not only increases competition for other uses but also loads of wastewater (Kondash et al. 2018). Agricultural communities are especially impacted as frack-sand mining and fracking takes place primarily in rural agricultural areas, where farmers lease out their land to the oil and gas industry and mining companies.

Some low-carbon technologies, such as wind and solar PV, require less water, but depending on the siting and size of solar generation systems, water consumption for cooling and cleaning of panels can be substantial. Thus, depending on the decarbonization pathway – for example, one that favours biofuels, concentrated solar, carbon capture or nuclear power, water implications can be very large, large, or limited. For example, the volume of water consumed globally for ethanol production was roughly equivalent to global water consumption for coal-fired power plants, even though global ethanol production represented approximately one hundredth the energy content of global coal-fired electricity production (Spang et al., 2014). However, in most climate change mitigation assessments, biofuels are given an important role for climate mitigation, including in the latest Special Report on the impacts of global warming of 1.5°C above pre-industrial levels and related global greenhouse gas emission pathways (Rogelj et al., 2018). Although regional variation is substantial, de Fraiture et al., 2008 estimate that on average it takes around 2,500 litres of crop evapotranspiration (green water) and 820 litres of water withdrawals (blue water) to provide one litre of biofuel. It is at the country or local level that the trade-offs between water for food and water for biofuels are felt (Varghese, 2007).

At the same time, the energy requirements of the water distribution sector – to abstract and distribute water, including for most forms of irrigation – are increasing. Higher pollution levels require more energy for treating water and the increasing need to transport water over longer distances also uses significant energy. Energy is also required for heating water for food production processes, for domestic hygiene and for food preparation. One of the major challenges for water for energy is that it must be provided at a high assurance of stability of supply. As a result, in times of low rainfall, water allocation for irrigation may be reduced in order to ensure supplies for energy production.

Groundwater extraction has increased dramatically as a source of irrigation water with the result that energy use for groundwater pumping is now often the largest use of energy in agriculture in semi-arid and arid countries of the global South, such as Pakistan (for example, Siddiqui and Wescoat, 2013). Thus, agricultural water use practices are contributing to the growth in energy demand. The introduction of cheap solar pumps may reduce fossil energy use for groundwater pumping in the future, but with uncertain implications for those aquifers that are already subject to depletion.

While there are important trade-offs between water, energy and food resources and uses, there are also large opportunities for synergies. For example, small run-of-the-river hydropower stations have been built on large irrigation canals in southern Vietnam to harness the energy created by canal flows,[2] and eThekwini municipality in South Africa is looking at hydropower generation on distribution pipelines on steep hillsides in its area of jurisdiction. Nutrients contained in point source wastewater, such as phosphorous, can also be harnessed and reused as fertilizer on agricultural fields, or slurry can be transformed into heating agents. There are thus many opportunities for jointly improved water, energy and food security. Much of this has yet to be implemented and there are significant challenges in managing competing trade-offs.

> **BOX 2.3 HYDROPOWER: SUPPORT OR CHALLENGE TO REGIONAL COOPERATION AND ENERGY SECURITY?**
>
> Hydropower is among the most controversial renewable energy options in use. While the construction of reservoirs not only supports hydro-electricity production but also provides important flood control, low-season flow augmentation and water storage for multiple use benefits, a series of far-reaching environmental and social impacts of hydropower have been well documented (see WCD, 2000 and UN WWAP, 2014). The technology is particularly challenged due to the large quantities of water required to be stored, uncertainties regarding the water consumed as evaporative losses from reservoirs, the release of methane emissions from submerged vegetation in tropical areas, and uncertainties related to changes in river temperatures and flows.
>
> Still, hydropower is often proposed as a climate-friendly option and as a key element of energy security in regional power sharing agreements, as reflected in various power pools, such as the Southern African Power Pool (SAPP). SAPP is an alliance of 12 countries in southern Africa, interconnected through an electricity grid to smooth spatial and temporal shortfalls in generating capacity. Other goals include harmonization of relationships and development of expertise across member states and utilities and the promotion of sustainable development. The SAPP generating mix is dominated by coal (around 70%) but also includes hydropower (less than 20%). South Africa hosts 77% of SAPP's installed power supply capacity, mostly coal, while hydropower contributes less than 2% of South Africa's electricity supply. On the other hand, hydro-electricity contributes more than 30% to capacity in Swaziland and Zimbabwe, and close to 100% in Lesotho, Malawi and Zambia. This exposes SAPP members to different levels of production risk during prolonged droughts, but also during extreme flood events, when dam safety is an additional risk. With much of the region expected to experience reduced water availability as a result of climate change, affecting hydro-electric production in most or the entire region, it is not clear to what extent SAPP will be able to fulfil its energy security role. What is known is that climate change, combined with increasing demand associated with

wider socio-economic development pathways, will intensify competition over energy and water resources in the region, particularly during climate-extreme events (Conway *et al.*, 2015). To ensure that power trade supports regional economic cooperation, according to Phillips *et al.* (2008), consideration should be given to the potential of hydropower, asymmetry in the volumes of water available in the co-riparians, the gap between electricity supply and demand, and the relative propensity to collaborate by the riparians in the basin or region in question. (See Chapter 4 for a discussion of the controversies of large dams in terms of food security.)

Changing consumption and production patterns

As living standards increase around the world, and with globalization, diets are changing. One of the major changes is the increasing consumption of vegetable oils and animal products. This has a significant impact on the water required to produce food. Yang and Cui (2014) suggest that to produce 1 kg of beef requires 15.4 m^3, as compared to 1 kg of cereals, which only needs 1.6 m^3. The authors further suggest that water use per capita might well overtake population growth as the main driver of growth in water use due to continued dietary changes (Yang and Cui, 2014).

China is often listed as an example of dietary changes that take place as countries develop, incomes increase and populations urbanize. In 2010, China accounted for 20% of the global population and had experienced a long period of growth driving increases in average food availability levels and also inducing a shift away from the consumption of cereals as direct food toward the increased consumption of meats, milk, vegetables and oils. As a result, overall calorie availability in China increased by 19% during 1990–2009. At the same time, direct intake of cereals declined from 64% to 48% of total calorie availability; while calories contributed from meats more than doubled, and those from vegetables almost tripled. Clearly, water use in agriculture in China (and elsewhere) increased not only as a result of the growing population and income-growth driven food accessibility, but also due to dietary changes related to income growth and urbanization (Ringler and Zhu, 2015). Similarly, OECD-FAO predicts a 1.5% annual increase from 2013 to 2022 for China's meat consumption, mirroring the production trend (FAO, 2014). Per capita poultry consumption in the country increased from barely 1kg to over 9kg per year over the past three decades and in 2011 China became the world's second largest poultry meat producer (Pi, Rou and Horowitz, 2014).

The ongoing growth of meat consumption is likely to add to the pressure on feed imports which are mainly from the United States (maize and soybean), Brazil (soybean) and Argentina (soybean) (Sharma, 2014). The challenge in the growing demand for meat is not only in relation to the volume of water required for growing feed for the livestock, but also the pollution arising from intensive stock farming.

In China, land and water have been polluted by the massive expansion of livestock production and the switching to large-scale industrialized facilities. A 2010 water survey by the Chinese Ministry of Environmental Protection listed livestock production as one of the largest contributors to water pollution (Gale, 2013).

Globally, total poultry meat consumption expanded from 66.4 million tonnes in 2000 to almost 91 million tonnes in 2009, and Asia accounts for 40% of this growth (The Poultry Site, 2013). India too saw its per capita poultry and egg consumption increasing from 0.8 kg to 2.8 kg and from 28 eggs to 56 eggs in the period 2000–2012, respectively.

But rapidly changing consumption patterns are not limited to rapidly growing economies. In the United States, for example, poultry consumption grew over a 30-year period from 27.31 kg per person in 1982 to 44.36 kg in 2012 (National Chicken Council, 2014). Moreover, as noted in the section on utilization of food, even within low-income countries, there are growing segments of more well-off people who consume more water-intensive diets, with large variations in the types of diets consumed as well as in the water usage of such diets. Thus, there are clear signs of diets too high in animal sourced foods and oils neither achieving important nutrition goals, nor environmental sustainability goals. Changing adult diets with excessive consumption levels of meats, sugar, refined grains and starchy vegetables into more sustainable diets could thus improve both nutrition and health outcomes and also improve water availability and security for marginal users. China and other rapidly developing economies have started to issue nutrition guidelines that are not only focused on improving diets for low-income, malnourished segments of its population, but also aim to curb excessive consumption levels in urban areas, for example, by reducing the average recommended daily food intake from 2600 kilocalories (kcal) in 1990 to 2200–2300 kcal in the 2014–2020 Food and Nutrition Development Outline (Chen and Wang, 2019).

The climate change discourse on livestock production often centres on further intensification of production processes to mitigate impacts. However, this discourse largely ignores other costs to the environment such as water, soil and air pollution resulting from intensified animal feeding operations common in the United States and increasingly adopted in their varied forms in other countries, including China. Key concerns regarding human and ecological health related to production in concentrated animal feeding operations (CAFOs) include contamination of ground and surface water with viruses, bacteria and parasites, which originate from the operations, as well as with nutrients and industrial and agricultural chemicals used in these operations (Pew Commission, 2008). Excessive nutrient loading leads to eutrophication of surface waters for instance, resulting in 'dead zones' in both inland and marine waters due to algal blooms and massive fish kills and declines in biodiversity (ibid.). Contamination of soil is also a key problem of such practices as a result of the deposition of nutrients, chemicals and pathogens around CAFOs, making it difficult to carry out other agricultural and non-agricultural activities (ibid.).[3]

Increasing demand for feed grains results in agricultural expansion into rainforests and fragile landscapes, contributing to land-use changes, which further alter already disturbed water flows. In some cases, expansion of feed production into so-called 'marginal' or forest lands displaces indigenous and marginalized populations, some of whom were already marginalized through subsistence-related livelihoods.

Today, 1 billion poor depend on livestock for food and income, according to the FAO (FAO, 2012b). Many of these livestock producers live on 20% of the world's pastures and rangelands. According to the FAO, 70% of the rangelands in dry areas have been degraded to some extent through overgrazing, compaction and erosion (FAO, 2013). Given growing land scarcity, there is also increasing conflict over water and land resources between pastoralists and crop farmers.

Pastoralist communities, moreover, are seldom integrated into the national, regional or global livestock value chains and the meat industry supplying the growing demand in low-income and emerging economies. It is, in fact, often small producers – including women who own one or two cows in a rural community – who get displaced as industrialized systems take their place for providing dairy or meat to wealthier consumers.

Importantly, these trends should not detract from the nutritional and related water challenges of the poor and marginalized who are often forced to rely on staple food diets providing insufficient calories and lacking in important macro and micronutrients. In particular, young children aged six months or more should eat more animal-sourced foods and not less in much of sub-Saharan Africa, parts of Asia (in particular South Asia) and parts of the Middle East, Latin America and Central Asia. Animal-source foods have high-quality proteins, multiple micronutrients and other important characteristics that support physical growth and cognitive development. Being fed a variety of animal-source foods is associated with a much lower risk of stunting (Headey et al., 2018). Access to animal-source foods in these countries and regions is often hindered by a lack of affordability of these foods, which is, in turn, affected by under-investment in agricultural research, poor rural infrastructure and weak market structures.

Food losses and waste

In the wake of the food price crisis of 2007/2008, development practitioners and donors started to resurrect a topic that had last been in the news following the oil price crisis (and associated food price crisis) of the mid-1970s: food losses and waste, also commonly known as Post Harvest Losses or PHL. The studies of the late 1970s and early 1980s found that some of the losses occurred because farmers in developing countries started to mechanize, which increased losses while improving economic profitability of production (for example Greeley 1982). Sheahan and Barrett (2017), focusing on PHL in sub-Saharan Africa, suggest four key objectives for the resurgence of research on

PHL: 1) to improve food security; 2) to improve food safety; 3) to improve unnecessary resource use; and 4) to increase profits in the value chain. Of importance for water–FSN linkages is the third objective, as a result of the vast amounts of water embedded in the food that was produced for human consumption but was never actually consumed. Assuming a conservative average of food water productivity of 1 kg/m^3, the total associated annual water wasted would be about 1300 km^3, over ten times the total discharge of the River Nile in one year.

HLPE (2014, p. 11) defines these losses as 'a decrease, at all stages of the food chain from harvest to consumption, in mass, of food that was originally intended for human consumption, regardless of the cause'. PHLs generally occur in two main settings: first between farmers' fields and the retail sector; these losses are generally assumed to be of particular importance in the global South due to limitations in post-harvest storage, processing and transportation, and overall poorly functioning markets. The second set of losses relates to consumers purchasing but not actually consuming foods. This second type of losses also includes wastage in the retail sector, such as wet and supermarkets and in restaurants. There are suggestions that the global North could generate large savings in this area. But how large are actual losses and what is the potential for loss reduction? The FAO estimates that about one third of food produced for human consumption is lost or wasted (FAO, 2011, and see also below). However, there is no consensus on the actual volume and value of food losses and waste. Clearly, published numbers in almost all cases remain estimates, methods used in measuring and assessing losses and wastes are contested and there is an important linkage between food safety and food losses, particularly in low-income settings. Rosegrant *et al.* (2015) note that not only is there no consensus in the literature on actual losses; there is even less certainty about the magnitude of costs associated with reducing such losses. While applying various methods and technologies to reduce PHL, such as improved storage and transportation, many of these technologies may require a scale of production that excludes smallholder farmers. Thus, while there is potential for reducing water use in agriculture through reducing PHL across the globe, much more careful research and evaluation is needed to provide insights on what is actually feasible and on what has been achieved, and at what cost.

Finally, it is also important to look at patterns of food wastage at the consumer level. According to the FAO annually

> consumers in rich countries waste almost as much food (222 million tonnes) as the entire net food production of sub-Saharan Africa (230 million tonnes). The amount of food lost or wasted every year is equivalent to more than half of the world's annual cereals crop (2.3 billion tonnes in 2009/2010). Per capita waste by consumers is between 95–115 kg a year in Europe and North America, while consumers in sub-Saharan Africa, south and south-eastern Asia, each throw away only 6–11 kg a year.[4]

While rich people can afford to throw away food, the poor continue to suffer from chronic malnourishment and food insecurity.

As discussed, even though these figures are estimates and may be contested, all this wasted food also has embedded water. While there is still much to learn and understand about PHL, efforts to reduce wastage and spoilage across the entire value chain and across the globe should be supported and expanded – as long as they are cost-effective and do not adversely harm the food security and food safety of the poor.

Corporatization of land and water resources

The food price crisis of 2007–2008 contributed to increased investments by some companies and countries in land resources and associated water resources for production of biofuels and in some cases, food (see Borras and Franco, 2010; Cotula *et al.*, 2009; Deininger, 2011; Deininger and Byerlee, 2011; De Schutter, 2011; Von Braun and Meinzen-Dick, 2009). This phenomenon was popularly known as 'land grabbing'. Many of the planned investments did not go forward or were later on cancelled as the complexity of large-scale land transactions had not been clear to all involved parties; some investments were seen as important for supporting rural growth and poverty alleviation (cf. Deininger, 2011; World Bank, 2010), while others were seen as displacing small land holders and marginal populations.

Importantly, all these negotiations over land also included a water dimension as the planned agricultural production processes required concomitant development of water resources for production (Franco *et al.*, 2013; Mehta *et al.*, 2012; Woodhouse, 2012). A Special Issue of Water Alternatives discusses several water implications of land deals on local food production and agriculture (Mehta *et al.*, 2012). The papers show how 'water grabbing' associated with land investments has led to a significant re-appropriation of water resources and water tenure relations with implications for basic human rights and local water and food security (see Chapter 4 for a full discussion of land and water grabbing).

A review by the *Financial Times* entitled 'A World Without Water' (FT, 2014) describes increasing corporate involvement in water management. Since 2011, global corporations have spent more than $84 billion on how they manage, conserve or obtain water. The reasons range from having to deal with physical water shortages and the need to appear concerned about water scarcity and water crises. While some argue that the growing corporate involvement in water management is negligible compared with conventional use by agriculture and is also to be welcomed because it will lead to new technological innovation (see FT, 2014), others argue that these have risks and implications for current and future water and food security (see Sojamo and Larson, 2012). These include the potential re-allocation of water to the 'highest economic value' having detrimental impacts on local lives, livelihoods, and water and food security (see Franco *et al.*, 2013). Importantly, risks are often unequally shared between companies and other local water uses and new water stresses may be created. Furthermore, companies are often more legally bound to be accountable to distant shareholders than to local stakeholders, who are often voiceless and powerless. Due to their structural, bargaining power and influence over global and national policies and processes, they shape and frame powerful discourses, subjecting water governance institutions to processes of capture (see Newborne and Mason, 2012; Sojamo and Larson, 2012). These issues will be further explored in the chapter on water governance.

Conclusions

Water and FSN are intrinsically linked and growing demands on both water and food are further strengthening these interlinkages. FSN challenges cannot be addressed without a comprehensive understanding of the myriad linkages between water and food, and it is also unlikely that water security goals can be achieved unless we change the ways we produce and consume food.

Dietary change has been identified as a major entry point for more sustainable water use, but in the short term pressures on water from food production will likely grow. This will – in turn – likely affect food security and nutrition negatively, from increased water scarcity, pollution and degradation as well as limited access to crucial land and water resources, especially for vulnerable and marginalized social groups. It is important to also bear in mind that the global scenarios provided in this chapter (with some regional, national and local examples) lack granularity. This is because global and national figures mask regional differences, differential access for poorer groups and gendered access and are subject to uncertainties arising due to climate variabilities and change.

These issues need to be borne in mind whilst trying to understand the extremely different water contexts across the world and what they mean for FSN. This discussion points to the need to highlight the importance of local perspectives and contexts, as well as diverse ways in which local women and men can develop resilient systems to deal with increasing uncertainties. How water for FSN can be managed amidst these uncertainties alongside governance challenges is considered in the following chapters.

Notes

1 The HLPE (2014) defines the food system as follows: 'A food system gathers all the elements (environment, people, inputs, processes, infrastructures, institutions etc.) and activities that relate to the production, processing, distribution, preparation and consumption of food, and the outputs of these activities, including socio-economic and environmental outcomes' (HLPE, 2014: 29). The complexity of food security requires a complex framework that encompasses social, political,

economic and ecological issues and must also include the 'activities, processes and outcomes' related to food.
2 Nguyen Vu Huy, personal communication, 2014.
3 Studies in the U.S. offer some lessons for consideration, as we explore how to meet increasing needs of ASF in a sustainable manner. According to Halden and Schwab (2014), 55% of soil and sediment erosion, 37% of pesticide use, 80% of antibiotic usage and more than 30% of nitrogen and phosphorus loading into national drinking water sources in the U.S. are estimated to originate from animal farming. Moreover, 16% of more than 300,000 miles of impaired rivers and streams in the U.S. are contaminated by animal feeding operations due to the lack of regulations for treatment of animal waste (Graham and Nachman, 2010). In 2008, the U.S. Government Accountability Office (GAO) found that even though 15 out of 68 peer-reviewed studies found direct linkages between air and water pollution problems and industrial animal production, the Environment Protection Agency lacked even the basic data on emissions from these operations and therefore was unable to assess the extent of public health and environmental damage (GAO, 2008).
4 www.fao.org/save-food/resources/keyfindings/en/(accessed May 2019).

References

Ayers, R.S. and Westcot, D.W. 1985. *Water Quality for Agriculture*. Rome: FAO.
Barrett, C., Garg, T. and McBride, L. 2016. Well-being dynamics and poverty traps. Centre for Climate Change Economics and Policy Working Paper No. 250 and Grantham Research Institute on Climate Change and the Environment Working Paper no. 222. Available at: www.lse.ac.uk/GranthamInstitute/wp-content/uploads/2016/01/Working-Paper-222-Barrett-et-al.pdf.
Borras, S. Jr. and Franco, J. 2010. From threat to opportunity? Problems with the idea of a 'code of conduct' for land-grabbing. *Yale Human Rights and Development Law Journal*, 13(2): 507–523.
CA (Comprehensive Assessment of Water Management in Agriculture). 2007. *Water for Food, Water for Life: A Comprehensive Assessment of Water Management for Agriculture*. London: Earthscan; Colombo, Sri Lanka: International Water Management Institute (IWMI).
Chatham House. 2012. *Resources Futures*. London: Chatham House.
Chen, K.Z. and Wang, Z. 2019. Agriculture and nutrition in China. In S. Fan, S. Yosef and R. Pandya-Lorch, eds. *Agriculture for Improved Nutrition: Seizing the Momentum*. Chapter 19. Wallingford, UK: International Food Policy Research Institute (IFPRI) and CABI. Available at: http://ebrary.ifpri.org/cdm/ref/collection/p15738coll2/id/133091.
Closas, A. and Rap, E. 2017. Solar-based groundwater pumping for irrigation: Sustainability, policies and limitations. *Energy Policy*, 104: 33–37.
Colenbrander, W. and van Koppen, B. 2013. Improving the supply chain of motor pumps to accelerate mechanized small-scale private irrigation in Zambia. *Water International*, 38(4): 493–503.
Comprehensive Assessment of Water Management in Agriculture. 2007. *Water for Food, Water for Life: A Comprehensive Assessment of Water Management for Agriculture*. London: Earthscan; Colombo, Sri Lanka: International Water Management Institute (IWMI).
Conway, D., Archer van Garderen, E., Deryng, D., Dorling, S., Krueger, T., Landman, W., Lankford, B., Lebek, K., Osborn, T., Ringler, C., Thurlow, J., Zhu, T.

and Dalin, C. 2015. Climate and southern Africa's water-energy-food nexus. *Nature Climate Change*, 5(9): 837–846.

Cotula, L., Vermeulen, S., Leonard, R. and Keeley, J. 2009. *Land Grab or Development Opportunity? Agricultural Investment and International Land Deals in Africa.* London/Rome: IIED (International Institution for Environment and Development)/FAO (Food and Agriculture Organization of the United Nations)/IFAD (International Fund for Agricultural Development).

Cumming, O. and Cairncross, S. 2016. Can water, sanitation and hygiene help eliminate stunting? Current evidence and policy implications. *Maternal and Child Nutrition*, 12 (S1): 91–105.

Danaei, G., Andrews, K.G., Sudfeld, C.R., Fink, G., McCoy, C.D., Peet, E., Sania, A., Smith Fawzi, M.C., Ezzati, M. and Fawzi, W.W. 2016. Risk factors for childhood stunting in 137 developing countries: A comparative risk assessment analysis at global, regional and country levels. *PLoS Med*, 13(11): e1002164.

Dangour, A.D., Watson, L., Cumming, O., Boisson, S., Che, Y., Velleman, Y., Cavill, S., Allen, E. and Uauy, R. 2013. Interventions to improve water quality and supply, sanitation and hygiene practices, and their effects on the nutritional status of children. *The Cochran Library*, Issue 8. Available at: researchonline.lshtm.ac.uk.

Davies, W. 2014. Brazil drought: Sao Paulo sleepwalking into crisis. BBC, 7 November 2014. Available at: www.bbc.com/news/world-latin-america-29947965. Accessed 2 February 2015.

de Fraiture, C. and Giordano, M. 2014. Small private irrigation: A thriving but overlooked sector. *Agricultural Water Management*, 131: 167–174.

de Fraiture, C., Giordano, M. and Liao, Y. 2008. Biofuels and implications for agricultural water use: Blue impacts of green energy, *Water Policy*, 10(Supplement 1): 67–81.

Debaere, P. and Li, T., 2017. "The effects of water markets: Evidence from the Rio Grande," 2017 annual meeting, July 30–August 1, Chicago, IL 259187, Agricultural and Applied Economics Association.

Deininger, K. 2011. Challenges posed by the new wave of farmland investment. *The Journal of Peasant Studies*, 38(2): 217–247.

Deininger, K. and Byerlee, D., with J. Lindsay, A. Norton, H. Selod and M. Stickler. 2011. *Rising Global Interest in Farmland: Can It Yield Sustainable and Equitable Benefits?* Washington, DC: World Bank.

Delgado, C., Rosegrant, M., Steinfeld, H., Ehui, S. and Courbois, C. 1999. Livestock to 2020. The next food revolution. In 2020 Vision for Food, Agriculture, and the Environment Discussion Paper 28. Washington, DC: IFPRI.

De Schutter, O. 2011. How not to think of land-grabbing: Three critiques of large-scale investments in farmland. *The Journal of Peasant Studies*, 38(2): 249–279.

Döll, P. 2009. Vulnerability to the impact of climate change on renewable groundwater resources: A global-scale assessment. *Environmental Research Letters*, 4: 035006.

Domènech, L. 2015. Improving irrigation access to combat food insecurity and undernutrition: A review. *Global Food Security*, 6(October 2015): 24–33.

Drechsel, P. and Evans, A.E.V. 2010. Wastewater use in irrigated agriculture. *Irrigation and Drainage Systems*, 24(1–2): 1–3.

European Commission. 2012. *The European Report on Development 2011/2012: Confronting Scarcity: Managing Water, Energy and Land for Inclusive and Sustainable Growth.* Brussels: EU.

Evans, A., Mateo-Sagasta, J., Qadir, M., Boelee, E. and Ippolito, A. 2019. Agricultural water pollution: Key knowledge gaps and research needs. *Current Opinion in Environmental Sustainability*, 36, February 2019, 20–27.

Falkenmark, F. and Widstrand, C. 1992. Population and water resources: A delicate balance. *Population Bulletin*, 47(3): 1–36.

Falkenmark, M. and Lannerstad, M. 2005. Consumptive water use to feed humanity – curing a blind spot. *Hydrology and Earth System Sciences*, 9: 15–28.

FAO. 2000. *The Four Dimensions of Food and Nutrition Security: Definitions and Concepts: Rainer Gross, Hans Schoeneberger, Hans Pfeifer, Hans-Joachim A. Preuss.* Available at: http://fpmu.gov.bd/agridrupal/sites/default/files/Four_Dimension_of_FS_0.pdf.

FAO. 2007. *Promises and Challenges of the Informal Food Sector in Developing Countries.* Rome: FAO.

FAO. 2011. *Global Food Losses and Food Waste – Extent, Causes and Prevention.* Rome: FAO.

FAO. 2012a. *Coping with Water Scarcity: An Action Framework for Agriculture and Food Security.* FAO Water Reports 38. Rome: FAO.

FAO. 2012b. *Livestock and Landscapes, Sustainability Pathways.* Rome: FAO. Available at: www.fao.org/3/ar591e/ar591e.pdf.

FAO. 2013. *Livestock and Environment.* Rome: FAO. Available at: www.fao.org/ag/againfo/themes/en/Environment.html.

FAO. 2014. *OECD–FAO Agricultural outlook 2013–2022.* Rome: FAO.

FAO. 2015. *The State of Agricultural Commodity Markets. Trade and Food Security: Achieving a Better Balance between National Priorities and the Collective Good.* Rome: FAO.

FAO, IFAD and WFP. 2015. *The State of Food Insecurity in the World 2015. Meeting the 2015 International Hunger Targets: Taking Stock of Uneven Progress.* Rome: FAO.

FAO, IFAD, UNICEF, WFP and WHO. 2018. *The State of Food Security and Nutrition in the World 2018. Building Climate Resilience for Food Security and Nutrition.* Rome: FAO.

Franco, J., Mehta, L. and Veldwisch, G.J. 2013. The global politics of water grabbing. *Third World Quarterly*, 34(9): 1651–1675.

Freeman, M.C., Garn, J.V., Sclar, G.D., Boisson, S., Medlicott, K., Alexander, K.T., Penakalapati, G., Anderson, D., Mahtani, A.G., Grimes, J.E.T., Rehfuess, E.A. and Clasen, T.F. 2017. The impact of sanitation on infectious disease and nutritional status: A systematic review and meta-analysis. *International Journal of Hygiene and Environmental Health* 220(6): 928–949.

FT (*The Financial Times*). 2014. A world without water. 14 July 2014. Available at: http://ig-legacy.ft.com/content/8e42bdc8-0838-11e4-9afc-00144feab7de#ft-article-comments (by Pilita Clark).

Gale, F. 2013. Livestock pollution: Women worried, dimsums.blogspot.com, 30 January 2013. Available at: http://dimsums.blogspot.com/search?q=water+pollution. Accessed 27 January 2014.

GAO (United States Government Accountability Office). 2008. *Concentrated Animal Feeding Operations: EPA Needs More Information and a Clearly Defined Strategy to Protect Air and Water Quality from Pollutants of Concern.* GAO-08-944. Washington, DC: GAO. Available at: www.gao.gov/products/GAO–08–944.

Gerbens-Leenes, P.W., Mekonnen, M.M. and Hoekstra, A.Y. 2013. The water footprint of poultry, pork and beef: A comparative study in different countries and production systems. *Water Resources and Industry*, 1–2: 25–36.

Graham, J.P. and Nachman, K.E. 2010. Managing waste from confined animal feeding operations in the United States: The need for sanitary reform. *Journal of Water and Health*, 8(4): 646–670.

Greeley, M. 1982. Farm-level post-harvest food losses: The myth of the soft third option. *IDS Bulletin*, 13: 51–60.

Grey, D., Garrick, D., Blackmore, D., Kelman, J., Muller, M. and Sadoff, C. 2013. Water security in one blue planet: Twenty-first century policy challenges for science. *Philosophical Transactions of the Royal Society A* 371: 20120406.

Grey, D. and Sadoff, C.W. 2007. Sink or swim? Water security for growth and development. *Water Policy*, 9: 545–571.

Halden, R. and Schwab, K. 2014. *Environmental Impact of Industrial Farm Animal Production*. Pew Commission on Industrial Farm Animal Production. Available at: www.pcifapia.org/_images/212-4_EnvImpact_tc_Final.pdf.

Hales, C.M., Carroll, M.D., Fryar, C.D. and Ogden, C.L. 2017. Prevalence of obesity among adults and youth: United States, 2015–2016. NCHS Data Brief No. 288. Available at: www.cdc.gov/nchs/data/databriefs/db288.pdf.

Harris, F., Green, R.F., Joy, E.J.M., Kayatz, B., Haines, A. and Dangour, A.D. 2017. The water use of Indian diets and socio-demographic factors related to dietary blue water footprint. *Science of the Total Environment*, 587–588: 128–136.

Headey, D., Hirvonen, K. and Hoddinott, J. 2018. Animal sourced foods and child stunting. *American Journal of Agricultural Economics*, 100(5): 1302–1319.

Headey, D. and Palloni, G. 2019. Water, sanitation, and child health: Evidence from subnational panel data in 59 countries. *Demography*, 56(2): 729–752.

HLPE. 2012. Food security and climate change. A report by the High Level Panel of Experts on Food Security and Nutrition of the Committee on World Food Security. Rome: HLPE.

HLPE. 2013. Biofuels and food security: A report by the high level panel of experts on food security and nutrition. HLPE Report 5. Rome: HLPE.

HLPE (High Level Panel of Experts on Food Security and Nutrition). 2014. Food losses and waste in the context of sustainable food systems. A report by the High Level Panel of Experts on Food Security and Nutrition of the Committee on World Food Security. Rome: HLPE.

HLPE. 2015. Water for food security and nutrition. A report by the High Level Panel of Experts on Food Security and Nutrition of the Committee on World Food Security, Rome: HLPE.

Humphrey, J.H. 2009. Child undernutrition, tropical enteropathy, toilets and handwashing. *Lancet*, 374(9694): P1032–11035.

International Energy Agency (IEA) 2016. Available at: www.eia.gov/electricity/data/browser/. Accessed October 2016.

IPCC, 2012. Managing the Risks of Extreme Events and Disasters to Advance Climate Change Adaptation. A Special Report of Working Groups I and II of the Intergovernmental Panel on Climate Change. Cambridge, UK and New York: Cambridge University Press.

IPCC, 2014. Climate Change 2014: Synthesis Report. Contribution of Working Groups I, II and III to the Fifth Assessment Report of the Intergovernmental Panel on Climate Change, IPCC. https://doi.org/10.1017/CBO9781107415324.

IPCC. 2018. Summary for policymakers. In V. Masson-Delmotte, P. Zhai, H.O. Pörtner, D. Roberts, J. Skea, P.R. Shukla, A. Pirani, W. Moufouma-Okia, C. Péan, R. Pidcock, S. Connors, J.B.R. Matthews, Y. Chen, X. Zhou, M.I. Gomis, E. Lonnoy, T. Maycock,

M. Tignor and T. Waterfield, eds. *Global Warming of 1.5°C. An IPCC Special Report on the Impacts of Global Warming of 1.5°C above Pre-Industrial Levels and Related Global Greenhouse Gas Emission Pathways, in the Context of Strengthening the Global Response to the Threat of Climate Change, Sustainable Development, and Efforts to Eradicate Poverty*, p. 32. Geneva, Switzerland: World Meteorological Organization.

Jawahar, P. and Ringler, C. 2009. Water quality is essential to food safety: Risks and drivers of global change. *Water Policy*, 11: 680–695.

Jiménez Cisneros, B.E., Oki, T., Arnell, N.W., Benito, G., Cogley, J.G., Döll, P., Jiang, T. and Mwakalila, S.S. 2014. Freshwater resources. In C.B. Field, V.R. Barros, D.J. Dokken, K.J. Mach, M.D. Mastrandrea, T.E. Bilir, M. Chatterjee, K.L. Ebi, Y.O. Estrada, R.C. Genova, B. Girma, E.S. Kissel, A.N. Levy, S. MacCracken, P.R. Mastrandrea and L.L. White, eds. *Climate Change 2014: Impacts, Adaptation, and Vulnerability. Part A: Global and Sectoral Aspects*. Contribution of Working Group II to the Fifth Assessment Report of the Intergovernmental Panel on Climate Change, pp. 229–269. Cambridge, UK and New York: Cambridge University Press. Available at: www.ipcc.ch/site/assets/uploads/2018/02/WGIIAR5-Chap3_FINAL.pdf.

Kacker, S.D. and Joshi, A. 2012. Pipe Dreams? The governance of urban water supply in informal settlements, New Delhi. *IDS Bulletin*, 43(2): 27–36.

Khennas, S. and Barnett, A. 2000. Best practices for sustainable development of micro hydro power in developing countries. ESMAP technical paper no. 6. Washington, DC: World Bank. Available at: http://hdl.handle.net/10986/20314.

Kondash, A.M., Lauer, N.E. and Vengosh, A. 2018. The intensification of the water footprint of hydraulic fracturing. *Science Advances*, 15 August 2018: 4(8), eaar5982.

Konzmann, M., Gerten, D. and Heinke, J. 2013. Climate impacts on global irrigation requirements under 19 GCMs, simulated with a vegetation and hydrology model. *Hydrological Sciences Journal*, 58(1): 1–18.

Lefore, N., Giordano, M., Ringler, C. and Barron, J. 2019. Sustainable and equitable growth in farmer-led irrigation in sub-Saharan Africa: What will it take? *Water Alternatives*, 12(1): 156–168.

Luby, S.P., Rahman, M., Arnold, L., Unicomb, L., Ashraf, S., Winch, P.J., Stewart, C.P., Begum, F., Hussain, F., Benjamin-Chung, J., Leontsini, E., Naser, A.M., Parvez, S.M., Hubbard, A.E., Lin, A., Nizame, F.A., Jannat, K., Ercumen, A., Ram, P.K., Das, K.K., Abedin, J., Clasen, T.F., Dewey, K.G., Fernald, L.C., Null, C., Ahmed, T. and Colford, J.M. 2018. Effects of water quality, sanitation, handwashing, and nutritional interventions on diarrhoea and child growth in rural Bangladesh: A cluster randomised controlled trial. *The Lancet Global Health*, 6: e302–e315.

McCartney, M. and Smakhtin, V. 2010. Water storage in an era of climate change: Addressing the challenge of increasing rainfall variability. Blue paper, IWMI Reports 212430. Colombo, Sri Lanka: International Water Management Institute (IWMI).

Malmquist, L. (2018). Water productivity and water requirements in food production – examples from Ethiopia, Tanzania and Burkina Faso. Swedish University of Agricultural Sciences: Department of Soil and Environment (Master of Science 2018:10).

Mehta, L. 2005. *The Politics and Poetics of Water: Naturalising Scarcity in Western India*. New Delhi: Orient Longman.

Mehta, L. 2013. *Ensuring Rights to Water and Sanitation for Women and Girls*, Interactive Expert Panel: Challenges and achievements in the implementation of the Millennium Development Goals for women and girls, 4–15 March 2013. New York: United Nations Commission on the Status of Women.

Mehta, L. 2014. Water and human development. *World Development*, 59: 59–69.

Mehta, L. 2016. Why invisible power and structural violence persist in the water domain. *IDS Bulletin*, 47(5): 31–42.

Mehta, L., Veldwisch, G.J. and Franco, J. 2012. Special Issue: Water grabbing? Focus on the (re)appropriation of finite water resources. *Water Alternatives*, 5(2): 193–207.

Mekonnen, M. and Hoekstra, A.Y. 2012. A global assessment of the water footprint of farm animal products. *Ecosystems*, 15: 401–415.

Merrey, D. and Lefore, N. (2018) Improving the availability and effectiveness of rural and "micro" finance for small scale irrigation in sub-Saharan Africa: A review of lessons learned. IWMI Working Paper 185. Colombo, Sri Lanka: International Water Management Institute (IWMI).

Miguel, E. and Kremer, M. 2004. Worms: Identifying impacts on education and health in the presence of treatment externalities. *Econometrica*, 72: 159–217.

Mitra, A. and Rao, N. 2019. Gender, water and nutrition in India: An intersectional analysis. *Water Alternatives*, 12(1): 169–191.

Movik, S. 2012. *Fluid Rights: South Africa's Water Allocation Reform*. Cape Town: Human Sciences Research Council Press.

Murphy, S. and Hansen-Kuhn, K. 2017. Counting the costs of agricultural dumping. Institute for Agriculture & Trade Policy. Available at: www.iatp.org/sites/default/files/2017-06/2017_06_26_DumpingPaper.pdf.

Myers, T. 2012. Potential contaminant pathways from hydraulically fractured shale to aquifers. Groundwater 50(6): 872–882.

Narula, K. and Lall, U. 2009. Challenges in securing India's water future. *Journal of Crop Improvement*, 24(1): 85–91.

National Chicken Council. 2014. *Per Capita Consumption of Poultry and Livestock, 1965 to Estimated 2014, in Pounds*. National Chicken Council [online]. Available at: www.nationalchickencouncil.org/about-the-industry/statistics/per-capita-consumption-of-poultry-and-livestock-1965-to-estimated-2012-in-pounds/.

Newborne, P. and Mason, N. 2012. The private sector's contribution to water management: Re-examining corporate purposes and company roles. *Water Alternatives*, 5(3): 603–618.

Nobre, A.D. 2014. The future climate of Amazonia scientific assessment report (*Portugese, Futuro Climático da Amazônia*). Available at: https://d2ouvy59p0dg6k.cloudfront.net/downloads/the_future_climate_of_amazonia_report.pdf.

Nobre, C.A., Marengo, J.A., Seluchi, M.E., Cuartas, L.A. and Alves, L.M. 2016. Some characteristics and impacts of the drought and water crisis in southeastern Brazil during 2014 and 2015. *Journal of Water Resource and Protection*, 8(2): 252–262.

Null, C., Stewart, C.P., Pickering, A.J., Dentz, H.N., Arnold, B.F., Arnold, C.D., Benjamin-Chung, J., Clasen, T., Dewey, K.G., Fernald, L.C.H., Hubbard, A.E., Kariger, P., Lin, A., Luby, S.P., Mertens, A., Njenga, S.M., Nyambane, G., Ram, P.K. and Colford, J.M. 2018. Effects of water quality, sanitation, handwashing, and nutritional interventions on diarrhoea and child growth in rural Kenya: A cluster-randomised controlled trial. *The Lancet Global Health*, 6(3): e316–e329.

Nunes, S.S., Jos Barlow, T.A., Gardner, J.V., Siqueira, M.R., Sales, A. and Souza, C.M. A 22 year assessment of deforestation and restoration in riparian forests in the eastern Brazilian Amazon. 2015. *Environmental Conservation*, 42(3): 193–203.

OECD. 2012. *OECD Environmental Outlook to 2050: The Consequences of Inaction*. OECD Publishing. Available at: www.oecd.org/env/indicators-modelling-outlooks/oecdenvironmentaloutlookto2050theconsequencesofinaction.htm.

Olivares, M. and Uauy, R. 2005. Essential nutrients in drinking water. In *Nutrients in Drinking Water*. Geneva: WHO.

Passarelli, S., Mekonnen, D., Bryan, E. and Ringler, C. 2018. Evaluating the pathways from small-scale irrigation to dietary diversity: Evidence from Ethiopia and Tanzania. *Food Security*, 10(4): 981–997.

Pew Commission on Industrial Farm Animal Production. 2008. Environmental impact of industrial farm animal production, A Report of the Pew Commission on Industrial Farm Animal Production (authored by Rolf U. Halden, and Kellogg J. Schwab). Available at: www.pcifapia.org/_images/212-4_EnvImpact_tc_Final.pdf.

Phillips, D.J.H., Allan, J.A., Claassen, M., Granit, J., Jägerskog, A., Kistin, E., Patrick, M. and Turton, A. 2008. The TWO Analysis: Introducing a Methodology for the Transboundary Waters Opportunity Analysis. Report Nr. 23. SIWI, Stockholm.

Pi, C., Rou, Z. and Horowitz, S. (eds). 2014. Fair or fowl? Industrialization of poultry production in China. Institute for Agriculture and Trade Policy. Available at: www.iatp.org/documents/fair-or-fowl-industrialization-poultry-production-china.

Renault, D. and Wallender, W.W. 2000. Nutritional water productivity and diets. *Agricultural Water Management*, 45(3): 275–296.

Ringler, C. 2017. Investment in irrigation for global food security. IFPRI Policy Note. Washington, DC: IFPRI.

Ringler, C., Biswas, A. and Cline, S.A. (eds). 2010. *Global Change: Impacts on Water and Food Security*. Berlin: Springer.

Ringler, C., Choufani, J., Chase, C., McCartney, M., Mateo-Sagasta, J., Mekonnen, D. and Dickens, C. 2018. Meeting the nutrition and water targets of the sustainable development goals: Achieving progress through linked interventions. Colombo, Sri Lanka: International Water Management Institute (IWMI). CGIAR Research Program on Water, Land and Ecosystems (WLE); Washington, DC, USA: The World Bank. 24p. (WLE Research for Development (R4D) Learning Series 7).

Ringler, C. and Zhu, T. 2015. Water resources and food security. *Journal of Agronomy*, 106: 1–6.

Rogelj, J., Shindell, D., Jiang, K., Fifita, S., Forster, P., Ginzburg, V., Handa, C., Kheshgi, H., Kobayashi, S., Kriegler, E., Mundaca, L., Séférian, R. and Vilariño, M.V. (2018). Mitigation pathways compatible with 1.5°C in the context of sustainable development. In V. Masson-Delmotte, P. Zhai, H.O. Pörtner, D. Roberts, J. Skea, P.R. Shukla, A. Pirani, W. Moufouma-Okia, C. Péan, R. Pidcock, S. Connors, J.B.R. Matthews, Y. Chen, X. Zhou, M.I. Gomis, E. Lonnoy, T. Maycock, M. Tignor and T. Waterfield, eds. *Global Warming of 1.5°C. An IPCC Special Report on the Impacts of Global Warming of 1.5°C above Pre-Industrial Levels and Related Global Greenhouse Gas Emission Pathways, in the Context of Strengthening the Global Response to the Threat of Climate Change, Sustainable Development, and Efforts to Eradicate Poverty*. Available at: www.ipcc.ch/site/assets/uploads/sites/2/2019/05/SR15_Chapter2_Low_Res.pdf.

Rosegrant, M.W., Cai, X. and Cline, S. 2002. *World Water and Food to 2025: Dealing with Scarcity*. Washington, DC: International Food Policy Research Institute.

Rosegrant, M.W., Magalhaes, E., Valmonte-Santos, R.A. and Mason-D'Croz, D. 2015. Returns to investment in reducing postharvest food losses and increasing agricultural productivity growth: Post-2015 consensus. Food Security and Nutrition Assessment Paper. Lowell, MA: Copenhagen Consensus Center. Available at: www.copenhagenconsensus.com/sites/default/files/food_security_nutrition_assessment_-_rosegrant_0.pdf.

Rosegrant, M.W., Ringler, C. and Zhu, T. 2014. Water markets as an adaptive response to climate change. In K.W. Easter and Q. Huang, eds. *Water Markets for the 21st Century:*

What Have We Learned?, pp. 35–65. Global Issues in Water Policy 11. Dordrecht: Springer.

Sadoff, C., Hall, J.W., Grey, D., Aerts, J.C.J.H., Ait-Kadi, M., Brown, C., Cox, A., Dadson, S., Garrick, D., Kelman, J., McCornick, P., Ringler, C., Rosegrant, M., Whittington, D. and Wiberg, D. 2015. Securing water, sustaining growth: Report of the GWP/OECD task force on water security and sustainable growth. University of Oxford, UK. Available at: www.gwp.org/Global/About%20GWP/Publications/The%20Global%20Dialogue/SECURING%20WATER%20SUSTAINING%20GROWTH.PDF.

Scott, C.A. 2011. The water-energy-climate nexus: Resources and policy outlook for aquifers in Mexico. *Water Resources Research*, 47, W00L04.

Sen, A. 1981. *Poverty and Famines: An Essay on Entitlement and Deprivation*. Oxford, UK: Clarendon Press.

Sharma, S. 2014. *The Need for Feed: China's Demand for Industrialized Meat and Its Impacts*, ITAP, Global Meat Complex, China Series [online]. Available at: www.iatp.org/files/2014_03_26_FeedReport_f_web.pdf.

Sharma, S. and Schlesinger, S. 2017. The rise of big meat: Brazils' extractive industry. Institute for Agriculture and Trade Policy. Available at: www.iatp.org/sites/default/files/2017-11/2017_11_30_RiseBigMeat_f.pdf.

Sheahan, M. and Barrett, C.B. 2017. Food loss and waste in Sub-Saharan Africa: A critical review. *Food Policy*, 70: 1–12.

Shiklomanov, I. 1999. International hydrological programme database. St Petersburg, Russia: State Hydrological Institute. Available at: http://webworld.unesco.org/water/ihp/db/shiklomanov/.

Siddiqui, A. and Wescoat, J.L. 2013. Energy use in large-scale irrigated agriculture in the Punjab province of Pakistan. *Water International*, 38(5): 571–586.

Siebert, S., Burke, J., Faures, J.M., Frenken, K., Hoogeveen, J., Döll, P. and Portmann, F. T. 2010. Groundwater use for irrigation – A global inventory. *Hydrology and Earth System Sciences*, 14(10): 1863–1880.

Sojamo, S. and Larson, E.A. 2012. Investigating food and agribusiness corporations as global water security, management and governance agents: The case of Nestlé, Bunge and Cargill. *Water Alternatives*, 5(3): 619–635.

Spang, E.S., Moomaw, W.R., Gallagher, K.S., Kirshen, P.H. and Marks, D.H. 2014. The water consumption of energy production: An international comparison. IOP Publishing Ltd. *Environmental Research Letters,* 9(10). Available at: https://iopscience.iop.org/article/10.1088/1748-9326/9/10/105002.

Thebo, A.L., Drechsel, P., Lambin, E.F. and Nelson, K.L. 2017. A global, spatially-explicit assessment of irrigated croplands influenced by urban wastewater flows. *Environmental Research Letters*, 12(7). Available at: https://iopscience.iop.org/article/10.1088/1748-9326/aa75d1.

Theis, S., Deribe Bekele, R., Lefore, N., Meinzen-Dick, R.S. and Ringler, C. 2018a. Considering gender when promoting small-scale irrigation technologies: Guidance for inclusive irrigation interventions. IFPRI-REACH Project Note. Washington, DC: International Food Policy Research Institute (IFPRI).

Theis, S., Lefore, N., Meinzen-Dick, R. and Bryan, E. 2018b. What happens after technology adoption? Gendered aspects of small-scale irrigation technologies in Ethiopia, Ghana and Tanzania. *Agriculture and Human Values*, 2018: 1–14

The Poultry Site. 2013. *Global Poultry Trends 2013: Asia Consumes 40 Per Cent of World's Chicken*. The Poulty Site [online]. Available at: www.thepoultrysite.com/articles/2929/global-poultry-trends-2013-asia-consumes-40-per-cent-of-worlds-chicken.

UNDESA (United Nations, Department of Economic and Social Affairs), Population Division. 2017. World population prospects: The 2017 Revision. DVD Edition.

United Nations Development Programme (UNDP). 2006. Beyond scarcity: Power, poverty and the global crises. Human Development Report 2006. New York: UNDP.

United Nations Environment Programme (UNEP). 2011. *Water Issues in the Democratic Republic of the Congo: Challenges and Opportunities*. Nairobi, Kenya. Available at: https://postconflict.unep.ch/publications/UNEP_DRC_water.pdf.

UN WWAP (UN World Water Assessment Programme). 2014. *UN World Water Development Report 2014: Water and Energy*. Paris: UNESCO.

US EPA. 2016. Hydraulic fracturing for oil and gas: Impacts from the hydraulic fracturing water cycle on drinking water resources in the United States (Final Report). Washington, DC: United States Environmental Protection Agency. EPA/600/R-16/236F.

Varghese, S. 2007. *Biofuels and Global Water Challenges*. Minneapolis, MN: IATP.

Von Braun, J. and Meinzen-Dick, R.S. 2009. "Land grabbing" by foreign investors in developing countries. Policy Brief. Washington, DC: IFPRI. Available at: www.ifpri.org/publication/land-grabbing-foreign-investors-developing-countries.

Watts, J. 2014. Brazil drought crisis leads to rationing and tension. *The Guardian*, 5 September, 2014. Available at: www.theguardian.com/weather/2014/sep/05/brazil-drought-crisis-rationing. Accessed 2 February 2015.

WCD (World Commission on Dams). 2000. *Dams and Development: A New Framework for Decision-Making*. London: Earthscan.

Webb, P. and Iskandarani, M. 1998. Water insecurity and the poor: Issues and research needs. Discussion Paper on Development PolicyNo. 2. Bonn: University of Bonn, Center for Development Research (ZEF).

Wenhold, F. and Faber, M. 2009. Water in nutritional health of individuals and households: An overview, *Water SA*, 35(1): 61–71.

WHO. 2012. Global costs and benefits of drinking-water supply and sanitation interventions to reach the MDG target and universal coverage. WHO/HSE/WSH/12.01. Geneva, Switzerland.

WHO. 2015. Progress on sanitation and drinking water – 2015 update and MDG assessment. Geneva, Switzerland: UNICEF and World Health Organization.

WHO/UNICEF. 2017. Progress on drinking water, sanitation and hygiene 2017. Update and SDG Baseline. Geneva: World Health Organization (WHO) and the United Nations Children's Fund (UNICEF).

Willett, W., Rockström, J., Loken, B., Springmann, M., Lang, T., Vermeulen, S., Garnett, T., Tilman, D., DeClerck, F. et al. 2019. Food in the Anthropocene: The EAT–Lancet Commission on healthy diets from sustainable food systems. *The Eat Lancet Commission. The Lancet*, 393(10170): 447–492.

Woodhouse, P. 2012. New investment. Old challenges. Land deals and the water constraint in African agriculture. *The Journal of Peasant Studies*, 39(3–4): 777–794

World Bank. 2010. *Rising Global Interest in Farmland: Can It Yield Sustainable and Equitable Benefits?*, Washington, DC: World Bank.

WWAP. 2012. *The United Nations World Water Development Report 4: Managing Water under Uncertainty and Risk*. Paris: UNESCO.

WWAP (United Nations World Water Assessment Programme). 2014. *The United Nations World Water Development Report 2014: Water and Energy*. Paris: UNESCO.

Xie, H. and Ringler, C. 2017. Agricultural nutrient loadings to the freshwater environment: The role of climate change and socioeconomic change. *Environmental Research Letters*, 12: 104008.

Yang, C. and Cui, X. 2014. Global changes and drivers of the water footprint of food consumption: A historical analysis. *Water*, 6: 1435–1452.

Zeng, R., Cai, X., Ringler, C. and Zhu, T. 2017. Hydropower versus irrigation – an analysis of global patterns. *Environmental Research Letters*, 12(2017): 034006.

3
AGRICULTURAL WATER MANAGEMENT

Water management in agriculture and food systems has been receiving increasing attention over the last several decades. However, due to changing demographic patterns and the emergence of a wealthier middle class in most developing regions combined with the high consumption levels in the global North, food, feed, fibre and fuel demands and their associated water impacts across the entire agriculture and food systems continue to grow.

At the same time, as discussed in Chapters 1 and 2, the water demands of other sectors, such as energy, municipal and industrial, have been growing even more rapidly (Rosegrant *et al.*, 2002). Across the world enough food is produced to theoretically feed the global population, but poorer people, who still may spend half or more of their income on food, cannot always afford food of sufficient quantity and quality, nor is the food distributed effectively to where it is needed. Thus, achieving food security for all requires both better use of existing resources, such as water, to produce better food at lower prices, better income opportunities to help afford food, and particularly healthier and culturally appropriate food choices. Also it requires improved institutions from the global to the local level to make food accessible to those facing temporary and chronic shortages (HLPE, 2012). As discussed in the previous chapter, even though issues of food security are mainly concentrated in water scarce and poor countries, access to food, and specifically nutritious food, is primarily affected by socio-economic factors, such as class, gender and race, even in the global North. Similarly, the inability to produce or to buy enough food is as linked to the risks of water shortages and drought as to institutional and socio-economic factors, as well as gender (CA, 2007).

Current efforts of water management for improved FSN are largely limited to conventional approaches, such as improvements of irrigation application efficiency through moving from traditional to advanced irrigation systems, more optimal use of complementary inputs, and direct interventions in the crop architecture, such as short-duration and semi-dwarf varieties of cereal crops. Modernizing irrigation systems may not add substantial or real water savings: while they increase field and farm irrigation efficiency, the overall water savings at the basin or landscape levels may not be proportional (see for example, Grafton et al., 2018; Perry, 2007). Moreover, as long as the yield to total biomass ratio does not improve or as long as total biomass increases as a result of yield improvement, then water use might not decline. In addition, contrary to the attempts in domestic and some industrial sectors, little progress has been made in water demand management in the agricultural sector through pricing, for a host of reasons, ranging from the overall low value but high use of water in agriculture to cultural factors (CA, 2007).

This notwithstanding some areas, including the Middle East and the North African region, have developed innovative water reuse technologies that have seen significant improvements in water productivity. Among those are the use of treated sewage water and brackish water sometimes mixed with fresh water, for selected cropping patterns and the decentralized treatment and recycling of grey water within the rural household for agriculture (Boufaroua et al., 2013; CA, 2007). Other regions are starting to improve monitoring of actual evapotranspiration levels and responses of various interventions, such as advanced irrigation technologies or water pricing on evapotranspiration. Farmer to farmer knowledge-exchange on agroecological systems and practices (such as multilayer intercropping that reduces evapotranspiration), is increasing wider adoption of such practices as well.

A major challenge is that future improvements in water management will need to respond to increasing risk and uncertainties associated with climate variability and change, which, in addition to changing rainfall patterns, impact biotic stressors, such as pests and disease. Other important uncertainties are associated with local and global economies. For instance, the grain price hikes of 2007/08 and associated shortages in international markets led to a flurry of short-term initiatives and government policies to help improve food security in many countries. These policy measures, generally the reduction or elimination of exports of grains, led to a much stronger price response as climate and other factors would have suggested. The price spikes of 2001/2008 may not have been necessary if there had been a predictable global policy environment in place to support the progressive realization of the right to food (Oweis, 2016).

Unfortunately, technological advancements are unpredictable and institutional/policy environments, especially at the country level (such as subsidies, land tenure and others) may, if inappropriately designed, present major risks that affect farmers' ability or desire to invest in and gain from improved water productivity. However, there are a number of responses to increased risk and uncertainty that include learning how to deal with uncertain variables such as precipitation, for example, through the development of storage; farmer insurance; diversification of crops; and international trade. A notable negative and technically inefficient response to the grain shortages and price hikes of 2007 was a strong movement towards achieving self-sufficiency in food production in many water scarce countries such as some of the Gulf Cooperation Council (GCC) countries. With a strategy for self-sufficiency, countries attempt to produce crops that require far more water than in more suitable environments in other countries to produce the same level of outputs. Trade of virtual water would be a more efficient option in this case.

This chapter sheds light on how water-related uncertainties affect efforts to meet global food demand and nutrition security, and suggests a shift in the water management paradigm, together with alternative approaches to reducing risk, increasing resilience and improving food security. It addresses water management challenges across scales: namely, from global to farms and crops. Given that most water for FSN is used in agriculture, the discussion largely focuses on the various dimensions of agroecosystems including rainfed, irrigated and agropastoral. It also describes the potential for reform in the processing and preparation stages and issues concerning managing water quality and wastewater. Finally, it looks at the challenges in water accounting before concluding with some policy and institutional implications.

Managing agricultural water at scale

Water is managed for agriculture at a range of scales from the global to the local levels, with different management, technology, and institutional options. The boundaries of these irrigated fields, systems, watersheds and river basins, generally differ from political or administrative boundaries. This introduces significant challenges in aligning agricultural water management with other sectors, such as energy or urban spaces, which typically operate according to the political or administrative boundaries. This section outlines some of the critical aspects of water management at various scales, and their implications for FSN.

Global level

Many processes at the global scale are relevant to water use in agriculture, such as trade in food and other commodities as well as global policies and international agreements on climate, energy, finance and development (see Chapter 5). Other international processes matter as well, such as on investment, sustainable development, and importantly, on the environment. Of particular importance has been the adoption of the Sustainable Development Goals in 2015, with a separate Goal on Water and Sanitation titled 'Ensure availability and sustainable management of water and sanitation for all'. While this is an important improvement over the Millennium Development Goals that only referred to drinking water and were limited to countries in the global South, SDG 6 is on Water and Sanitation, and is global in nature. Still, this too does not refer to water use in agriculture, despite its overwhelming role in freshwater use. On the positive side, in January 2017, 83 ministers of agriculture accounting for most agricultural water use globally, jointly declared that they 'will work to ensure that agriculture shoulders its share of responsibility in achieving and maintaining good status of water bodies, including water quality and quantity' and 'acknowledge the need to take conservation, protection and sustainable use and management of water into account in agricultural and related policies'. The ministers then identified 18 measures in the areas of enhancing access to water, improving water quality, reducing water scarcity risks and managing surplus water, with the overall goal of more sustainable agricultural water management (GFFA Communique, 2017). There are several other new initiatives that are geared toward improved agricultural water management with a global focus: they include The Global Framework on Water Scarcity in Agriculture and the OECD Water Governance Initiative, among others. The other notable agreement at the global level is the 2015 Paris Climate Agreement that invited countries to submit Nationally Determined Contributions to address climate change. Many of the measures submitted and ongoing efforts will also help reduce water use in agriculture and other sectors. However, some efforts submitted under the Paris Climate Agreement, such as expanded use of biofuels as a renewable energy source, could substantially increase agricultural water use.

One concept that has helped illustrate water use and, particularly, water flows at the global level is the concept of virtual water. The virtual-water content of a product is the volume of freshwater used to produce the product. Virtual water trade refers to the hidden flow of water if food or other commodities are traded from one place to another. The use of the virtual water concept illustrates the important linkages between agricultural water use locally and the global economy. It shows how existing water shortages can be at least partially alleviated by a combination of economic factors including importation of food (Allan, 2011), and policy incentives that help shift water allocation away from water intensive crops/industries that contribute to increasing water scarcity in the region. In water scarce areas, the concept of virtual water allows countries to assess the value of producing a specific crop locally vs importing it. Similarly, countries might opt to import electricity, or explore alternative low-water footprint energy sources, rather than use limited water resources to generate their own electricity.

By importing agricultural or other commodities a nation saves the amount of water it would have required to produce these domestically. As an example, the water-scarce Middle East and North Africa region has had net imports of nearly 50 million tons of grain every year (FAOSTAT, 2014). If produced locally, the region would have had to dedicate over 50 billion cubic metres of water to these grains, water that is not available. At the same time, exporting water-intensive agricultural crops contributes to local water scarcity, and national water deficit. For example, India, with 18% of the world's population and 4% of its water, is considered to be a water-stressed country with many parts of the country experiencing water scarcity. Dominant framings focus on rapid population growth and a relatively warm and hot monsoon regime that is substantially affected by climate change. Other reasons that are not adequately addressed in official statements include unequal access to water, ineffective governance and management, as well as an over-reliance on large-scale and top-down options, rather than more locally appropriate ones (see Chapter 4). Finally, the focus on export-oriented agricultural policies also undermines water security (see Box 3.1).

BOX 3.1 INDIA'S AGRI-TRADE IMPLICATIONS FOR ITS WATER SECURITY

A 2018 study mapping water productivity of ten major Indian crops paints a bleak picture when it comes to implications of India's agri-trade for its water security: 'India is the largest exporter of rice in the world with an export volume of more than 10 million tonnes per year. One kg of rice inherently needs about 5000 litres of water for irrigation in a region like Punjab-Haryana, and about 3000 litres in water abundant regions. Taking an average of say 4000 litres per kg of rice, export of 10 million tonnes amounts to exporting 40 billion cubic metres of water. On the other hand our largest agri-import is of edible oils and pulses. Oilseeds and pulses are water saving, except oil palm which needs high rainfall and moisture. Overall, our agri-trade structure is turning out to be hydrologically and economically unsustainable with low productivity of water resources. These trends need to be reversed for creating a water positive agriculture' (Sharma *et al.*, 2018: 179).

In sum, national agricultural trade policies play an important role in the water security of a country. They can even help by reducing virtual water export from water scarce regions and by encouraging virtual water import in water stressed countries.

Basin level

Water resources are generally best managed according to watershed, basin or catchment boundaries. A watershed, basin or catchment is an area of land that drains all the streams and rainfall falling on it to a common outlet, usually into a water body. Groundwater basins often interact with surface water basins but might have different boundaries. Watersheds or basins can be defined in a series of nested levels from relatively small sub-basins within a larger basin, to entire basins, which may cover large areas of land, often expanding across several countries. The scale at which water management technologies and institutional setups are addressed affects very much the choices available.

The four principles of watershed management, according to the US Environmental Protection Agency (EPA), are: 1) Watersheds are natural systems that we can work with; 2) watershed management is continuous and needs a multidisciplinary approach; 3) a watershed management framework supports partnering, using sound science, taking well-planned actions and achieving results; and 4) a flexible approach is always needed (EPA, 2017). As discussed in Chapter 1, most government planning, however, is done according to administrative boundaries (national, state and municipal). This requires that water management, while focused on the hydrological system, must, at the same time, align with political imperatives defined within different administrative boundaries. To add to this complexity, many basins are transboundary, either at the state or country level, and water management must deal with transboundary issues such as water sharing between countries, benefit sharing, water quality issues and water-related disaster planning and management (see Chapter 5). The focus on the hydrological system requires, inter alia, an understanding of the impacts of upstream land use and activities on downstream water availability and quality. As a result, basin management must engage with other sectors that impact on water resources, particularly agriculture, energy, mining, urbanization and conservation, highlighting the need for cooperation between water managers and key players in other sectors.

National level

At the national scale, water resource managers need to coordinate a wide range of ministries across which water is usually spread. These can include a Ministry of Water Resources or Irrigation, as well as Ministries of Agriculture, Construction, Environment, Livestock and Fisheries, Mines and Energy, but also Ministries of Health, and Finance. In many cases, the Ministry using most fresh water resources, i.e. the Ministry of Agriculture, is not in charge of managing water resources. And only in very few cases do governments include coordinating bodies that reduce the fragmentation of water management through regular management, information on bills and regulations under development and by coordination of investments, such as those in energy with those in irrigation or agriculture (see Chapter 4 for a further discussion on the politics of water allocation and problems of integration).

Local level

Local organizations of farmers and water users are crucial for the adaptive management of water resources and related ecosystems. Examples include local watershed management organizations, fishing associations, farmer field schools, and water user groups. Local organizations are particularly well placed to monitor and respond adaptively to environmental change. This is important because variation within and among the environments in which water resources are located is enormous.

Uncertainty, spatial variability and complex non-equilibrium and non-linear ecological dynamics require flexible responses, mobility and local-level adaptive water resource management in which farmers, pastoralists, fisher folk and forest dwellers are central actors in analysis, planning, negotiations and action (Gunderson *et al.*, 1995). Such adaptive management is mediated by local groups that co-ordinate planning and action at different spatio-temporal scales, often through polycentric networks of local organizations (Borrini, 2011). Local organizations facilitate the emergence of institutions that are key for the adaptive management of water resources and the ecosystems that sustain them – from agreements on rights of access and use of water resources to sanctions for transgressing locally decided 'rules of the game'. These forms of local governance usually include a network of often overlapping institutions, negotiated agreements on the roles, rights and responsibilities of different actors, leadership, cultural practices, labour allocation, religious beliefs and so forth (Borrini, 2011). They also help enforce the locally (or nationally) negotiated agreements, rules, incentives and penalties needed for the sustainable management of landscapes and environmental processes on which the availability, quality and renewal of water resources depend.

By bringing together relevant actors and their local organizations into polycentric networks, such local governance regimes are key for mobilizing capacity for social learning, negotiation, and collective action for the adaptive management of water and critical ecological services at different scales – from farm plots and the wider agro-ecosystem to whole watersheds and landscapes (Pimbert, 2010). Collective action, based on social learning and negotiated agreements among relevant actors, is often a condition for the sustainable management of water resources and the ecosystems they depend on. However, even at the local level as we outline in some detail in the next chapter, differential power relations inform who controls or influences water allocation and management decisions, and in many cases, women continue to be disadvantaged even at the local level.

Agroecosystem level

Applying ecological principles into agroecosystems can suggest novel management approaches that would not otherwise be considered. Agroecosystem assessment identifies how, when and if technology can be used in conjunction with natural, social and human assets. Agroecologists may study questions related to the four system properties of agroecosystems: productivity, stability, sustainability and equitability. As opposed to disciplines that are concerned with only one or some of these properties, agroecologists see all four properties as interconnected and integral to the success of an agroecosystem. To improve agroecosystem outcomes, they use an interdisciplinary lens, including natural sciences to understand elements of agroecosystems such as soil properties and plant–insect interactions and social sciences to understand the effects of farming practices on rural communities, economic constraints to developing new production methods, and cultural factors determining farming practices (CBD, 1992). Approaches of studying agroecologies include Agro-population ecology, Indigenous agroecology and Inclusive agroecology. The approach was first adopted by the UN Convention on Biological Diversity (UN CBD) but its implementation has been impeded by lack of policy support.

However, there have been many agroecological practices that have been developed (Wezel *et al.*, 2014) by smallholder farming communities across the world, often in response to the specific local challenges they face. In the context of FSN, the agroecological approach requires that the concept of agroecology is applied to the whole food system. Due to its transdisciplinary nature, it embraces the science, the on-the-ground practices as well as the crucial role of food producers' movements. The decision by UN FAO's Committee (COAG/2018/5) on Agriculture (FAO, 2018c) to support agroecology as one of the approaches to promote sustainable agriculture and food systems, particularly for smallholders and family farmers, was a turning point. The '*Scaling up Agroecology Initiative*' is seen as

> an opportunity for UN partners and related bodies (FAO, IFAD, WFP, UNEP, UNDP and CBD) to work in a coordinated way to scale up agroecology through policies, science, investment, technical support and awareness, according to their mandate and expertise, and extending the knowledge to all actors in an effort to address various challenges, including climate change elements of the 2030 Agenda, protection and preservation of biodiversity, and conservation and recovery of degraded forests and soils.
>
> *(FAO, 2018a: 3)*

Given that the member governments and other stakeholders of the UN Committee on Food Security are also in the process of developing possible policy options around agroecology, it is likely that more and more countries will adopt policies that incentivize agroecological practices (see Box 3.2).

BOX 3.2 FAO'S SCALING UP AGROECOLOGY INITIATIVE: TEN ELEMENTS TO GUIDE THE TRANSITION TO SUSTAINABLE FOOD AND AGRICULTURAL SYSTEMS

The Scaling up Agroecology Initiative endorses ten elements of agroecology that are based on the seminal scientific literature on agroecology – in particular, five principles of agroecology (Altieri, 1995) and five levels of agroecological transitions (Gliessman, 2015), as well as inputs from various FAO regional and international multi-stakeholder symposiums (2015–2018), and inputs from international and FAO experts.

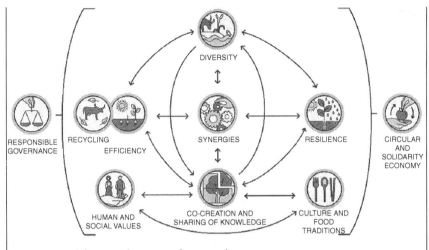

FIGURE 3.1 The ten elements of agroecology
Source: FAO: www.fao.org/3/i9037en/I9037EN.pdf

> As an analytical tool, the ten elements can help countries to operationalize agro-ecology actions on the ground. By identifying key considerations in developing an enabling environment for agroecology, the ten elements also serve as a guide for policymakers, practitioners and stakeholders in planning, managing and evaluating agroecological transitions. Source: www.fao.org/3/i9037en/I9037EN.pdf

Agroecological practices, as is evident from the above, are based on a series of principles: management should be decentralized to the lowest appropriate level; the approach should be undertaken at the appropriate spatial and temporal scales; the conservation of ecosystem structure and functioning should be a priority target; ecosystems must be managed within the limits of their functioning and all relevant sectors of society and scientific disciplines need to be included (Roy et al., 2011).

Collective action is a common ecosystem approach, for example, around water management, but also for common grazing lands or community forests (CBD, 1992). Although it is concerned with increasing productivity, this approach equally seeks to ensure the achievement of the right to food at the household level including through improved nutritional content. It focuses on the entire agroecosystem in specific socio-economic contexts (Altieri et al., 2012b). The agroecological approach stresses the right of people to define their own food and agriculture systems, allows producers to play a lead role in innovation and places those who produce, distribute and consume food at the centre of decisions on food systems and policies. Some benefits include dietary diversity and nutrition security through preserving macro- and micronutrients in the soil; protecting natural resources through using fewer artificial inputs; promoting agricultural resilience through use of diverse farming systems and providing a sustainable and scalable path to food security through allowing smallholder farmers to lead (IAASTD, 2009). Agroecological approaches also recognize the important role women play in agriculture by respecting and honouring women's knowledge as seed keepers, and cultivators. This knowledge is explicitly sought and built on in agroecological approaches (Altieri et al., 2012b).

Such an approach to food security also seeks to protect available natural resources, including water. Farming techniques with fewer inputs protect water from degradation due to chemical pesticides and fertilizers, and agroecological methods maximize the productivity of available resources through context-specific soil, water and biodiversity management regimes informed by traditional knowledge. Agroecology's focus on maintaining crop diversity also allows farmers to appropriately utilize available water resources (Altieri et al., 2012a). An example of such approaches in more drought prone and marginal environments are water and land management practices that make use of indigenous technology, such as water harvesting, micro-irrigation, mulching and the construction of hill-side terraces lined with shrubs and trees which enhance the ability of the soil to catch and store water. While agroecology is rooted in the rationale of traditional peasant farming systems (Altieri et al., 2012b), agroecological transition processes include innovative forms of collaboration between farmers and researchers, building primarily on functionalities given by ecosystems and traditional knowledge and know-how but combining it with the best use of modern agroecological science (Parmentier, 2014).

Another approach of potential importance for agroecology is ecological sanitation or eco-san. This takes an ecosystem approach to sanitation by making use of human excreta to improve soil nutrients and increase food production (Esrey et al., 2001). Promotion of ecological sanitation methods can contribute to closing the gap between the agriculture sector's perception of phosphorous as a valuable fertilizer resource and the WASH sector's perception of phosphorous as a water pollutant. Although hygiene guidelines should be followed when handling human excreta for agriculture, both urine and faeces are high-quality, complete fertilizers that have been shown to improve crop production when appropriately applied (Jönsson et al., 2004). Tapping into this resource, therefore, could have important implications for both food security and water use if food safety and human health considerations are adequately addressed.

Livestock are an important part of agroecological approaches that are multi-functional in nature, providing milk, meat, eggs, cash income, farm power and manure that can enhance soil fertility, while being nurtured by hay and other crop residues. They also have important cultural values, are a means for poor people to accumulate wealth and provide some resilience to drought and other harsh environments. The growing demand for meat and milk in urban areas in particular is largely being met not through integrated animal–crop production systems, but increasingly through concentrated animal feeding operations (CAFOs) that create substantial demand for animal feed production, the component of the livestock cycle that constitutes the bulk of water use (Peden et al., 2007). Concentrated animal feeding operations, in many areas, has significant localized impacts on water quality with the resulting excessive nutrient loading leading to eutrophication of surface waters for instance, creating 'dead zones' in both inland and marine waters due to algal blooms and resulting in massive fish kills and declines in biodiversity.

Agricultural ecosystems

Agricultural systems range from fully rainfed to fully irrigated with several combinations in between, such as supplementary irrigated, pastoral, urban and peri urban systems. Following is a brief description of the important systems:

Rainfed systems

Rainfed agriculture is the primary source food for poor communities in the developing world and most of these countries depend primarily on it for their food grains. Almost all land in sub-Saharan Africa (93%), three quarters of cropland in Latin America, two thirds of cropland in the Middle East and North Africa region, and more than half of cropland in Asia is rainfed. Women, who make up some 70% of the world's poor, play a key role in rainfed agriculture (FAO, 2012b). While the yield from rainfed agriculture varies widely across regions, average rainfed agricultural productivity (t/ha) is globally less than half of that of irrigated agriculture (Rockström et al., 2010). The highest yields from rainfed agriculture are found in the predominantly temperate regions, with relatively reliable rainfall and inherently productive soils, particularly in Europe and North America. However, even in tropical regions, agricultural yields in commercial rainfed agriculture exceed 5–6 metric tons per hectare (CA, 2007). The dry sub-humid and semiarid regions experience the lowest yields and weakest yield improvements per unit of land.

The main rainfed challenge, especially in dry areas (and more so with climate change), is to manage the risk of rainfall variability, but key constraints vary from one region to another. In the arid regions, physical water availability constitutes the major limiting factor. In the semiarid and dry sub-humid tropical regions, variability and amount of rainfall is the main issue and coping with extreme rainfall variability over time and space is the main challenge. In the wetter parts of the semi-arid and the dry sub-humid zones, the volume of rainfall is not a problem, but extreme rainfall events and the high frequency of dry spells and droughts. However, the large observed differences between farmers' yields and attainable yields may also be a result of management problems rather than only rainfall characteristics (Wani et al., 2009). In rainfed farming systems, agroecological approaches can help building healthy soils with higher water storage capacity, which improves crop productivity (Kremen and Miles, 2012).

Farmers generally realize the high risk associated with rainfall variability and resulting yield losses so they are cautious with investments in labour, improved seed, and fertilizers. Yield fluctuations and risk avoidance strategies makes it hard for poor farmers in semiarid areas to capture opportunities in emerging markets, trade and globalization. Management therefore first needs to address reducing rainfall-induced risks, such as through encouraging agro-ecological practices as they help build climate resilient farms, and make investment decisions that are less risky (Fraser et al., 2011).

Irrigated system

In irrigated systems, blue water (surface water and groundwater that can be abstracted for use) is the main source of water to support agricultural production. The main issue is to sustainably manage both land and water, which includes appropriate irrigation and cropping systems and related investments, the efficiency and productivity of water use, and the availability of the resource.

As discussed earlier, globally, irrigation accounts for about 70% of water withdrawals and about 80% of consumptive water use.[1] These figures vary heavily from country to country (World Bank, 2006), are generally higher in the global South. Irrigation covers about 20% of all cultivated lands and contributes about 40% of agricultural production. Globally, about 350 million hectares of cropland are irrigated. Two-thirds of this area is located in Asia, 15% in the Americas, 9% in Europe and 6% in Africa. Key irrigated areas include the rice–wheat belt of the Indo-Gangetic Plains; the Hai He, Yellow and Yangtze basins in China, the Eastern Nile basin and the corn belt of the United States (Faurès et al., 2007).

Irrigation has been essential in achieving the productivity gains and food price reductions seen all over the world over the last three decades. Irrigation is also associated with significant multiplier effects, such as employment in the lean season, widening of livelihood opportunities through household gardens, livestock rearing, aquaculture and handicrafts, and benefits for health and nutrition (Domenech and Ringler, 2013; Rosegrant et al., 2009a; Box 3.3).

BOX 3.3 THE GENDERED NATURE OF IRRIGATION AND WATER MANAGEMENT

Women make up about 43% of the on-farm labour force in developing countries (Doss, 2011), but own a much smaller share of agricultural land. Sex-disaggregated data on land ownership is still limited, but in sub-Saharan Africa and Asia, data available for several countries show that women own substantially less land than men do (Doss et al., 2015; Kierean et al., 2015). Limited access to and ownership of land is a key factor limiting participation of women in irrigation activities.

But there are many other factors that matter. Men and male engineers dominate the irrigation sector and the implementation of water and sanitation projects (Zwarteveen, 2008). Even where the involvement of women is a requirement of the implementing agency, it is often either

> tokenistic or women and girls are expected to devote their voluntary labour rather than have any clear influence on decision making or develop particular skills. For example, as a rule, men are trained to manage wells, pumps and sanitation facilities and women are required to maintain and clean them, drawing on the traditional imagery of women as the keepers of cleanliness and purity in their families and local communities. Women's participation in decision making is hampered by cultural barriers and traditional gender roles and they are often excluded from irrigation or water management committees. Nationally and internationally very few women are represented in relevant ministries and international agencies or bodies (Zwarteveen, 2008).
>
> Empowering women will impact on the way irrigation is managed as they will have the chance to share decision making with men. Studies have shown that when women are included in irrigation project design and implementation, the projects are more effective and sustainable (FAO, 2012a). See also Chapter 2, Box 2.1.

However, public investments in large-scale irrigation have declined substantially over the last two decades in much of the world; only sub-Saharan Africa has seen strong increases in investment, albeit from a small base (Rosegrant et al., 2009b). As aptly put by CA (2007: 4), 'The era of rapid expansion of large-scale public irrigated agriculture is over: for most regions a major new task is adapting yesterday's irrigation systems to tomorrow's needs'. This includes a focus on farmer-financed and managed irrigation, chiefly supported by motor pumps, smarter surface systems; judicious investment in selected, large-scale systems linked with reservoirs that are often built for multiple purposes; and reforming water management institutions toward maintaining the ecological integrity of systems while improving productivity and profitability (Rosegrant et al., 2009a; Wichelns, 2014).

Salts may exist in agricultural lands due to natural geological causes but large irrigated areas in many arid and semi-arid regions face problems of reduced soil productivity as a result of secondary soil salinization. As an example, 50% of the fertile land in Iraq has been salinized over the last two decades due to mismanagement or lack of drainage facilities (Wu et al., 2014), and in Central Asia, the lack of proper maintenance of drainage systems is causing substantial salinization of irrigated lands. Salts accumulate in the irrigated soils as a consequence of continuous addition of salts with irrigation water or due to a rising water table (water logging) bringing salts to the surface through capillary rise. Tens of thousands of hectares of productive irrigated land are salinized every year to various degrees, affecting the livelihoods of communities that are dependent on this land.

Two strategies are available to deal with secondary salinization: a) 'living with salinity' by allowing the land to salinize and then cultivating salt tolerant crops and halophytes with special management; or b) 'controlling salinity' through leaching and maintaining highly productive land. It is estimated that 40–60% of irrigated areas require drainage to avoid soil salinization (Tanji and Kielen, 2002). This is the recommended strategy in irrigated areas, which requires investment in drainage facilities and irrigation management with appropriate institutions and policies.

Saltwater intrusion (salinity ingress) is another problem that impacts both agricultural and domestic water use negatively. Gujarat, an Indian state with the longest coastal line, has had growing saltwater intrusion along the coastal line of Kutch and Saurashtra, as a result of excessive ground water withdrawals. The lack of a cohesive and comprehensive water strategy over the last few decades has resulted in diminishing freshwater flow into river estuaries as a result of diversion of fresh water for other areas and uses upstream. One consequence has been spreading of saltwater intrusion further south, even into the estuary of Gujarat's largest river, Narmada (Gururaja et al., 2012).

The challenge for irrigated agriculture in this century is to improve equity, reduce environmental damage, strengthen ecosystem functions and enhance water and land productivity in existing and new irrigated systems. This is possible through linking existing irrigation systems to national socio-economic conditions and especially by supporting farmers with improved small irrigation systems and input, particularly in sub-Saharan Africa and Southeast Asia (Faurès et al., 2007). The System of Rice intensification (SRI) is an example of such nature friendly approaches, especially in the case of small-scale operators practising organic or minimal application of external inputs while achieving high levels of yields and water productivity.

Pastoral system

The agro-pastoral ecosystems are mainly rangelands occupying substantial areas around the world. These systems receive varying amounts of rainfall, but this is largely lost as evaporation or flow into salt sinks, especially in dry and hot environments (Oweis et al., 2012). Where surface or groundwater resources are available, people practice intensive agriculture through irrigation. Communities in this ecosystem primarily practise livestock herding and activities built on their products such as milk and meat.

Local conditions differ substantially from one region to the other, depending on prevailing climatic as well as socio-economic activities. One common challenge, however, is that these ecosystems are largely degraded, especially in dry environments and steep slopes. Reasons include exposure to both human interventions such as overgrazing, cultivation, wood cutting and overuse of water resources, and climate factors such as drought and weather extremes (Evenari et al., 1982).

In the Middle East, the main dry rangeland ecosystem functions sustained communities and supported their livelihoods until 50–100 years ago when overgrazing and drought substantially reduced vegetation cover. Severely degraded rangelands can sustain animals for only one to two months a year. People and animals migrate to wetter areas for the rest of the year looking for feed supplements and water supplies. Similar conditions exist in most of the dry rangelands (Gintzburger and Le Houérou, 2005).

In African rangelands, indigenous grasses were replaced by crops, such as maize and millet, changing the system's equilibrium and biodiversity (Vohland and Barry, 2009). With fragile soil surfaces exposed to the direct impact of raindrops, the water erosion process continued for years before the fertile soils began moving downstream, depriving the rangelands of their productivity. These fertile soils settled in dams and salt sinks, further degrading the land. Degraded and cultivated soils are also exposed to strong winds, causing further erosion and loss of surface soil. Dust, as a result of wind erosion, affects people in the rural areas, and moves to urban areas causing health and transportation problems in urban areas as well.

Degraded pastoral areas in Inner Mongolia and the Gobi Desert cause dust that affects the western parts of Japan and other countries in the region (Wang et al., 2004). A mega dust storm hit seven countries in the Middle East in 2015, leaving several people dead, sending thousands to hospitals with respiratory problems and disrupting transportation services, especially at airports (Howard, 2015). The cost of land degradation in the rangeland ecosystems is considerable (Nkonya et al., 2016).

Urban systems

Urban agriculture has the potential to contribute to food security both directly through producing nutritionally rich food for home consumption and indirectly by providing livelihoods to the urban poor through producing food for the market (Zezza and Tasciotti, 2010). However, while urban agriculture has been shown to be important to urban poor households' food security by contributing to dietary diversity and calorie availability, these benefits are limited, particularly for the poorest households. Participation in urban agriculture is correlated with wealth and landholdings since it requires access to land and inputs (Frayne et al., 2014), limiting its potential as a solution to food security issues for the truly poor. However, in the Kibera slums in Nairobi, Kenya, sack gardening has become increasingly common since it can be practised with limited space (Gallaher et al., 2013). It has been demonstrated to have a positive impact on household food security as well as increasing households' sense of food security, but its impacts are limited by household access to inputs, including water. Limited access to water for irrigation in urban areas can also have negative health consequences if polluted water resources are used, a common problem for urban and peri-urban agriculture (Cofie and Drechsel, 2007).

In other contexts, however, urban agriculture has been seen to provide positive impacts on community food security. A report on urban agriculture in London called for planning that would encourage agriculture in the capital in order to improve food security and meet the demand for locally grown food

(London Assembly, 2010). The report suggests using city wastewater for irrigating these agricultural spaces in order to counter the impact of increased demands on the city's water supply. In this context, problems faced by urban agriculture tend to be issues with competition over high priced land (and the water associated with it), access to irrigation infrastructure, getting food to the market, and soil and air pollution. Peri-urban agriculture has also received attention from city planners since peri-urban regions shape cities. Maintaining farmland in peri-urban regions can provide benefits to urban centres, such as environmentally processing waste, ecosystem management and job creation through agri-tourism. Peri-urban farmland has a direct impact on urban water in that, by protecting ecological systems, it filters water and preserves water quality.

In many peri-urban areas, particularly in Southeast Asia (Holm *et al.*, 2010), wastewater is used for growing food that is then sold in both the urban fringe and in urban centres. Use of wastewater for irrigation provides water in areas of scarcity, disposes of waste and decreases the need for other inputs such as fertilizer because of the higher availability of plant nutrients in wastewater. However, wastewater use for irrigation can also lead to higher concentrations of metals in agricultural products, especially vegetables, and in the soil. Consuming food with heavy metal-contamination can deplete nutrients in the body, leading to health problems associated with malnutrition. Studies of levels of food contamination through use of wastewater in production in Vietnam, Cambodia and India have found limited health risks but noted that some foods, like spinach, have higher concentrations of toxicity (Ghosh *et al.*, 2012). Much more research is needed on the linkage between water pollution and human health.

Impact of climate change on major agroecosystems

As discussed earlier, climate change may cause increases in rainfall intensity and variability and the frequency of extreme events such as drought, floods and hurricanes (IPCC, 2014) with the potential to cause agricultural losses estimated at 10–20% of production area, with some 1–3 billion people possibly affected by 2080 (Fischer *et al.*, 2002). Hilhost and Muchena (2000) estimate that cultivation potential in sub-Saharan Africa could decline by 12%, particularly in the Sudano-Sahelian zone. Moreover, by increasing the volatility of crop yields, climate risk provides a disincentive for investments in agricultural technologies such as improved varieties and inputs. Climate change impacts are interactive and their effects are likely to be multiplicative, with changes in one area likely to either mute or amplify changes in another (Vargas Hill and Viceisza, 2011).

Generally, ecosystems will be directly affected by climate change in three ways (HLPE, 2015):

- Increased temperature and CO_2 levels will increase evapotranspiration and reduce soil water (Wreford *et al.*, 2010), which will put more stress on all

plants in dry ecosystems, shortening the crop growing periods and reducing yields,
- Rainfall characteristics are likely to change though predictions lack precision. The Intergovernmental Panel on Climate Change (IPCC) indicates that it is likely that total rainfall in the Mediterranean and subtropics will decrease by up to 20% by the end of the century (IPCC, 2014), and
- Most important to dry ecosystems are the intensity and distribution of the rainfall. However, methods to estimate trends in precipitation extremes at the local level are still challenging (Willems et al., 2012).

Assessing the impacts of climate change, not only at the regional, but also at the local level, would help better understand how rainfall patterns are affected by these factors. Methods available for downscaling the outputs of global climate models to local scales have improved substantially, but still need more research (Lasage and Verburg, 2015; Willems et al., 2012). Increased intensity will increase runoff with higher soil erosion and lower opportunity for infiltration into the soil, especially in degraded drylands. This will cause more moisture stress on plants and reduced recharge of groundwater (HLPE, 2015). While this may increase the availability of surface water it may also result in increased floods with associated soil water erosion. Changes in rainfall distribution are likely to intensify drought spells and the duration of droughts, exposing vegetation to increased moisture stress (IPCC, 2014). As a result, there will be less support for vegetation and further land degradation.

The potential impacts of climate change on the major agricultural systems are very complex and vary from one region to another. For example, rising temperatures and CO_2 levels may harm crop productivity in warm and water-scarce environments, while they may help crops in many cool and water abundant environments in the short term, with significant reductions from 2030 onwards.

> This should be seen in the context of already existing malnutrition in many regions, a growing problem also in the absence of climate change, due to growing populations, increasing economic disparities and the continuing shift of diets towards animal protein.
>
> *(IPCC, 2014)*

A more recent IPCC report (IPCC, 2018) denotes a higher earth system sensitivity and reviews recent evidence on regionally differentiated risks to food security, water resources, drought, heat exposure and coastal submergence and finds substantial benefits from limiting global warming to 1.5°C compared to 2°C.

Rainfed agroecosystems will be directly affected by climate change in three ways (Wreford et al., 2010):

- Increased temperature and CO_2 levels will increase evapotranspiration and reduce soil water, putting stress on plants in dry ecosystems, shortening

crop growing periods and reducing yields. In wet and cool agroecosystems the same changes may prolong crop growing periods and increase yields.
- Rainfall patterns are likely to change in many dry and wet regions though predictions of changes lack precision. More serious will be the increased intensity and changes in distribution of rainfall in many areas. Increased intensity will, especially on degraded sloping lands, result in more runoff with higher soil erosion and lower soil infiltration, causing more moisture stress on plants and reduced recharge of groundwater. This is especially important in sub-Saharan Africa and Southeast Asia where people have little adaptive capacity. While this may increase the availability of surface water and the potential for rainwater harvesting, it may also result in increased floods. More intense and/or longer droughts will expose crops to moisture stress, and reduce rainfed yields and quality.
- Impacts of climate change on crop and livestock diseases and pests is yet to be assessed. However, it is likely that these impacts will be substantial. More research is needed in this area.

Irrigated agroecosystems will be affected by climate change in three ways (IPCC, 2014; Wreford *et al.*, 2010):

- Blue surface water supply may be higher in some regions as more runoff will be generated as a result of increased rainfall intensity, but less groundwater is likely to be available due to reduced opportunity for water infiltration. The overall impact on blue water resources is difficult to predict, especially taking into consideration the variations between regions and the upstream–downstream consequences of changing agricultural demands and investments in improving green water use. More modelling work is needed in this area.
- Faster melting of glacial bodies in the north will, in addition to higher flood risks, require building larger storage facilities for the additional water flow rate.
- Increased temperature will increase evaporation and transpiration so that more water will be required by crops, even as water availability from lakes, rivers and reservoirs decreases. Higher CO_2 levels usually act as a fertilizer for crops and may increase transpiration efficiency and thus water productivity but this is only possible if more soil water is available. Impacts of climate change on soil–water–plants relations require more research.

Pastoral agroecosystems are more fragile than other ecosystems and their resources are limited. These ecosystems are poor in soil organic carbon and have lost a lot by degradation, but they still have the potential to recover and contribute to the mitigation of climate change impacts (Sowers *et al.*, 2011). The potential impacts of climate change on this ecosystem are very complex and vary from one region to the other (Albalawneh *et al.*, 2015). The main changes that affect pastoral ecosystems include decreasing annual precipitation, increasing rainfall variability and higher intensity and frequency of extreme events, such as droughts, rainstorms/floods and hurricanes (IPCC, 2014). These changes may not be uniform because of local topography and other aspects, but hold true in general, including (HLPE, 2015):

- More intensive rainstorms will lead to higher runoff rates, especially on degraded lands, with more soil water erosion. As the total rainfall in dry environments will likely be lower, more intense storms imply shorter storm durations, hence less opportunity time for infiltration and less moisture storage in the soil profile. This would encourage further degradation as vegetation will decrease.
- Greater variability of rainwater would increase the duration of drought spells and allow more stress on the vegetation that is already stressed and create greater risk for the restoration efforts especially in drier environments.
- As runoff is expected to be higher with greater rainwater intensity, an opportunity to store surface water will be higher. Potential for artificial recharge from those structures may be increased.

Producing more food and nutrition with less water

The role of measurement in water management

Various metrics have been developed to understand progress in water use in agriculture. Key among these are water efficiency, water productivity, water footprint and virtual water. The term water application efficiency or irrigation efficiency is a ratio of water stored and used to water applied and is widely used in irrigation system design, evaluation and management. Farm irrigation performance is based on four fundamental and interrelated efficiency terms – conveyance, application, distribution and storage. Water conveyance efficiency is the ratio of water delivered to the farm to that diverted from the source. It reflects water losses from the conveyance system mainly through seepage, evaporation and consumptive use by weeds. Irrigation application efficiency is the ratio of the water stored in the plant root zone to that applied to the field. It mainly reflects losses of water through deep percolation and runoff. (Oweis, 2016). Water 'losses' implied in the above efficiency terms are mostly 'paper' not 'real' ones. Seepage from irrigation canals and field level deep percolation losses are largely recoverable as they normally join adjacent groundwater and springs. Runoff losses end up in fields downstream. Drainage water can also be recycled and used several times before becoming too saline, as is the case in Egypt. Although most of these losses are recoverable, engineers strive to minimize them as their recovery implies some costs to the user and probably there are other implications (Van Steenbergen and Abdel Dayem, 2007). Importantly, increasing application and conveyance efficiencies saves water at the farm level, but not necessarily at the scheme or basin level, as 'lost' water can be recycled and reused downstream. And higher irrigation efficiency implies better irrigation performance – but not necessarily higher agricultural production (Kijne *et al.*, 2002).

Water productivity is the ratio of the net benefits from crop, forestry, fishery, livestock, and mixed agricultural systems to the amount of water required to produce those benefits. In its broadest sense it reflects the objectives of producing more food, income, livelihood and ecological benefits at less social and environmental cost per unit of water consumed. Higher water productivity, both biophysical and economic, contributes to improved food security, especially in countries of the global South. The denominator of the water productivity equation is expressed as water depletion. Water is depleted when it is consumed by evapotranspiration, is incorporated into a product, flows to a location where it cannot be readily reused, or becomes heavily polluted (Seckler, 1996).

The water footprint of a product is defined as 'the total volume of fresh water that is used directly or indirectly to produce the product' (Hoekstra *et al.*, 2011). For food it includes water consumed in all steps of the food chain and processing and water required to assimilate pollutants to ambient water quality standards (Hoekstra, 2009). The term is mainly technical and indicates the biophysical relationships between water and products/processes. As outlined in Chapter 1, there are challenges with different kinds of metrics, including water footprints. The determination of water needed for a specific product is, however, challenging as production chains become more complex, and also it is difficult to distinguish between products produced under industrial agriculture with negative impacts on the local economy and environment and those done by smallholders with rain or green water.

The concept, however, can help raise public awareness regarding the huge water consumption to produce certain products, especially important in water scarce regions. Knowing that 0.5 litre of soft drink may need over 200 litres of water to produce and one kilogram of beef requires over 15,000 litres of water would help set up priorities for food production in many places. Values of water footprints of a specific product differ from one situation to another, depending on the production efficiency, the source of water, green or blue, and the agro-climatic conditions of the production chain. So, when estimating water footprints, the conditions around the process need to be indicated (Mekonnen and Hoekstra, 2010).

Finally, virtual water reflects the amount of water 'embedded' in a produce or 'consumed' to produce a commodity. The concept was developed to highlight the significant amounts of water used in food production and the great variations between water needs for different products. The concept can help link and compare the trading of food products (and their embedded water) to national water resources used in agriculture. Importing products that need significant amounts of water for production may compensate for national water scarcity (Allan, 2003). The concept may be used to help water-scarce countries achieve food security by importing food from water- abundant countries (Wichelns, 2010).

Although trade is not a new practice, the quantification of water savings associated with imports and linking it to the opportunities to use the available water in other activities or products is the new approach. This, however, has limitations in its simple aggregation and partial nature. Aggregating volumetric values of water use in very different products with different underlying opportunity and environmental costs can distort policy recommendations resulting from the analysis (Gawel and Bernsen, 2011). The partial nature of the concept renders the concept insufficient to determine the net benefits from water scarcity, as other factors such as labour and capital also matter for economic growth and social welfare (Wichelns, 2001). However, as we saw earlier, if these underlying factors – including regional and agroecosystem specific variations in water productivity – are factored in, then estimating virtual water content of traded commodities can help inform trade policy formulation. For example, a country might decide that it is not in their long-term strategic interest to have a surplus in virtual water export (i.e. exports higher than imports), and redirect its agricultural and trade policies.

Importing virtual water, although logical and more water use efficient, means that the importing country faces certain risks, such as reflected in the 2007/08 global food price crisis. Countries depending on imports face implications of potential shortages on international markets or political sanctions by the exporting countries. Overdependence on imports may weaken local production systems and disturb social values based on traditional agricultural production in rural areas (Gawel and Bernsen, 2011). From a food systems approach there are strong arguments that support local production as important for the social and economic development of rural areas. Table 3.1 provides a summary of the main metrics currently in use with their discription, purposes, advantages and limitations.

Towards a paradigm change in agricultural water management

Over the last few decades, substantial resources have been spent to increase food production in water-scarce areas. The main strategies used to cope with water scarcity are no longer adequate or effective. Conventional strategies included:

i   Increasing yield: requires more water

The Green Revolution transformed food production by increasing grain yields several-fold through improved cultivars, better fertility and improved water management. Ample examples illustrate large yield increases through the proper management of water and cropping systems. However, higher crop yields, if equated with higher crop biomass, generally consume more water. This is evidenced by the established linear relationship between biomass and evapotranspiration (Passioura, 1977; Passioura and Angus 2010; Zhang and Oweis, 1999). This is not to say that there is no room for increasing a specific crop yield per unit of land without additional water, as this is possible by improving the harvest index and transpiration efficiency and suppressing evaporation. Other breeding efforts have focused on semi-dwarf and short-duration

TABLE 3.1 Comparison of metric tools for water management and use (adapted from HLPE, 2015)

Tools	Description	Purpose	Main users	Advantages	Limitations
Water efficiency	Indicator of water used by a system with respect to water as input.	Evaluate systems' performance in capacity to satisfy crop needs, and reduce losses	Engineers Practitioners Farmers	Simplicity and well adapted to its specific public	Needs to be clearly characterized. Indirectly linked to outputs
Water productivity	Indicator of output (physical, economic social etc.) of a system with respect to water as input.	Measure the benefits provided by a unit of water in a certain system, in order to compare options and improve its performance.	Engineers Practitioners Farmers decision makers	Focused on output, and as such clearly of interest for FSN.	Diverse approaches, especially at multiple dimensions. Data needs.
Water footprint	Indicator of the total volume of fresh water that is used directly or indirectly to produce a product	Evaluate aggregated water consumption of countries, individuals and the impact of the consumption of a certain product.	Consumers	Simplicity. Concept aligned with other indicators. Popular	Does not properly account for local-specific impacts. Very data-intensive
Virtual Water	Measure of the water 'embedded' in produce.	Describe indirect consumption of water by countries, through trade, exports and imports.	Analysts	Simple, popular	Does not properly take into account local specific impacts.

varieties that have reduced plant water consumption needs. More recently, improvements have been more limited and have not contributed substantially to water saving (Oweis, 2017).

Breeders adopt three strategies to improve water use efficiency; reducing evaporation from the soil surface, deep percolation and residual water in the root zone; improving the crop's transpiration efficiency and; increasing the harvest index. The three processes are not independent, as targeting specific traits to improve one process may have detrimental effects on the other two, but there may also be positive interactions (Farquhar et al., 2004). Except for increasing the transpiration efficiency, the other processes require more water to increase yields. Drought tolerant varieties, for example, yield better under drought conditions than water responsive varieties, but their higher yields may not be without more water use. This means that by increasing yields we do not necessarily have proportional water saving. Generally, substantial increases in crop yields require larger supplies of water, which may not be available. Thus, a yield-targeting strategy, alone, cannot solve the water shortage problem, especially in water scarce regions (Oweis, 2017). However, recent investments in agricultural research are strengthening a focus on improving transpiration efficiency and other means to reduce plant water use at equal or higher yield.

ii Improving irrigation efficiency: minor savings at scale

As indicated earlier, improving irrigation efficiency addresses losses in seepage from irrigation canals and field level deep percolation losses which are largely recoverable as they normally join adjacent groundwater and springs. Runoff losses flow to fields downstream and can be used again. Drainage water can also be recycled and used several times before becoming too saline, as is the case in Egypt (Van Steenbergen and Abdel Dayem, 2007). Although most of these losses are recoverable, engineers strive to minimize them as their recovery implies some costs to the user and probably there are other implications (FAO, 2017).

iii Modernizing irrigation systems: the fallacy

Many countries strive to convert traditional irrigation to modern drip and sprinklers systems which achieve higher irrigation efficiency. The lower efficiency of traditional surface systems is mainly due to low application efficiency. As indicated above, these losses occur at the field level, but often are partially or fully recovered at the scheme or basin levels. Reducing field losses by converting to modern systems will not create substantial additional water resources. In Egypt, individual farmers along the Nile and over the Delta lose on average about 55% of the water they apply through surface irrigation systems in runoff and deep percolation. However, the lost water is continuously recycled through the drainage system and groundwater pumping with only about 10–15% lost to the sea. Understanding the surface irrigation system losses needs to be put it in the context of scale to evaluate the real and the paper losses across the system (Oweis, 2012).

Modern systems can achieve higher crop productivity through better control, higher irrigation uniformity, reduced irrigation frequency, better fertilization and other factors. In some modern systems, such as drip systems, real water saving can be achieved by reduction of evaporation losses, where the wetted soil surface is limited and may be covered by mulches (FAO, 2017). The increased land productivity, however, comes at a cost including capital, energy and maintenance. Successful conversion requires a developed industry, skilled engineers, technicians, and farmers, and regular maintenance (Oweis, 2016). Modern systems can be efficient only if they are managed properly. It has been reported, for example, that the modern drip systems in the Jordan valley were operated at an efficiency of about 56%. Surface systems can perform better if designed and operated properly (Shatanawi et al., 2005). Surge flow furrow irrigation can achieve over 75% application efficiency (Oweis and Walker, 1990). Selection of the appropriate irrigation system may not depend solely on its efficiency, but on other physical and socio-economic conditions at the site.

Modern systems are relevant in water-scarce areas as farmers can recover the system cost by reducing irrigation losses and increasing productivity. When water is cheap and abundant, farmers have little incentive to convert to modern systems. Improving surface irrigation systems through land levelling and better controls may be more appropriate for most farmers in the global South. Investing in improving surface irrigation may be emphasized while encouraging the use of modern systems when conditions are favourable (Oweis, 2012).

iv Managing demand: the social constraints

It is widely accepted that water pricing would improve efficiency and increase investment in irrigation projects. Water for agriculture is generally supplied free of charge or at low and highly subsidized rates (Cosgrove and Rijsberman, 2000). As a result, farmers have little incentive to invest in technologies and practices that improve water use. Everyone is advocating pricing schemes for irrigation water based on recovery of total or partial costs but with little success, especially in developing countries. The concept presents enormous practical, social and political challenges (Meinzen-Dick, 1997).

Traditionally, in many cultures water is considered a gift of God, to be available free to everyone. Additionally, farmers pressure for subsidized inputs. There is also a fear that once water is established as a market commodity, prices will be determined by the market, leaving the poor unable to buy water even for household needs. Downstream riparian countries fear that upstream countries may use international waters as a market commodity in the negotiations on water rights. As those are real concerns, innovative solutions are needed to put a real value on water in order to improve efficiency, but also to be sensitive to cultural norms and ensuring that people have sufficient water for their basic needs of food production. Subsidies for poor farmers may be designed to support farmers but also to encourage efficiency. Water pricing and other tools of demand management will reduce the demand for water in agriculture, but may not improve production and/or poor farmers' livelihoods. This may benefit other water use sectors, but will contribute a little to increasing food security.

Improving agricultural water productivity

Increasing water productivity is particularly appropriate where water is scarce compared with other resources involved in production. Reasons to improve agricultural water productivity include: (i) to meet the rising demand for food from a growing, wealthier, and increasingly urbanized population, in light of water scarcity, (ii) to respond to pressures to reallocate water from agriculture to cities and to ensure that water is available for environmental uses, and (iii) to contribute to poverty reduction and economic growth. For the rural poor, more productive use of water can mean better nutrition for families, more income, and productive employment. Targeting high water productivity can reduce investment costs by reducing the amount of water that has to be withdrawn. Increasing physical water productivity in agriculture reduces the need for additional water and land in irrigated and rainfed systems and is thus a critical response to growing water scarcity, including the need to leave enough water to sustain ecosystems and to meet the growing demands of cities and industries (Molden *et al.*, 2007).

Areas where ecosystem functions greatly depend on water availability such as groundwater mining and reduction in environmental flow is of major concern. The world will need to substantially increase withdrawals of water for agriculture to satisfy increased food demand. However, this can be achieved with available water and land resources through increasing water and land productivities. Upgrading rainfed and irrigated systems, optimizing virtual water flows between countries based on its impact on environmental sustainability, and reducing food demand by adjusting diets, reducing food losses and waste and improving the efficiency of food processing and distribution are among the most promising venues (CA, 2007). However, drivers for improving water productivity vary from one scale to the other (Oweis, 2016):

- At the global level, drivers include coping with water scarcity, reducing poverty, adaptation to climate change, sustainable transboundary ecosystems and alleviating international disputes over water.
- At the basin level, drivers to improve water productivity include alleviating transboundary conflicts, equitable allocation of water, trading virtual water, allocation of water resources among sectors, including energy and cooperation for optimizing water use.
- At the national level, drivers include enhancing food security and/or self-sufficiency, strengthening agricultural trade/hard currency to satisfy socio-political interests in the country.
- At the farm level, the main farmers' interest is increasing income from every unit of water used, hence maximizing economic water productivity. However, in many regions where farmers still practise subsistence farming, nutritional water productivity is important so farmers can get a balanced diet on the farm.

- At the field level, improving biophysical water productivity of the crops/livestock dominates the scene. Breeders for example try to increase grains per unit of water consumed.
- Finally, at the plant level, improving nutrient and quality aspects are the main drivers for increasing water productivity.

There are several venues to improve water productivity for better food security and nutrition. According to Molden et al. (2010) these are:

1. Increasing the productivity per unit of water consumed through cultivating alternative crops and varieties, such as switching to crops with lower water demand, or with higher economic or physical productivity provided, the societal cost of diverting water to a high value crop is not too high (in terms of health, food and nutrition security, local water availability for basic needs etc.).
2. Deficit, supplemental, or precision irrigation; improved water management with better timing of irrigation; optimizing non-water inputs including better agronomic practices, policy reform and public awareness.
3. Reducing non-beneficial water depletion by reducing evaporation from soil surfaces in irrigated fields and from fallow land; reducing water flows to sinks (such as salt lakes and the sea); minimizing salinization of return flows and shunting polluted water to sinks to avoid the need to dilute with freshwater; reusing return flows through gravity and pump diversions to increase the irrigated area. Mechanisms to shift vapour consumption from non-productive 'evaporation' to productive 'transpiration' increases biophysical WP.
4. Reallocating water among uses can dramatically increase the economic productivity of water; tapping uncommitted outflows to be used for productive purposes and improving the management of existing facilities; policy, design, management and institutional interventions to reduce delivery requirements; adding storage facilities to store and regulate the use of uncommitted outflows.
5. Improving management of existing irrigation facilities and reusing return flows by controlling, diverting and storing drainage flows and using them again.
6. Plant and livestock breeding approaches have helped to reduce crop water use and will be an important tool to address future water and other biotic and abiotic stresses.
7. Using C4 crops (such as maize and sorghum) and CAM crops (Crassulacean Acid Metabolism) such as cactus, which has higher transpiration efficiency than C3 crops (wheat and rice) can increase water productivity. There are attempts to genetically convert C3 crops to more water use efficient C4 crops but still no breakthroughs occurred in this regard.

Greater potential with economic water productivity

Increasing economic net benefits or value per unit of water has key implications for farmer decisions, economic growth, poverty reduction, equity and the environment. There is much more scope for increasing value per unit of water use in agriculture (economic water productivity) than in physical water productivity, which is becoming increasingly constrained. Yet, the methodology for assessing economic water productivity rarely incorporates the concept of 'cost of water to society' incurred by irrigating the crop/field under study. Strategies for increasing the value of water used in agriculture include (CA, 2007):

- Increasing yield per unit of blue or green water.
- Changing cropping pattern from low to high value crops.
- Reallocating water from low to higher valued uses.
- Lowering the costs of inputs to increase economic water productivity.
- Increasing health benefits (such as nutritional and energy WP) and the value of ecological services of agriculture.
- Decreasing social, health and environmental costs (for example, minimizing degradation of other ecosystems).
- Obtaining multiple benefits per unit of water including agriculture, fisheries and/or power.
- Increasing social benefits such as livelihood support and more jobs and income for the same amount of water.

Having listed these, we note that research that incorporates assessment of 'cost of water to society' in calculating economic water productivity will have a better chance of shifting policy priorities so as to help decrease environmental costs, increase the health benefits and provide livelihood support for the same amount of water. This is especially important with increasing water scarcity, and ever-present demand for diverting water away from 'low value food crops' to high value uses, including high value crops.

Investments in improving water management are important in increasing water productivity, but many people question whether these practices promote real water savings (Perry et al., 1997; Seckler, 1996). Releasing water from irrigated agriculture can make it available to other, higher value uses in cities, industries, ecosystems or more agriculture. However, practices that reduce applications such as improving efficiency also reduce outflows such as runoff and drainage. Farmers downstream may be using these outflows or they may be supporting important ecosystems. Reducing deliveries and drainage works well in situations where drainage flows damage, pollute or flow into salt sinks (Molden et al., 2007). In other cases, a basin scale analysis can determine whether savings are real.

In water scarce regions, as the amount of water available for agriculture is declining due to competition with other sectors, food security is increasingly threatened. If the non-agricultural consumption of water continues to grow at present rates, the share of water for agriculture in several North African countries will drop to 50% in 25 years. In several countries, such as Jordan, marginal-quality water will soon become the major source of irrigation water. Despite its scarcity, water continues to be misused. New technologies allow farmers to extract groundwater at rates far in excess of recharge, rapidly depleting centuries-old aquifers. Water scarcity and mismanagement will also accelerate environmental degradation, through soil erosion, soil and water salinization and waterlogging. These are global problems, but they are especially severe in the dry areas (Pereira et al., 2002).

Practices to increase water productivity include improved irrigation uniformity/distribution through better irrigation systems and management, adopting water-use efficient practices such as supplemental irrigation, deficit irrigation and water harvesting, and improved cultural practices such as fertility and conservation agriculture. Using agricultural crop residues in animal feed and open grazing or rangeland farming may provide a several-fold increase in livestock water productivity.

Technologies can be more effective if introduced in an integrated system. Switching to higher value agricultural uses or reducing costs of production; better integration of livestock in irrigated and rainfed systems and using irrigation water for household and small industries can increase water productivity. Such integrated farming systems with better recycling of nutrients (using animal waste for energy generation or fertilizing crops; using crop residue as animal feed or for energy generation; using energy generated for use in processing of crops/animal products) not only contribute to improved nutrient content in farm products, but also help to lower the climate footprint of farming systems.

According to the CA (2007), higher physical and economic water productivity can reduce poverty in two ways: water saved can be accessed by poor or marginal producers to produce food and generate income; and additional production can reduce food prices and increase employment through multiplier effects. This is only possible, however, if water savings are made accessible to the poor. With the rapid increase in consumption of animal products, water use in the livestock sector is likely to increase in the near future. Globally, the water use of the livestock production systems (2,422 Gm^3/y, in the 1996–2005 period) accounted for 29% of the total water use in agriculture (Mekonnen and Hoekstra, 2012). Of this, only 2% is used for servicing and maintaining the operations or directly as drinking water. Animal-feeding in varied production systems – pasture raised, mixed and industrial operations or Concentrated Animal Feeding Operations (CAFOs) – accounts for the remaining 98%. Mekonnen and Hoekstra (2012) estimate that of this 98%, feed from grazing accounts for only 38%, with water use in CAFOs and mixed production systems accounting for the remaining 60% of the water use in livestock production systems. The rise of industrial livestock production has resulted in nearly 30% of all cereals used as feed for livestock production. By 2050, nearly half of all cereals grown are expected to feed pigs and poultry – unless we dramatically transform the economic and political drivers that lead to mass production and over consumption (Sharma, 2018).

Savings in animal water use are mainly associated with feed consumption. There is considerable scope for increasing both physical and economic livestock water productivity through, for example, improving feed sourcing through integrated crop–livestock systems, enhancing animal production or output, improving animal health and adopting proper grazing practices such as adaptive multi-paddock grazing (AMP) to reduce rangelands degradation (Peden et al., 2007). Using natural rangelands and enhancing the production of comparatively more water-efficient livestock can help to reduce the pressure on water for feed production. Poultry for example has a high water productivity level and is increasingly replacing beef and lamb meat in many countries of the global South.

Gerbens-Leenes et al. (2013) note that the water footprint of pork is two times larger than that of pulses and four times that of grains. To produce 1 kg of beef requires 15.4 m^3, as opposed to 1 kg of cereals, which only needs 1.6 m^3. They further suggest that increased water use per capita due to continued dietary changes might well overtake population growth as the main driver of growth in water use. This assumes that the meat is being sourced from animals raised in CAFOs rather than in pastures. The size and characteristics (e.g. blue, green or grey water) of the water footprint depend on animal types and production systems; moreover, the three factors that influence the water footprint of an animal – feed conversion efficiency of the animal, feed composition, and origin of the feed – vary, depending on the type of production system (pasture raised, mixed and industrial operations or CAFOs) used (Mekonnen and Hoekstra, 2010).

Thus, meat or milk from pasture raised cattle in a rainfed region would only have green water use; it is more complicated to estimate the water use of animals from mixed or industrial (CAFOs) operations: born in a mixed operation, shipped to another CAFO in a different country, fattened on feed grown in other regions and finally slaughtered, processed and packaged in yet another place, its meat will not only have green and blue water footprints, but also a substantial grey water footprint. A comparative, context specific assessment of water footprints of food products from animals raised in these production systems is necessary to help guide policy decisions to ensure that public and private sector efforts in animal based food systems are indeed sustainable.

Further research is needed to assess livestock water productivity and how to improve it. Research may include better evaluation of water productivity along the value chain of livestock products, and improving/changing feed sources to reduce water consumption. Better integration of fisheries and aquaculture with water management systems can also improve water productivity. The two major components of water use in aquaculture are the water required to produce feed, and the water required for the aquaculture itself. Water needs range from 0.5 to

45 m^3 per kilogram of produce depending on the intensity/extensity of the system used (Verdegem *et al.*, 2006). Fish can often be integrated into water management systems with the addition of little or no water (Prein, 2002). Aquatic ecosystems provide many other services and benefits beyond fisheries such as biodiversity. Considering only the value of fish produced per unit of water is an underestimation of water productivity in these systems (Dugan *et al.*, 2006).

Achieving meaningful improvement in water productivity, however, cannot be done through technological advancement alone. It requires enabling policies and a healthy institutional environment to align users' incentives at various scales, to encourage the uptake of new techniques and to deal with trade-offs (CA, 2007).

Water and land productivities: trade-offs and complementarities

In conventional agriculture, water is used to maximize crop yield (maximizing production per unit of land). This is relevant in the case when water is ample and land is the most limiting resource. In the dry areas, the most limiting factor to production is usually water not land. It is, therefore, more relevant maximizing the return per unit of water instead of unit of land. Strategies to maximize water productivity may differ from that of maximizing yield. High water productivity does not come always with high yields. Deficit irrigation for example can increase water productivity but with reduced yields. As saved water can be used to irrigate new lands with higher returns, the intervention should yield higher overall benefits for the farmer (Zhang and Oweis, 1999).

Fortunately, both water and land productivities increase at the same time as improvement to on-farm management is introduced, but this does not continue all the way. At some high level of yield, incremental yield increase requires higher amounts of water to achieve. This means that water productivity drops as yield increases beyond certain levels. Figure 3.2 shows the relation between land productivity and water productivity for durum wheat in the Mediterranean basin. Generally, maximum water productivity occurs at sub-optimal crop yield per unit area (Zhang and Oweis, 1999).

The association of high water productivity values with high yields has important implications for the crop management for achieving efficient use of water resources in water-scarce areas (Oweis *et al.*, 1998). However, attaining higher yields with improved water productivity should ensure that increased gains in crop yield are not offset by increased costs of inputs and running costs. The curvilinear water–land productivity relationship emphasizes the importance of attaining relative high yields for efficient use of water. A policy for maximizing yield and/or net profit should be looked at very carefully under water scarcity conditions. Guidelines for recommending

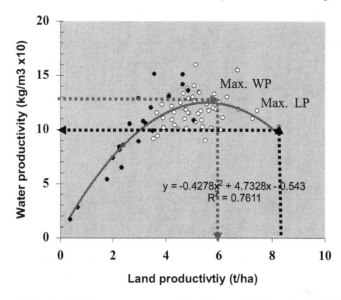

FIGURE 3.2 Relationship between water productivity and land productivity for durum wheat in a Mediterranean environment
Source: Zhang and Oweis, 1999

irrigation schedules under normal water availability may need to be revised when applied in areas with limited water resources.

Irrigation is traditionally scheduled to satisfy full crop water requirements to achieve maximum crop yield but in water-scarce areas deficit irrigation is more applicable where irrigation is deliberately reduced below crop water requirements, exposing the plants to some moisture stress. Stress lowers the crop yield but the percentage reduction from the reduced irrigation should be smaller than that of the associated water saving. This means that more yield per unit of water used is achieved with deficit irrigation and higher water productivity (Figure 3.2). The water saved could be used to expand in irrigated areas and achieve further increase in benefits or reallocated to other potential uses.

In farmers' fields in northern Syria, significant improvement in water productivity was achieved with deficit than with full supplemental irrigation. This is especially clear as farmers, in general, tend to over irrigate. The highest water productivity for applied irrigation was obtained at rates between one-third and two-thirds of that achieved with full irrigation, in addition to rainwater (Pereira et al., 2002). One important merit of deficit irrigation in rainfed systems is that it allows space for soil water storage to accommodate occasional rainwater, otherwise being lost in deep percolation. However, guidelines for crop water requirements and irrigation scheduling to maximize water productivity are yet to be developed for the important crops. In particular, it is necessary to develop further the water production functions for various crops and work with economists on evaluating the feasibility of deficit irrigation and its optimization. National policies, however, need to be adjusted to reward farmers using deficit irrigation by maximizing their returns with improved water productivity.

Generally, when land is more limiting than water, then yield increases contribute to higher economic returns, where in water-scarce areas such as dry areas where water is more limiting than land, maximizing water productivity should be the strategy. This will require structural changes to water management and agricultural practices (Oweis and Hachum, 2009).

Unlocking the potential of rainfed systems

Enhancing green water productivity

If the adoption rates of improved technologies are low and rainfed yield improvements do not materialize, the expansion in rainfed cropped area required to meet rising food demand would be around 53% by 2050. There is, however, little suitable agricultural land left; and further expansion would encroach on remaining natural forest areas, with large adverse environmental impacts (Wani et al., 2009).

According to Rockström et al. (2010), attention should be focused on enhancing rainfed productivity through improved water management. Despite successes in upgrading rainfed agriculture through soil water and crop management practices, supplemental irrigation and water harvesting, tend to be adopted on a small scale for some reasons including: low profitability, often a result of fluctuating international markets and/or surplus commodities, or due to lack of local processing facilities; poor access to storage or markets; relatively high labour costs; and high risks. Supplemental irrigation water may complement rainwater for enhancing soil moisture and help in reducing yield loss during dry spells. This gives the farmers additional security to risk investing in other inputs such as fertilizers and high-yielding varieties and allows farmers to grow higher value market crops, such as vegetables or fruits.

Although rainfed systems dominate world food production, investments in rainfed agriculture have been neglected in favour of irrigated agriculture over the past 50 years. A number of studies show the huge potential for improving water productivity in smallholder rainfed agriculture, through adoption of agroecological approaches, with water savings of 15–20% possible over the coming decade. Small investments will enable farmers to provide supplemental irrigation to rainfed crops, increasing yield and yield stability, and allowing better use of inputs. In combination with soil fertility management and improved varieties, supplemental irrigation can more than double water productivity and yields (Oweis and Hachum, 2009).

Integrating supplemental irrigation and water harvesting

Supplemental irrigation (SI) is a key strategy in rainfed agriculture for improving rainfed yields and water productivity. It can substantially increase production and income by using limited amounts of irrigation water, applied during dry spells, to alleviate soil moisture stress. The critical importance of supplemental irrigation lies in its capacity to bridge dry spells and thereby reduce risks in rainfed agriculture. Irrigation with 50–200 mm during the season is sufficient to double or more the rainfed yields. Such small amounts can be collected using water in local springs, shallow groundwater, water harvesting or conventional water resource schemes. SI allows modifying crop calendars to escape climatic extremes and adapt to climate change. By reducing risk, SI may provide the necessary incentive for investments in other production factors such as improved crop varieties, fertilizer, labour, and tillage techniques, and for diversification (Oweis, 2013).

In addition to improved yields and water productivity, it may help stabilize farmers' production and income. For the greatest benefit, supplemental irrigation should be accompanied by a package of soil and crop management practices. In areas where groundwater is used deficit supplemental irrigation can reduce pumping and sustain the functionality of aquifers (World Bank, 2006).

Supplemental irrigation supports adaptation to climate change (IPCC, 2014; Sommer *et al.*, 2011; Box 3.4). There are, of course, external consequences to applying water upstream in the rainfed areas, including reduced flow amounts and quality to downstream irrigated areas. Trade-offs are necessary to optimize the upstream conjunctive use of water and that flowing downstream with green water for full irrigation and other uses (Hessari *et al.*, 2012).

BOX 3.4 SUPPLEMENTAL IRRIGATION PACKAGE MAY TRIPLE RAINFED SYSTEMS PRODUCTIVITY

Research and field application in the Mediterranean environments have shown that wheat yields and water productivity can be tripled by timely application of only 100 to 200 mm of supplemental irrigation. While the limited amount of water available would not support a fully irrigated crop it substantially increases wheat land and water productivities when conjunctively used with rainwater (Oweis and Hachum, 2009).

The area of wheat under supplemental irrigation in northern and western Syria increased from 74,000 hectares (1980) to 418,000 hectares (2000), which substantially increased both yields and total production (Figure 3.3). Net imports of Syria were shifted to net exports starting in the 1990s when supplemental irrigation was applied at large scale (Figure 3.4). This can only happen when SI is combined with improved varieties and nitrogen application (Figure 3.5)

98 Agricultural water management

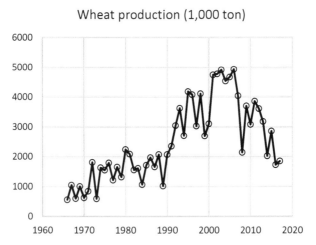

FIGURE 3.3 Total national wheat production in Syria from years 1980 to 2016
Source: MAARS, 2018

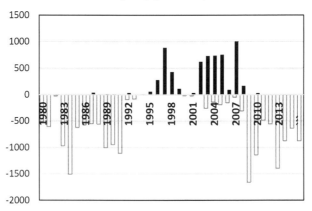

FIGURE 3.4 Syria imports and exports of wheat from 1980 to 2016
Source: MAARS, 2018

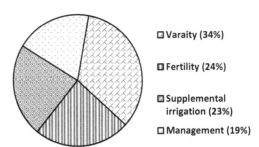

FIGURE 3.5 Contribution of agricultural inputs and management to wheat yield increase in Syria
Source: Adapted from Mazid et al., 2003

The estimated mean increase in net profit between rainfed and supplemental irrigation for wheat is US$300 per hectare. Supplemental irrigation with deficit irrigation led productivity in northwest Syria to increase from 0.84 to 2.14 kilograms of grain per cubic meter of water. (Oweis and Hachum, 2003).

In Burkina Faso and Kenya it was demonstrated that SI of 60 to 80 mm can double and even triple grain yields from the traditional 0.5–1 ton per hectare (sorghum and maize) to 1.5–2.5 tons per hectare. However, the most beneficial effects of supplemental irrigation were obtained in combination with soil fertility, and improved variety and management (Mazid et al., 2003). The major constraint to supplemental irrigation development in Africa is farmers' capacity, both technical and financial, to develop storage systems for runoff water (Rockström et al., 2003).

Rainwater harvesting (RWH) helps recovering of otherwise lost water in evaporation and flow to salt sinks, and provides opportunities for decentralized community-based management of water resources. Substantial amounts of rainwater are lost annually through runoff as a result of a lack of structures to collect and use. Through RWH, runoff is collected, diverted and stored for beneficial use. Storage can be in surface storage reservoirs, in the soil profile or by recharging of groundwater aquifers. Stored water can be used later if retained in surface or groundwater storage for human, animal or agriculture. Often micro catchment RWH halts soil erosion and improves soil fertility. Farm ponds or aquifers are often used as a source of supplemental irrigation for rainfed agriculture (Falkenmark et al., 2001).

RWH can play a role in adapting to climate change and increasing the resilience of ecosystems to drought and other extreme events. By slowing down or halting runoff, it allows more infiltration, increased soil water storage and better groundwater recharge. As RWH efficiency is dependent on runoff, climate change, by increasing rainfall intensities may in fact provide an opportunity instead of a disadvantage (Oweis *et al.*, 2012).

Investment in rainfed agriculture helps in reducing the ecosystem vulnerability to risks and improving productivity, equity and sustainable development. Rainfed systems do not require costly investment like that of irrigated systems; on the other hand, returns on investment are usually higher in rainfed agriculture. Practices including RWH and SI, however, require new infrastructure and equipment which may not be afforded by poor farmers, especially women, who still struggle to access financial resources (CA, 2007). Methods to mitigate risks for farmers, and enhance the sustainability and productivity of rainfed agriculture while maintaining ecosystem benefits include (Rockström *et al.*, 2010):

- Storage of rainwater and making it available to crops when it is most needed especially during drought spells.
- Enhancing the capacity of individuals and institutions working in rainfed systems.
- Applying an integrated approach for rainwater management both upstream and on-farm.
- Scaling up technologies and practices using principles such as Learning and Practice Alliances and suitability mapping.

Enhancing the productivity of irrigated agriculture

From efficiency to productivity

Although still needed, investment in irrigation must become more strategic to take into account the full social, economic and environmental costs and benefits, and development should be selected appropriately from a range of options, from small-scale, individual-farmer managed systems to large-scale, reservoir based systems (Faurès *et al.*, 2007; Wichelns, 2014).

At the same time, rehabilitation of existing systems, chiefly through irrigation management reform has started to show promise. Conjunctive use systems, such as those in parts of South Asia have superseded surface-only systems to achieve higher productivity and efficiency. In yet other systems, multiple-uses of irrigation water provide greater benefits than irrigation alone (Meinzen-Dick, 1997).

In the global South, women have less access to technology, extension and advisory services, which are key to modernization (FAO, 2012a). Consideration must be given to women's differentiated needs, capacities and priorities when new systems are introduced and implemented. Technology may not bring sought improvements if it is not made accessible to all the stakeholders involved in the sector. Water-savings are expected more in existing irrigation systems and achieving substantial expansion requires serious measures both at the technical as well as the socio-economic and institutional levels. Irrigation systems are expected to provide greater water control to overcome erratic precipitation patterns. This will come at a cost and, given that much of the infrastructure is aging, it is necessary to revitalize large-scale surface irrigation systems (CA, 2007).

Canal irrigation built in the second part of the last century constitutes most of the world large-scale systems. Canals played a pivotal role in increasing food production but their efficiency and effectiveness have deteriorated over the years and they need revitalization. Lack of investment in maintenance and operation and weak institutions are the main reasons. Governments in many countries failed to establish acceptable cost recovery schemes to keep the systems operating at high efficiency (Malik *et al.*, 2014). As said, 'if you can't measure it you can't manage it', and especially at the farm level, revitalization of irrigation systems requires investment in automation and measurement and an increase in the reliability of water supply. Upgrading infrastructure and increased investment is needed to maintain existing drainage systems and build new ones. One should not underestimate the role of water user associations in managing the irrigation system; however, they encounter many challenges due to conflicting social, cultural and institutional interests (see Chapter 4).

The issue of irrigation efficiency is often subject to controversy and misinterpretation. Because only 30–50% of the water withdrawn from a resource is actually evapo-transpired by crops in a typical irrigation system, many conclude that substantial gains in water volumes can be obtained by increasing application efficiency in irrigation. However, as Seckler *et al.* (2003) state, irrigation efficiency improvements at the system level might yield little real water savings as water is reused many times in river basins; and the concept of water efficiency is therefore site-, scale- and purpose-specific. It is, therefore, important to understand the hydrology of the entire catchment or basin before suggesting investments in water use efficiency. Other issues to consider when devising irrigation efficiency improvements include the irrigation design, operation and management, equity in access, energy savings and levels of waterlogging and salinization (Faurès *et al.*, 2007).

Many countries strive to convert traditional surface irrigation to modern systems, such as drip and sprinklers, which achieve higher water application efficiency and yields. The lower efficiency of surface systems is mainly a consequence of low application efficiency, but while these losses occur at the field level, they are often partially or fully recovered at the scheme or basin level by recycling drainage and runoff water or by pumping deep percolation losses from groundwater aquifers. In some occasions these losses are not recovered as they may join salt sinks or be stored in unreachable locations. While farm level losses are important to the farmer as water and pumping bring costs to bear, these are usually not total losses at the larger scale (Oweis, 2013).

Reducing field losses by converting to modern systems will increase yields and save some water but will not create substantial additional water resources. In Egypt, farmers along the Nile and around the delta lose on average about 55% of the water they apply through surface irrigation systems in runoff and deep percolation (an application efficiency of 45%). However, the lost water is continuously recycled through the drainage system and groundwater pumping. Only about 10–15% of the Nile water in Egypt enters the sea, which brings the system's overall efficiency to about 85%. So, understanding surface irrigation system losses needs to be put in the context of scale to evaluate the real vs paper losses across the system (Molden et al., 2010).

It is well established that modern irrigation systems can achieve higher crop productivity, but this is achieved not by reducing system losses in deep percolation and runoff, but rather through better control, higher irrigation uniformity, reduced irrigation frequency (less crop moisture stress between irrigations), better fertilization (fertigation) and other factors. In some modern systems, such as drip systems, real water saving can be achieved by reduction of evaporation losses, where the wetted soil surface is limited and mulches can be used to further reduce evaporation. The increased land productivity, however, comes at a cost – higher capital, higher energy consumption and more maintenance requirements. Successful conversion requires a developed industry, skilled engineers, technicians and farmers, and regular maintenance (Oweis, 2012).

Modern systems are meant to be efficient. However, they can be efficient only if they are managed properly and often they are no more efficient than traditional surface irrigation systems because of poor management which can perform better if designed and operated properly. The vast majority of irrigation systems worldwide are surface irrigation; this is unlikely to change in the near future (FAO, 1997). Selection of the appropriate irrigation system may not depend solely on its application efficiency, but on other physical and socio-economic conditions at the site (Keller and Keller, 2003).

Modern systems are most successful in areas where water is scarce and expensive so that farmers can recover the system cost by reducing irrigation losses and increasing productivity. When water is cheap and abundant, farmers, especially in the global South, have little incentive to convert to modern systems. Improving surface irrigation systems through land levelling and better control may be more appropriate for most farmers in the global South than modernizing the irrigation systems.

The System of Rice Intensification (SRI) responds to water scarce conditions by making crops more productive and water use more efficient through better management practices, despite initial poor soil conditions. In SRI, soil physical properties are enhanced by amendments with organic matter, compost and mulch. This helps maintain and magnify the beneficial soil microorganisms' life in the soil in terms of their abundance, diversity and activity. This in turn enhances the structure and functioning of soil systems through fixing nitrogen, solubilizing phosphorus, immobilizing various macro- and micro-nutrients, storing them in the soil and releasing them to meet plants' needs (Uphoff, 2017). In essence, through the adoption of practices rooted in agroecological principles, even smallholder farmers are able to raise crop yields, despite cutting back on inputs including seeds, synthetic fertilizers and irrigation water. SRI helps even in cases where acidic conditions of the soil previously intervened in crop growth (Ferichani and Prasetya, 2017).

In many countries water for irrigation is highly subsidized. Farmers have little incentive to restrict their use of water or to invest in new technologies to improve the use of available water. Although it is widely accepted that water pricing would improve efficiency and increase investment in irrigation projects, the concept of pricing presents enormous practical, social and political challenges, including the difficulties in measuring water and monitoring its use by farmers and the pressures for subsidized inputs. There is also a fear that once water is established as a market commodity, prices will be determined by the market, leaving the poor unable to buy water even for household needs. Downstream riparian countries fear that upstream countries may use international waters as a market commodity in the negotiations on water rights (Altinbilek, 2014)

One cannot ignore these very real concerns. Innovative solutions are therefore needed to put a real value on water in order to improve efficiency, while at the same time recognizing cultural norms and ensuring that people have sufficient water for basic needs. Subsidies for poor farmers may be better provided in areas other than water, so that the subsidies do not encourage inefficient use of water. Countries must strengthen the recent trend to recover the running costs of irrigation supply systems. However, water pricing may reduce the demand for water in agriculture or divert it to high-value or luxury crops but may not improve agricultural production for food and nutrition security and/or poor farmers' livelihoods, thus benefitting other water use sectors with little contribution to increasing FSN (Perry et al., 1997).

Water user associations can play a central role in managing water at the irrigation scheme level and below, but although attempts to build these institutions were successful in a few places, they were a failure in many others partly because of communities' low capacity to manage irrigation systems and partly because governments are not willing to give up decision making powers to the water user associations (Metawie, 2002).

A review of several irrigation management transfer programs has shown that there is no blueprint for enhanced irrigation water management. Instead the approaches need to be tailored to local conditions. Water user associations are pivotal in reforming large surface irrigation systems, but require the empowerment of water users, especially women, mechanisms to resolve local conflicts, and improved mechanisms for involving women in running the water user associations. However, when such systems are built on the basis of traditional arrangements of collective ownership or sharing of water resources they function better (Garces-Restrepo et al., 2007).

Use and management of marginal quality water

As discussed, the use of marginal quality water has become an important source of water especially in water-scarce arid and semi-arid regions and in peri-urban agricultural developments. Marginal water includes brackish water, agricultural drainage water, and treated sewage effluent. In many areas farmers cannot afford but to use a low quality water for irrigation. Concerns regarding negative impacts of marginal water use on people and the environment are real but can be minimized through appropriate measures. The UN has identified four strategies to cope with these concerns: pollution prevention; treatment to higher quality; safe use of waste water; and restoration and protection of ecosystems. Close monitoring of water use together with appropriate institutional and policy environment can ensure productive use without affecting the health of the people or the ecosystem (FAO, 2002b).

Most of brackish water is available in groundwater aquifers with varying qualities. A number of fresh water aquifers have become brackish due to mining and seawater intrusion where others are naturally brackish. When salinity is not too high it is used directly for crop production or for salt tolerant crops. After desalination it is supplied for human, industrial or general agricultural use. The desalination cost of brackish water is lower than that for sea water and farmers in many countries, such as the Middle East, are desalinating water on-farm for agricultural purposes. Using brackish water in agriculture can contribute to increased food production and for the environment, but it requires special management to prevent land salinization and degradation of ecosystems. Currently saline water is being used innovatively to produce products with a special taste and texture with higher market value (Byczynski, 2010). Overexploitation of brackish water, however, would increase salinity.

Considerable research has been done on the reuse of drainage water in agriculture and the impacts on the environment. Drainage water quality is affected by irrigation application efficiency and can be suitable for most crops before becoming too saline. Farmers at the tail end of the canals use it when fresh water is scarce and sometimes mix the two to accommodate some sensitive crops. In Egypt, the drainage water from agricultural lands is collected by an extensive drainage network and recycled after being mixed with freshwater downstream, until it becomes too saline for productive use. In 2013 reused agricultural drainage water was estimated at 5.5 billion m^3 (Abdel-Shafy and Mansour, 2013). Currently the annual reuse amount exceeds 10 billion m^3 of water.

Treated sewage effluent is increasingly becoming an alternative source of irrigation water. Generally, about 70% of water used for domestic purposes can be recycled after treatment to be used for agriculture or environmental purposes. In Jordan, where the per capita annual share of water is currently about 130 m^3, over one third of agricultural water comes from treated sewage. Unfortunately, millions of small-scale farmers in urban and peri-urban areas of the global South irrigate with wastewater from residential, commercial and industrial sources, often with no treatment before use. In some areas there is scope for expanding irrigation on this basis, while in others the challenge is to get more productivity from existing infrastructure. Factors prevent the expansion of wastewater reuse include social barriers, technical, institutional and political issues. Utilizing treated sewage water is essential, especially in water-scarce areas but requires developing policies to properly control quality and use in the field (UNDP, 2013). Given the significant health risks associated with wastewater reuse, CA (2007) suggests three approaches to addressing marginal water: reduce the volume of wastewater generation; address risks in agricultural use of wastewater; and improve handling of food irrigated with wastewater. It is essential that sewage effluent is treated to the standards and guidelines set by WHO and other UN organizations for each use. Countries should develop their own cropping patterns guidelines regarding this water source. In general, treated sewage water (TSW) is best used for irrigation of landscape areas, non-edible crops or those not consumed fresh.

Groundwater for irrigation

Thanks to access to new drilling technologies and cheaper pumps, a quiet groundwater revolution took place between the 1970s and 1980s or later (Custodio, 2010), and this has helped millions of farmers and pastoralists in Asia improve their livelihoods and food security (Table 3.2). Groundwater development has been particularly rapid in the Indo-Gangetic plains of South Asia and the North China plains, both areas with high concentrations of poor farmers. The Gulf Countries rely almost entirely on groundwater, although with increasing production of freshwater through desalination.

There are estimates that groundwater accounts for 38% of the total irrigated area and 43% of total irrigation volumes (Siebert *et al.*, 2010). While in parts of South Asia groundwater expansion was directly associated with higher water tables arising from leaky public surface irrigation systems (Indo-Gangetic Plains) in other places groundwater use developed due to the lack of available surface systems (e.g. in the Vietnamese Central Highlands for coffee production). In yet other places, easily accessible aquifers have resulted in over-exploitation of

TABLE 3.2 Global survey of groundwater irrigation

Region	Groundwater irrigation		Groundwater volume used	
	Mha	propn total (%)	km^3/a	propn total (%)
Global total	112.9	38	545	43
South Asia	48.3	57	262	57
East Asia	19.3	29	57	34
Southeast Asia	1.0	5	3	6
Middle East & North Africa	12.9	43	87	44
Latin America	2.5	18	8	19
sub-Saharan Africa	0.4	6	2	7

Source: GWP (2012), derived from Siebert *et al.* (2010)

groundwater (for example the Ogallala in the US; parts of Northwest India, parts of China and parts of Pakistan).

Importantly, there is evidence from Asia to suggest that groundwater irrigation promotes greater interpersonal, inter-gender, inter-class and spatial equity than does large scale surface irrigation systems (CA, 2007).

The energy–groundwater nexus has created a curious political economy paradox: soaring energy prices may help save the aquifers. Increased energy costs can reduce the amount of pumping done, thus reducing over-abstraction of groundwater, in places where energy for pumping is not (highly) subsidized and where groundwater-based livelihood systems are currently under threat from over-abstraction. However, recent developments of affordable solar pumps may significantly change the energy–groundwater relationship.

In areas with good aquifers and recharge and a high prevalence of poverty, such as the Eastern Gangetic plains, the groundwater potential could be further exploited. Groundwater irrigation remains an important development strategy, especially in countries where it is still underutilized such as in parts of Central Asia (Rakhmatullaev et al., 2010) and much of sub-Saharan Africa (MacDonald et al., 2012).

Sustainable groundwater management requires balancing supply and demand, and needs effective interventions on both the supply and demand side. Supply-side measures may include artificial recharge, aquifer recovery or the development of alternative surface water sources, while demand-side measures generally focus on water use rights and permits, collective management, water pricing, legal and regulatory control and water saving crops and appropriate technologies (CA, 2007). However, supply-side measures may be easier to implement than demand-side measures due to local socio-economic and political factors. The only way to maintain aquifer systems to an acceptable degree may be to control the expansion of irrigated areas, improve practices and adopt water-use efficient crops (Shah, 2007).

Diversifying with fisheries and aquaculture

The role of fish and fisheries in food security and nutrition has been extensively dealt with in the HLPE Report on Sustainable Fisheries and Aquaculture for Food Security and Nutrition (HLPE, 2014). Fisheries and aquaculture play a very important role in the water productivity of fish and aquaculture is high compared to other sources of protein and nutrients: high technology cage fisheries can produce up to 100 kg of fish for each cubic meter of water (Dugan et al., 2006). Aquacultural operations are often run by small farmers with wide participation at all levels and scales, including farming, processing and marketing.

Inland fisheries are often critical to local food security and social structures and have vital gender dimensions based on the role of women in the fisheries. Lack of understanding of this importance by people outside the sector often causes non-inclusion or non-consideration of fisheries in basin water management and investment plans. It is critical that the role of fisheries and aquaculture in meeting the nutritional needs of poor rural communities in many areas, but also of the world at large, is considered in water policy and practice (FAO, 2002a).

Unfortunately, several freshwater fish species are seriously threatened due to poor water quality and habitat destruction. As competition for water resources increases fish, fisheries and aquaculture often suffer most as water allocation priorities are focused on other sectors. For example, drought in California saw salmons competing for water with farmers (Bland, 2014).

Inland fishery challenges include sustaining the current levels of production and other ecosystem functions while improving the management of capture fisheries. A wider adoption of improved methods to increase production levels is needed, which requires building partnerships between fishers, aquaculturists and other interest groups concerned with how to increase the overall benefits of water productivity to food security and poverty reduction and to achieve a higher level of integration in agricultural systems (CA, 2007; Dugan et al., 2006).

Sustaining agro-pastoral systems

Potential of rangelands and livestock

The dry agro-pastoral ecosystems are mainly rangelands occupying the majority of the arid environments of the world. Their aridity index ranges from 0.03 to 0.35 with a growing season length of less than 90 days and an environmental risk coefficient of variation greater than 25%. These systems receive rainfall amounts up to 250 mm in cool winter regions and up to 400 mm in hot summer regions with 50–100% variability. Although limited in depth, the vast area receives huge volumes of rainwater that are largely lost as evaporation or flow into salt sinks at times when rainwater is desperately needed to support vegetation (Owei, 2017). The CGIAR Dryland Systems (2013) distinguished two categories of dryland: those at the wetter side and suitable for intensive agriculture and those at the drier side which are mainly agro-pastoral.

Where surface or groundwater resources are available, intensive agriculture through irrigation is usually practiced in this environment. Some other areas on the drier side are deserts with sand dunes covering most of the land. However, the majority of the area is still rangelands with communities primarily practising livestock herding and associated activities. Figure 3.2 shows the target regions classified as arid.

Local conditions differ substantially from one place to the other. One common challenge, however, is that those ecosystems are mainly degraded. Reasons include exposure to both human interventions (overgrazing, cultivation, wood cutting, and overuse of water resources) and climate factors (drought and weather extremes) which have caused systematic degradation over the years (Evenari et al., 1982). Reports indicate that generally the dry ecosystems were in better shape not so long ago and sustained local population livelihoods by providing needed ecosystem services, such as animal feed and water resources all year round (Louhaichi and Tastad, 2010).

Ecosystem degradation caused the fall of several ancient civilizations. In the Middle East the 'badia', the main dry rangeland, provided sustainable ecosystem services for communities' livelihoods until 50 to 100 years ago. Now it is severely degraded with sparse vegetation developing after the rainy season sufficient to feed animals for only one to two months. People migrate with their animals to wetter areas for the rest of the year looking for feed and water supply. Similar conditions exist in most of the dry rangelands (Gintzburger and Le Houérou, 2005). With fragile soil surfaces exposed to the direct impact of raindrops, the process of water erosion continues year after year, taking most of the fertile soils downstream and depriving the rangelands of their productivity. They end up deposited in dams and salt sinks, further degrading the land.

With degraded and cultivated soil exposed to strong winds, erosion by wind causes further loss of surface soil and creates new problems of dust moving to urban areas, causing health and transportation problems. The dust originating from the degraded grasslands of Inner Mongolia and the Gobi Desert adversely affects the western parts of Japan and other countries in the region (Wang *et al.*, 2004). National Geographic reported on the mega dust storm that hit seven countries of the Middle East in 2015, leaving several people dead, sending thousands of people to hospitals with respiratory problems and disrupting transportation services, especially at airports (Howard, 2015). New socio-economic realities emerged when communities lost ecosystem services. Many migrated to rural areas, but also new developments were introduced including groundwater exploration and land cultivation which has further aggravated the degradation process.

Pastoralism provides a prime example of flexibility and the ability to adapt to changing conditions, and livestock provide a major source of livelihoods in dryland regions. In Chad, pastoral animals make up over one third of exports and feed 40% of the population. The story is similar in Uganda where pastoralist and smallholder livestock producers contribute 8.5% of total GDP, and in Mauritania livestock contributes 70% of total agricultural GDP. Pastoralism and livestock production can also be a major foreign exchange earner. In 2006, Ethiopia earned US$121 million from livestock and livestock products and Mali exported live animals worth US$44.6 million, while in Kenya, livestock raised by pastoralists is worth US$800 million a year (Thornton, 2010).

Pastoralists tend to move in search of the best quality forage. Consequently, pastoralist cattle are often in better heath than sedentary or ranched cattle as shown by comparisons of productivity and value in Botswana, Zimbabwe, Kenya and Ethiopia (FAO, 2018b). However, pastoralism is increasingly coming into conflict with modern governance systems. In many countries sedentarization policies dominate and even though legislation in many areas of West Africa is now designed to accommodate the needs of pastoralists, it may not be fully implemented. The African Union is now encouraging dialogue on the issues. Discussions with Pastoralists in East Africa indicate that these communities feel they are not fully consulted either about policies that affect them or about aid packages that are designed to assist them in times of hardship, but which may in fact exacerbate the situation through lack of consideration for local social networks and practices (ibid.).

Although drylands support some 50% of the world's livestock, they are threatened by desertification. Globally, more than 12 million hectares of arable land are lost to desertification every year and the rate is likely to increase as a result of climate change. To address such losses, improved farming techniques and greater understanding of the underlying ecosystem services provided by biodiversity will be needed (Gintzburger and Le Houérou, 2005). Understanding and maintaining the provision of ecosystem services, and the capacity of the local environment to support livelihoods is key to the sustainability of dryland farming and pastoralism. Further research will be important in this regard.

Restoration of degraded systems

Restoration of degraded dry ecosystems to their original status may be difficult, if at all possible. Most of the lands in these ecosystems have crossed the so-called 'threshold of irreversibility'. Efforts to rehabilitate them to new ecosystem equilibrium may be a more realistic goal (Aronson *et al.*, 1993). This will require bringing back indigenous components, including the biodiversity (Behnke and Kerven, 2013). There is a consensus, however, that either restoration or rehabilitation would enhance the resilience of the ecosystem and help provide socio-economic support to the dependent communities (Vohland and Barry, 2009).

Grazing management is a huge challenge for pastoral ecosystem restoration. Traditional rangeland systems are weakened due to rapid societal changes with existing community institutions no longer effective. Current policies and institutional setups often encourage increasing animal population which results in over grazing. Efforts to slow down or stop degradation, leave aside restoration, may not be successful without proper policies and strong institutions in place to regulate grazing (Oweis, 2017).

Attempts to restore degraded dry ecosystems traditionally followed conventional approaches – through protection and some reseeding without major integrated interventions. This approach is a passive one and has achieved limited success because degradation has completely changed the biophysical and socio-economic processes within these ecosystems. Rainwater that used to infiltrate and be stored in healthy and vegetated lands, supporting sustainable vegetation growth, now runs off taking fertile soils downstream with it (Oweis *et al.*, 2012).

Biodiversity that enhanced the system is no longer there. So, even if protected, the system may not recover to its original status, but take a long time just to show some improvement in vegetative cover. Protection is not an easy task for severely degraded ecosystems as it has shown limited improvement over long periods (CGIAR, 2000). A more progressive approach is to intervene using approaches that are more intensive. Aronson *et al.* (1993) indicated that ecosystems that have passed the 'threshold of irreversibility' will require structural interventions combined with revised management techniques for even limited restoration. Those may include land reallocation, reconstruction of seed bank and alteration of soil physical and chemical properties (Siegert, 1994).

Integrating rainwater harvesting

Integrative rainwater harvesting carries great potential to achieve a meaningful level of restoration of degraded pastoral ecosystems, especially in dry environments. Conventional passive approaches to restoring/rehabilitating degraded pastoral ecosystems including protection and reseeding are either too slow to show an obvious impact or not progressing satisfactorily. A major constraint to successful restoration of vegetation cover of degraded dry rangelands is insufficient moisture in the soil profile for plant growth. This is because currently most of the rainwater runs off downstream and is lost in salt sinks and evaporation. It requires serious interventions to alter the current process of surface runoff and soil erosion to allow a gradual build-up of soil moisture, fertility and seedbank necessary for revegetation (Oweis, 2017).

Rainwater harvesting can alter the rain runoff process, allowing more opportunity time for the water to infiltrate the soil and be stored for plant use. Furthermore, the practice can control soil erosion by water and provide a better environment for indigenous seeds to collect, germinate, emerge and grow in the target areas. The large-scale restoration of degraded dry rangeland ecosystems requires more progressive approaches to ensure modification of the biophysical and socio-economic processes concomitant with land degradation. If coupled with an integrated technical and socio-economic package during and after restoration, it can be a viable option to support degraded dry rangeland rehabilitation and enhance resilience to climate variability and change (Oweis et al., 2012).

Rainwater harvesting is one intervention that has a cost to pay, but the cost of doing nothing to maintain functioning ecosystems is much higher than the needed investment to sustain them (Nkonya et al., 2016). Although RWH remains relevant, there have been few efforts in recent decades to modernize old practices, develop new ones, or create an enabling environment to unlock its full potential. Many rural communities have become overly attached to old practices and all too often the concept of rainwater harvesting is blamed for failure when in reality mismanagement and poor design are most at fault (Van Dijk and Reij, 1994).

There are several opportunities and constraints to successful integration of RWH in restoring pastoral ecosystems (Box 3.5). Opportunities include (Oweis et al., 2012): enhancing vegetation growth, increasing water productivity, reducing land degradation, adapting to climate change and supporting conjunctive use of water resources. However, challenges and constraints to wide implementation remain substantial and include: climate uncertainties and risk especially in drought prone areas, storage limitations and cost of building new facilities, limitations of indigenous practices and the local capacity to modernize, upstream–

downstream conflicts, integration and lack of enabling environments such as appropriate policies and support for environmental development. One key limitation is that the technical aspects of water harvesting structures are not simple for unskilled labour and require special training (Vohland and Barry, 2009).

> **BOX 3.5 RESTORING DEGRADED PASTORAL 'BADIA' SYSTEM IN JORDAN**
>
> Although there is renewed interest in indigenous rainwater harvesting, traditional practices and technologies are rarely suitable or feasible. A practical and cost-effective alternative that combines indigenous knowledge with mechanization to enhance effectiveness and strengthen resilience was tested and implemented in the badia of Jordan.
>
> In an effort to overcome these constraints, ICARDA scientists worked with two communities in Jordan's badia – Mhareb and Majdieh – to design, test and promote a practical rainwater harvesting package. The package combines indigenous knowledge with mechanization and a contour laser guiding system to enhance the accuracy of ridges and bunds (Figure 3.6). Efforts were also taken to improve the selection of restoration sites, design appropriate structures, select the right shrubs and, most importantly, implement sustainable grazing strategies and ensure on-going maintenance.
>
>
>
> **FIGURE 3.6** Mechanized MICWH: (a) laser guided vallerani bunds maker, (b) mechanized intermittent contour bunds, (c) bunds planted with shrubs after a rain storm, (d) sheep grazing shrubs and vegetation from restored landscape
> Source: Adapted from Oweis (2017). Photos by: Theib Oweis

> With support from Jordan's National Center for Agricultural Research and Extension (NCARE), 80% and 90% of farmers in Mhareb and Majdieh used the package. Jordan's Ministry of Environment also adopted it, allocating funds for its implementation across 2000 hectares so far – an area the Ministry is planning to extend even further. The result? Rapid vegetation growth, more animal feed, less soil erosion, and enhanced biodiversity. The package is also cost-effective: it costs a mere USD 32/hectare – which includes the production, planting and maintenance of shrub seedlings – and the economic internal rate of return is estimated at some 13% (Oweis, 2017).
>
> While the positive impacts of the rainwater harvesting package are clear, additional financial support is needed to extend the intervention over a wider area and ensure its long-term sustainability. Given that local communities are unable or unwilling to fully cover the costs of implementation, public funding is essential. However, to extend benefits and reduce costs even further, public–private partnerships should be initiated to pay for the building of water harvesting structures. This would enhance the intervention's viability across the dry areas and ensure that many more rural communities could benefit from land restoration and enhanced resilience to climate variability and change.

There are several important lessons learned from efforts in the restoration of pastoral ecosystems and integration of rainwater harvesting. Those include (Oweis, 2017):

- Restoration schemes will have limited success unless new legislation is introduced and existing institutions are reformed to preserve collective conservation systems, limit subsidized feed and corresponding increase in animal populations and overgrazing.
- Local community should be involved from the start of the research and development of the restoration packages to ensure higher adoption rate.
- Rainwater harvesting should be part of an integrated package including technical, socio-economic and management aspects.
- New institutional setups are required to facilitate regulated rangelands grazing with emerging changes in land tenure and ecosystem equilibrium.
- Precision is the key in the selection, design and implementation of RWH. Mechanization helps overcome problems of unskilled farmers, but specialists should be involved in the early stages of the development.
- Local communities cannot afford to pay for the RWH works and associated activities. As most of the benefits are environmental or social, public support finances large-scale adoption. However, incentives, including subsidies, should be directed to restoration not to supplemental feed.

Conclusions

Increasing water scarcity for agriculture with unsustainable production patterns and allocations adversely affect food security and nutrition, especially of the poor. Adverse impacts include inequitable allocation of and corresponding access to water resources, food shortages as well as unbalanced diets.

This chapter has argued that to overcome the problems of food security and nutrition a paradigm change in the way water is used in agriculture is needed. As water is increasingly the most limiting resource for production, national policies need to shift toward the maximization of agricultural water productivity in terms of food, economic, nutrition and environmental outcomes. Agroecological approaches can help ensure that such a shift in focus is sustainable.

Increasing agricultural production alone does not ensure food security and nutrition. Cropping patterns should be increasingly diversified toward more fruits, vegetables and nuts in order to support more balanced diets. At the same time, food consumption habits, such as wastage of produce at the end user level and over-consumption of water-intensive calories should be addressed through demand management measures.

Addressing water in agriculture at scale would allow for a more water-productive, equitable and efficient use. Investment in modernizing irrigation systems may not always save water and bring higher water productivity and livelihoods. The real interest of the local farmers and their capacity to benefit from the investment should be considered in such investments.

To address the negative impacts from climate change on water and agriculture requires interventions in both adaptation and mitigation. More efforts are particularly needed on agricultural research and development that addresses the impacts from increased crop water requirements, increased heat and drought stress and from shorter-duration, more-intensive precipitation events that are linked to flash floods, soil erosion and reduced soil water storage.

While many technologies and practices to address these challenges are available or under development, they need to be better aligned with projected climatic changes, building on local knowledge and experience. They also need to be more strongly targeted toward the most affected and disadvantaged areas.

In sum, a multi-scalar approach that allows for embracing both hydrological and social complexities while also taking into account local users' needs and perspectives will ultimately be what makes water management practices sustainable over time. Here local co-management and local ownership are critical. Technological innovation alone is not enough to improve water and food security. Instead, there needs to be a combination of improving water and land productivity alongside institutional change and local ownership. Water management practices invariably interact with social, power and gender relations and with wider issues concerning policy and decision making across a range of scales which determine on-the-ground outcomes. The next chapter which focuses on water governance, highlights the complexities, challenges and potential of institutions managing and governing water across a range of scales alongside competing discourses, actors and policies around water.

References

Abdel-Shafy, H.I. and Mansour, M.S.M. 2013. Overview on water reuse in Egypt: Present and future. *Sustainable Sanitation Practice*, 14: 17–25.

Albalawneh, A., Chang, T., Huang, C. and Mazahreh, S. 2015. Using landscape Metrics Analytic Hierarchy process to assess water harvesting potential sites in Jordan. *Environments*, 2: 415–434.

Allan, J.A. 2003. Virtual water: The water, food, and trade nexus useful concept or misleading metaphor? *Water International*, 28(1): 4–11.

Allan, T. 2011. *Virtual Water: Tackling the Threat to Our Planet's Most Precious Resource*. London: I.B. Tauris & Co.

Altieri, M., Funes-Monzote, F.R. and Peterson, P. 2012a. Agroecologically efficient agricultural systems for smallholder farmers: Contributions to food sovereignty. *Agronomy for Sustainable Development*, 32(1): 1–13.

Altieri, M., Nicholls, C. and Funes, F. 2012b. The scaling up of agroecology: Spreading hope for food sovereignty and resiliency. Sociedad Científica Latinoamericana de Agroecología. Rome: FAO.

Altieri, M.A. 1995. *Agroecology: The Science of Sustainable Agriculture*. Boulder, CO: CRC Press.

Altinbilek, D. 2014. Development and management of the Euphrates–Tigris basin. *International Journal of Water Resources Development*, 20(1): 15–33.

Aronson, J., Floret, C., Le Floc'h, E., Levali, C. and Pontanier, R. 1993. Restoration and rehabilitation of degraded ecosystems in arid and semiarid lands. I. A review from the south. *Restoration Ecology*, 1(3): 8–17.

Behnke, R. and Kerven, C. 2013. Counting the costs: Replacing pastoralism with irrigated agriculture in the Awash Valley, north-eastern Ethiopia. IIED Climate Change Working Paper No. 4. Climate resilience, productivity and equity in the drylands. London.

Bland, A. 2014. California drought has wild salmon competing with almonds for water. NPR, The Salt. Available at: www.npr.org/blogs/thesalt/2014/08/21/342167846/california-drought-has-wild-salmon-competing-with-almonds-for-water.

Borrini, B.F. 2011. Co-management and shared governance – the 'effective and equitable option' for natural resources and protected areas? Grazia Borrini-Feyerabend, in *Proceedings of the National Workshop on Co-management Concept and Practice in Viet Nam Soc Trang*, 17–19 March 2010.

Boufaroua, M., Albalawneh, A. and Oweis, T. 2013. Assessing the efficiency of grey-water reuse at household level and its suitability for sustainable rural and human development. *British Journal of Applied Science & Technology*, ISSN: 2231-0843 3: 962–972.

Byczynski, L. 2010. New strategies for great-tasting tomatoes. Growing for Market. Available at: www.growingformarket.com/articles/Improve-tomato-flavor.

CA (Comprehensive Assessment of Water Management in Agriculture). 2007. *Water for Food, Water for Life: A Comprehensive Assessment of Water Management in Agriculture*. London: Earthscan; Colombo: International Water Management Institute (IWMI).

CBD (Convention on Biological Diversity). 1992. Convention on Biological Diversity. 5 June 1992, Rio de Janeiro (Brazil).

CGIAR. 2000. *System-wide Initiative on Livestock programme*. Biennial report 1999–2000. Aleppo, Syria: ICARDA.

CGIAR Dryland Systems. 2013. *CRP 1.1 Dryland Systems. Integrated agricultural production systems for improved food security and livelihoods in dry areas.* A proposal submitted to the CGIAR Consortium Board. Beirut, Lebanon: ICARDA.

Cofie, O. and Drechsel, P. 2007. Water for food in the cities: The growing paradigm of irrigated (peri)-urban agriculture and its struggle in sub-Saharan Africa. *African Water Journal,* 1(1): 26–50.

Cosgrove, W. and Rijsberman, F. (eds). 2000. *World Water Vision: Making Water Everybody's Business.* London: Earthscan Publications.

Custodio, E. 2010. Intensive groundwater development: A water cycle transformation, a social revolution, a management challenge. In L. Martínez-Cortina, A. Garrido and E. López-Gunn, eds. *Rethinking Water and Food Security,* pp. 259–277. Boca Raton, FL: CRC Press.

Domenech, L. and Ringler, C. 2013. The impact of irrigation on nutrition, health, and gender. A review paper with insights for Africa south of the Sahara. IFPRI Discussion Paper No. 1259. Washington, DC: IFPRI.

Doss, C. 2011. If women hold up half the sky, how much of the world's food do they produce? ESA Working Paper No. 11-04. Rome: Food and Agriculture Organization. Available at: www.fao.org/3/a-am309e.pdf.

Doss, C., Kovarik, C., Peterman, A., Quisumbing, A. and van Den Bold, M. 2015. Gender inequalities in ownership and control of land in Africa: Myth and reality. *Agricultural Economics,* 46(3): 403–434.

Dugan, P., Dey, M.M. and Sugunan, V.V. 2006. Fisheries and water productivity in tropical river basins: Enhancing food security and livelihoods by managing water for fish. *Agricultural Water Management,* 80(1–3): 262–275.

Environmental Protection Agency (EPA) of the USA. 2017. Principles of watershed management. Available at: https://cfpub.epa.gov/watertrain/moduleFrame.cfm?parent_object_id=512.

Esrey, S., Anderson, I., Hillers, A. and Sawyer, R. 2001. Closing the loop: Ecological sanitation for food security. Swedish International Development Cooperation Agency (SIDA) Publications on Water Resources No. 18. Available at: www.ecosanres.org/pdf_files/closing-the-loop.pdf.

Evenari, M., Shanan, L. and Tadmor, N. 1982. *The Negev: The Challenge of a Desert.* Cambridge, MA: Harvard University Press.

Falkenmark, M., Fox, P., Persson, G. and Rockström, J. 2001. Water harvesting for upgrading of rainfed agriculture: Problem analysis and research needs. Report number 11. Stockholm International Water Institute (SIWI), Stockholm, Sweden.

FAO. 1997. *Modernization of Irrigation Schemes: Past Experiences and Future Options.* Water Report 12. Rome.

FAO. 2002a. *The State of World Fisheries and Aquaculture.* Fisheries Department. Rome: FAO.

FAO. 2002b. *Agricultural Drainage Water Management in Arid and Semi Arid Areas,* by K.K. Tanji and N.C. Kielen. Irrigation and Drainage Paper No 61. Rome: FAO.

FAO. 2012a. *Improving Gender Equality in Territorial Issues.* Land and Water Division Working Paper 3. Rome: FAO. Available at: www.fao.org/docrep/016/me282e/me282e.pdf.

FAO. 2012b. *Coping with Water Scarcity: An Action Framework for Agriculture and Food Security.* Water Report 38. Rome: FAO.

FAO. 2017. Does improving irrigation technology save water? A review of the evidence. Discussion paper on irrigation and sustainable water resources management in the Near East and North Africa. Chris Perry and Pasquali Steduto. Rome: FAO.

FAO. 2018a. Scaling up agroecology to achieve the sustainable development goals. *Proceedings of the Second FAO International Symposium*, 3–5 April, 2018, Rome, Italy.

FAO. 2018b. *Pastoralism in Africa's Drylands*. Rome: FAO, 52 pp. Licence: CC BY-NC-SA 3.0 IGO.

FAO. 2018c. Scaling up agroecology initiative, transforming food and agricultural systems in support of the SDGs. A proposal prepared for the *International Symposium on Agroecology, 3–5 April 2018*. Available at: www.fao.org/3/I9049EN/i9049en.pdf.

FAOSTAT. 2014. *Import and Export Statistics*. Available at: http://faostat.fao.org. FAO Gender, Equity and Rural Employment Division, 2012.

Farquhar, G., Condon, A., Richards, R. and Rebetzke, G. 2004. Breeding for high water-use efficiency. *Experimental Botany*, 55(407): 2447–2460.

Faurès, J.-M., Svendsen, M. and Turral, H. 2007. Reinventing irrigation. In D. Molden, ed. *Water for Food, Water for Life: A Comprehensive Assessment of Water Management in Agriculture*, pp. 315–352. London: Earthscan; Colombo, Sri Lanka: International Water Management Institute (IWMI).

Ferichani, M. and Prasetya, D.A. 2017. System of rice intensification increases rice productivity on saline soil. *Paddy and Water Environment*, 15(3): 649–657.

Fischer, G., Shah, M. and van Velthuizen, H. 2002. Climate change and agricultural vulnerability. Special report for the UN World Summit on Sustainable Development, 26 August–4 September, Johannesburg, Laxenburg, Austria: International Institute for Applied Systems Analysis.

Fraser, E.D.G., Quinn, C. and Sendzimir, J. (eds). 2011. Resilience and vulnerability of arid and semi-arid social ecological systems. *Ecology and Society* (Special Feature), 16(3). Available at: www.ecologyandsociety.org/issues/view.php?sf=52.

Frayne, B., McCordic, C. and Shilomboleni, H. 2014. Growing out of poverty: Does urban agriculture contribute to household food security in Southern African cities? *Urban Forum*, 25: 177–189.

Gallaher, C.M., Kerr, J.M., Ngjenga, M., Karanja, N.K. and WinklerPrins, A. 2013. Urban agriculture, social capital and food security in the Kiberia slums of Nairobi, Kenya. *Agriculture and Human Values*, 30: 389–404.

Garces-Restrepo, C., Vermillion, D. and Muñoz, G. 2007. Irrigation management transfer: Worldwide efforts and results. FAO water report no. 32. Rome: FAO.

Gawel, E. and Bernsen, K. 2011. What is wrong with virtual water trading? UFZ Discussion paper 1/2011. Leibniz Information Centre for Economics (ZBW).

Gerbens-Leenes, P.W., Mekonnen, M.M. and Hoekstra, A.Y. 2013. The water footprint of poultry, pork and beef: A comparative study in different countries and production systems. *Water Resources and Industry*, 1–2: 25–36.

GFFA (Global Forum for Food and Agriculture). 2017. GFFA Communiqué 9th Berlin Agriculture Ministers' Conference 2017. Agriculture and Water—Key to Feeding the World. Available at: www.gffa-berlin.de/en/programmuebersicht-2017/berliner-agrarministerkonferenz/.

Ghosh, A.K., Bhatt, M.A. and Agrawal, H.P. 2012. Effect of long-term application of treated sewage water on heavy metal accumulation in vegetables grown in Northern India. *Environmental Monitoring and Assessment*, 184: 1025–1036.

Gintzburger, G. and Le Houérou, F. 2005. The steppes of middle Asia: Post-1991 agricultural and rangeland adjustment. *Land Research and Management*, 19(3): 215–239.

Gliessman, S.R. 2015. *Agroecology: The Ecology of Sustainable Food Systems*. 3rd edn. Boca Raton, FL: CRC Press, Taylor & Francis.

Grafton, R.Q., Williams, J., Perry, C.J., Molle, F., Ringler, C., Steduto, P., Udall, B., Wheeler, S., Wang, Y., Garrick, D. and Allen, R.G. 2018. The paradox of irrigation efficiency. *Science*, 361(6404): 748–750.

Gunderson, L.H., Holling, C.S. and Light, S. 1995. *Barriers and Bridges to the Renewal of Ecosystems and Institutions*. New York: Columbia University Press.

Gururaja, R., Khandelwa, S.A. and Sharma, D.K. 2012. Salinity ingress in costal Gujarat; Appraisal of control measures. *Journal of Soil Salinity and Water Quality*, 4(2): 102–113.

GWP. 2012. *Groundwater Resources and Irrigated Agriculture: Making a Beneficial Relation More Sustainable*. Stockholm: GWP.

Hessari, B., Bruggeman, A., Akhoond-Ali, A., Oweis, T. and Abbasi, F. 2012. Supplemental irrigation potential and impact on downstream flow of Karkheh River Basin of Iran. *Hydrology and Earth System Sciences Discussion Paper*, 9: 13519–13536.

Hilhost, T. and Muchena, F. 2000. *Nutrients on the Move: Soil Fertility Dynamics in African Farming Systems*. London: International Institute for Environment and Development.

HLPE. 2012. *Social Protection for Food security*. A report by the High Level Panel of Experts on Food Security and Nutrition of the Committee on World Food Security. Rome: FAO.

HLPE. 2014. Sustainable fisheries and aquaculture for food security and nutrition. A report by the High Level Panel of Experts on Food Security and Nutrition of the Committee on World Food Security. Rome: FAO.

HLPE. 2015. Water for food security and nutrition. report # 9. L. Mehta, O. Cordeiro-Netto, T. Oweis, C. Ringler and B. Schreiner S. Varghese. Rome: FAO. Available at: www.fao.org/fileadmin/user_upload/hlpe/hlpe documents/HLPE_Reports/HLPE-Report-9_EN.pdf.

Hoekstra, A.Y. 2009. Human appropriation of natural capital: A comparison of ecological footprint and water footprint analysis. *Ecological Economics*, 68(7): 1963–1974.

Hoekstra, A.Y., Chapagain, A.K., Aldaya, M.M. and Mekonnen, M.M. 2011. *The Water Footprint Assessment Manual: Setting the Global Standard*. London: Earthscan.

Holm, P.E., Marcussen, H. and Dalsgaard, A. 2010. Fate and risks of potentially toxic elements in wastewater-fed food production systems – the examples of Cambodia and Vietnam. *Irrigation Drainage Systems*, 2: 127–142.

Howard, B. 2015. Explaining the monster dust storm sweeping the Middle East. *National Geographic*. 8 September. *National Geographic Magazine*, Washington, DC. Available at: http://news.nationalgeographic.com/2015/09/150908-middle-east-dust-storm-haboob-weather/.

IAASTD (International Assessment of Agricultural Knowledge, Science and Technology for Development). 2009. *Agriculture at a Crossroads*. Washington, DC: Island Press.

IPCC. 2014. Climate change: Impacts, adaptation, and vulnerability. In V.R. Barros, *et al.* eds. *Part B: Regional Aspects*. Contribution of Working Group II to the Fifth Assessment Report of the Intergovernmental Panel on Climate Change. Cambridge, UK and New York: Cambridge University Press.

IPCC. 2018. Summary for Policymakers. In V. Masson-Delmotte, P. Zhai, H.O. Pörtner, D. Roberts, J. Skea, P.R. Shukla, A. Pirani, W. Moufouma-Okia, C. Péan, R. Pidcock, S. Connors, J.B.R. Matthews, Y. Chen, X. Zhou, M.I. Gomis, E. Lonnoy, T. Maycock, M. Tignor and T. Waterfield, eds. *Global Warming of 1.5°C: An IPCC Special Report on the Impacts of Global Warming of 1.5°C above Pre-Industrial Levels and Related Global Greenhouse Gas Emission Pathways, in the Context of Strengthening the Global Response to the Threat of Climate Change, Sustainable Development, and Efforts to Eradicate Poverty*, 32 pp. Geneva, Switzerland: World Meteorological Organization.

Jönsson, H., Stinzing, A.R., Vinneras, B. and Salomon, E. 2004. Guidelines on the use of urine and faeces in crop production. EcoSanRes Publication Report 2004-2. Stockholm: Stockholm Environmental Institute. Available at: www.ecosanres.org/pdf_files/ESR_Publications_2004/ESR2web.pdf.

Keller, J. and Keller, A.A. 2003. Affordable drip irrigation systems for small farms in developing countries. *Proceedings of the Irrigation Association Annual Meeting.* San Diego, CA, 18–20 November 2003.

Kierean, C., Sproule, K., Doss, C., Quisumbing, A. and Kim, S.M. 2015. Examining gender inequalities in land rights indicators in Asia. *Agricultural Economics*, 46(S1): 119–138.

Kijne, J., Tuong, T., Bennett, J., Bouman, B. and Oweis, T. 2002. *Ensuring Food Security via Improvement in Crop Water Productivity. Background Paper 1: Challenge Program on Water and Food*. Colombo, Sri Lanka: International Water Management Institute (IWMI).

Kremen, C. and Miles, A.F. 2012. Ecosystem services in biologically diversified versus conventional farming systems: Benefits, externalities, and trade-offs. *Ecology and Society*, 17 (4): 40.

Lasage, R. and Verburg, P.H. 2015. Evaluation of small scale water harvesting techniques for semi-arid environments. *Journal of Arid Environments*, 118: 48–57.

London Assembly. 2010. *Cultivating the Capital: Food Growing and the Planning System in London*. London: Greater London Authority, Planning and Housing Committee. Available at: http://legacy.london.gov.uk/assembly/reports/plansd/growing-food.pdf.

Louhaichi, M. and Tastad, A. 2010. The Syrian steppe: Past trends, current status, and future priorities. *Rangelands*, 32(2): 2–7.

MAAR (Ministry of Agriculture and Agrarian Reforms). 2018. Annual Agricultural Statistical Abstracts (1980–2017). Damascus: MAAR.

MacDonald, A.M., Bonsor, H.C., Dochartaigh, B.É.Ó. and Taylor, R.G. 2012. Quantitative maps of groundwater resources in Africa. *Environmental Research Letters*, 7(2).

Malik, R.P.S., Prathapar, S.A. and Marwah, M. 2014. Revitalizing canal irrigation: Towards improving cost recovery. IWMI Working Paper 160. Colombo, Sri Lanka: International Water Management Institute (IWMI).

Mazid, A., Martinin, M., Tutwiler, R., Al-Ahmed, H. and Maya, F. 2003. *Impact of Modern Agricultural Technologies on Durum Wheat Production in Syria*. Aleppo, Syria: International Center for Agricultural Research in the Dry Areas (ICARDA).

Meinzen-Dick, R. 1997. Valuing the multiple uses of irrigation water. In M. Kay, T. Franks and L. Smith, eds. *Water: Economic, Management and Demand*, pp. 50–58. London: E&FN Spon.

Mekonnen, M.M. and Hoekstra, A.Y. 2010. The green, blue and grey water footprint of farm animals and animal products. Value of Water Research Report Series 48. Delft, The Netherlands: UNESCO-IHE Institute for Water Education.

Mekonnen, M.M. and Hoekstra, A.Y. 2012. A global assessment of the water footprint of farm animal products. *Ecosystems*, 15(3): 401–415.

Metawie, A. 2002. Egypt: The role of water users' associations in reforming irrigation. Global Water Partnership. Available at: www.gwp.org/en/learn/KNOWLEDGE_RESOURCES/Case_Studies/Africa/Egypt-The-role-of-water-users-associations-in-reforming-irrigation-110/

Molden, D., Oweis, T., Steduto, P., Bindraban, P., Hanjra, M. and Kijne, J. 2010. Improving agricultural water productivity: Between optimism and caution. *Agricultural Water Management*, 97(4): 528–535.

Molden, D., Oweis, T., Steduto, P., Kijne, J., Hanjra, M. and Bindraban, P. 2007. Pathways for increasing agricultural water productivity. In D. Molden, ed. *Water for Food, Water for*

Life: A Comprehensive Assessment of Water Management in Agriculture, pp. 279–310. London: Earthscan; Colombo, Sri Lanka: International Water Management Institute (IWMI).

Nkonya, E., Mirzabaev, A. and von Braun, J. (eds). 2016. *Economics of Land Degradation and Improvement: A Global Assessment for Sustainable Development*. Cham, Switzerland: Springer International Publishing.

Oweis, T. 2012. The fallacy of irrigation modernization in water around the Mediterranean. *Revolve Magazine*. Available at: www.revolve-magazine.com/home/ 2012/01/19/irrigation-modernization/.

Oweis, T. 2013. Agricultural water management under scarcity: A need for a paradigm change. *Revista Cientifica de Producao Animal*, 15(1): 22–30.

Oweis, T. 2016. Adapting agricultural water management to water scarcity in dry environments. In A. Garrido and A. Rabi, eds. *Managing Water in the 21st Century: Challenges and Opportunities. Proceedings of the 8th Rosenberg International Forum on Water Policy*. The Regents of the University of California.

Oweis, T. and Hachum, A. 2003. Improving water productivity in the dry areas of West Asia and North Africa. In W.J. Kijne, R. Barker and D. Molden, eds. *Water Productivity in Agriculture: Limits and Opportunities for Improvement*, pp. 179–197. Wallingford, UK: CABI Publishing.

Oweis, T. and Hachum, A. 2009. Optimizing supplemental irrigation: Tradeoffs between profitability and sustainability. *Agricultural Water Management*, 96: 511–516.

Oweis, T., Oberle, A. and Prinz, D. 1998. Determination of potential sites and methods for water harvesting in central Syria. *Advances in GeoEcology*, 31: 83–88.

Oweis, T., Prinz, D. and Hachum, A. 2012. *Rainwater Harvesting for Agriculture in the Dry Areas*. London: CRC Press/Balkema,Taylor & Francis Group.

Oweis, T. 2017. Rainwater harvesting for restoring degraded dry agro-pastoral ecosystems: A conceptual review of opportunities and constraints in a changing climate. *Environmental Reviews*, 25(2): 135–149.

Oweis, T.Y. and Walker, W.R. 1990. Zero-inertia model for surge flow furrow irrigation. *Irrigation Science*, 11(3): 131–136.

Parmentier, S. 2014. Scaling-up agroecological approaches: What, why and how? Brussels, Oxfam-Solidarity. Swedish International Development Cooperation Agency (SIDA) Publications on Water Resources No. 18.

Passioura, J.B. 1977. Grain yield, harvest index, and water use of wheat. *Journal of the Australian Institute of Agricultural Science*, 43: 117–121.

Passioura, J.B. and Angus, J.F. 2010. Improving productivity of crops in water-limited environments. *Advances in Agronomy*, 106: 37–75.

Peden, D., Tadesse, G. and Misra, A.K. 2007. Water and livestock for human development. In D. Molden, ed. *Water for Food, Water for Life: A Comprehensive Assessment of Water Management in Agriculture*, pp. 485–514. London: Earthscan.

Pereira, L.S., Oweis, T. and Zairi, A. 2002. Irrigation management under scarcity. *Agricultural Water Management*, 57: 175–206.

Perry, C. 2007. Efficient irrigation; inefficient communication; flawed recommendation. *Irrigation and Drainage*, 56(4): 367–378.

Perry, C.J., Rock, M. and Seckler, D. 1997. Water as an economic good: A solution, or a problem? IIMI Research Paper 14. Colombo.

Pimbert, M.P. 2010. Towards food sovereignty: Reclaiming autonomous food systems. Ch. 4: The role of local organisations in sustaining local food systems, livelihoods and environments. London and Munich: IIED, RCC, CAWR. Available at: www.iied.org /towards-food-sovereignty-reclaiming-autonomous-food-systems.

Prein, M. 2002. Integration of aquaculture into crop–animal systems in Asia. *Agricultural Systems*, 71: 127–146.
Rakhmatullaev, S., Huneau, F., Kazbekov, J., Le Coustumer, P., Jumanov, J., El Oifi, B., Motelica-Heino, M. and Hrkal, Z. 2010. Groundwater resources use and management in the Amu Darya River Basin (Central Asia). *Environmental Earth Sciences*, 59(6): 1183–1193.
Rockström, J., Barron, J. and Fox, P. 2003. Water productivity in rain fed agriculture: Challenges and opportunities for smallholder farmers in drought-prone tropical agroecosystems. In J.W. Kijne, R. Barker and D. Molden, eds. *Water Productivity in Agriculture: Limits and Opportunities for Improvement*, pp. 145–162. Wallingford, UK: CABI Publishing.
Rockström, J., Karlberg, L., Wani, S.P., Barron, J., Hatibu, N., Oweis, T., Bruggeman, A., Farahani, H. and Qiang, Z. 2010. Managing water in rainfed agriculture: The need for a paradigm shift. *Agricultural Water Management*, 79(4): 543–550.
Rosegrant, M.W., Cai, X. and Cline, S. 2002. *World Water and Food to 2025: Dealing with Scarcity*. Washington, DC: International Food Policy Research Institute. 325 pp.
Rosegrant, M.W., Ringler, C. and De Jong, I. 2009b. Irrigation: Tapping potential. In V. Foster and C. Briceño-Garmendia, eds. *Africa's Infrastructure: A Time for Transformation*, pp. 287–297. A co-publication of the Agence Française de Développement and the World Bank.
Rosegrant, M.W., Ringler, C. and Zhu, T. 2009a. Water for agriculture: Maintaining food security under growing scarcity. *Annual Review of Environment and Resources*, 34: 205–222.
Roy, D., Barr, J. and Venema, H.D. 2011. Ecosystem approaches in integrated water resources management (IWRM), A review of transboundary river basins. United Nations Environmental Programme and the International Institute for Sustainable Development (IISD). Available at: www.iisd.org/pdf/2011/iwrm_transboundary_river_basins.pdf.
Seckler, D. 1996. The new era of water resources management: From "dry" to "wet" water savings. Research Report 1. Colombo, International Irrigation Management Institute.
Seckler, D., Molden, D. and Sakthivadivel, R. 2003. The concept of efficiency in water resources management and policy. In J.W. Kijne, R. Barker and D. Molden, eds. *Water Productivity in Agriculture: Limits and Opportunities for Improvement*, pp. 37–51. Wallingford, UK, and Colombo: CABI Publishing and International Water Management Institute (IWMI).
Shah, T. 2007. Issues in reforming informal water economies of low-income countries: Examples from India and elsewhere. In B. Van Koppen, G. Mark and J. Butterworth, eds. *Community-Based Water Law and Water Resource Management Reform in Developing Countries*, pp. 65–95. Comprehensive Assessment of Water Management in Agriculture Series 5. Wallingford: UK, CABI Publishing.
Sharma, B.R., Gulati, A., Mohan, G., Manchanda, S., Ray, U. and Amarasinghe, U. 2018. Water Productivity Mapping of Major Indian Crops, NABARD Mumbai, and ICRIER, New Delhi.
Sharma, S. 2018. Livestock's contribution to 1.5 pathway: Where transformation is needed. Available at: www.iatp.org/sites/default/files/2018-11/2018_11_28_COP_FactSheet_f.pdf.
Shatanawi, M., Fardous, A., Mazahreh, N. and Duqqa, M. 2005. Irrigation system performance in Jordan. In N. Lamaddalena, F. Lebdi, M. Todorovic and C. Bogliatti, eds. *Irrigation System Performance*, pp. 128–131. Options méditerranéennes, Series B No 52. Bari, Italy: CIHEAM.
Siebert, S., Burke, J., Faures, J.M., Frenken, K., Hoogeveen, J., Döll, P. and Portmann, F. T. 2010. Groundwater use for irrigation: A global inventory. *Hydrology & Earth System Science*, 14: 1863–1880.

Siegert, K. 1994. Introduction to water harvesting. Some basic principles for planning. In *Proceedings of the FAO Expert Consultation: Water Harvesting for Improved Agricultural Production*, Cairo, Egypt, 21–25 November 1993. FAO, Rome, Italy, pp. 9–21.

Sommer, R., Oweis, T. and Hussein, L. 2011. Can supplemental irrigation alleviate the effect of climate change on wheat production in Mediterranean environments? Oral presentation at the ASA, CSSA, SSSA Annual Meetings "Fundamental for Life: Soil, Crop, & Environmental Sciences", 16–19 October 2011, San Antonio, TX.

Sowers, J., Vengosh, A. and Weinthal, E. 2011. Climate change, water resources, and the politics of adaptation in the Middle East and North Africa. *Climatic Change*, 104(3): 599–627.

Tanji, K. and Kielen, N.C. 2002. Agricultural drainage water management in arid and semi-arid areas. Irrigation and Drainage Water Paper no. 61. Rome: FAO.

Thornton, P.K. 2010. Livestock production: Recent trends, future prospects. *Philosophical Transactions of the Royal Society B*, 365: 2853–2867.

UNDP. 2013. *Water Governance in the Arab Region: Managing Scarcity and Securing the Future.* New York: UNDP.

Uphoff, N. 2017. SRI: An agroecological strategy to meet multiple objectives with reduced reliance on inputs. *Agroecology and Sustainable Food Systems*, 41(7): 825–854.

Van Dijk, J. and Reij, C. 1994. Indigenous water harvesting techniques in sub-Saharan Africa: Examples from Sudan and the West African Sahel. In *Proceedings of the FAO Expert Consultation: Water Harvesting for Improved Agricultural Production*, pp. 101–112. Cairo, Egypt, 21–25 November 1993. FAO, Rome, Italy.

Van Steenbergen, F. and Abdel Dayem, S. 2007. Making the case for integrated water resources management: Drainage in Egypt. *Water International*, 32(Supplement 1): 685–696.

Vargas Hill, R. and Viceisza, A. 2011. A field experiment on the impact of weather shocks and insurance on risky investment. *Experimental Economics*, 15(2): 341–371.

Verdegem, M.C.J., Bosma, R.H. and Verreth, J.A.J. 2006. Reducing water use for animal production through aquaculture. *International Journal of Water Resources Development*, 22(1): 101–113.

Vohland, K. and Barry, B. 2009. A review of in situ rainwater harvesting (RWH) practices modifying landscape functions in African drylands. *Agriculture, Ecosystems & Environment*, 131(3–4): 119–127.

Wang, X., Dong, Z., Zhang, J. and Liu, L. 2004. Modern dust storms in China: An overview. *Journal of Arid Environments*, 58(4): 559–574.

Wani, S., Rockström, J. and Oweis, T. (eds). 2009. *Rainfed Agriculture: Unlocking the Potential*. Comprehensive Assessment of Water Management in Agriculture Series 7. London: CABI Publishing.

Wezel, A., Casagrande, M., Celette, F., Vian, J.-F., Ferrer, A. and Joséphine, P. 2014. Agroecological practices for sustainable agriculture. A review. *Agronomy for Sustainable Development. Springer Verlag/EDP Sciences/INRA*, 34(1): 1–20.

Wichelns, D. 2001. The role of 'virtual water' in efforts to achieve food security and other national goals, with an example from Egypt. *Agricultural Water Management*, 49(2): 131–151.

Wichelns, D. 2010. An Economic Analysis of the Virtual Water Concept in Relation to the Agri-Food Sector. Paris: OECD. Available at: www.oecd-ilibrary.org/agriculture-and-food/sustainable-management-of-water-resources- in-agriculture/an-economic-analysis-of-the-virtual-water-concept-in-relation-to-the-agri-food- sector_978926 4083578-8-en.

Wichelns, D. 2014. Investing in small, private irrigation to increase production and enhance livelihoods. *Agricultural Water Management*, 131(1): 163–166.

Willems, P., Arnbjerg-Nielsen, K., Olsson, J. and Nguyen, V. 2012. Climate change impact assessment on urban rainfall extremes and urban drainage: Methods and shortcomings. *Atmospheric Research*, 103: 106–118.

World Bank. 2006. *Shaping the Future of Water for Agriculture: A Sourcebook for Investment in Agricultural Water Management*. Washington, DC: World Bank.

Wreford, A., Moran, D. and Adger, N. 2010. *Climate Change and Agriculture: Impacts, Adaptation and Mitigation*. Paris: OECD.

Wu, W., Al-Shafie, W.M., Mhaimeed, A.S., Ziadat, F., Nangia, V. and Payne, W. 2014. Salinity mapping by multi-scale remote sensing in Mesopotamia, Iraq. *IEEE Journal of Selected Topics in Applied Earth Observations and Remote Sensing*, 7(11).

Zezza, A. and Tasciotti, L. 2010. Urban agriculture, poverty, and food security: Empirical evidence from a sample of developing countries. *Food Policy*, 35: 265–273.

Zhang, H. and Oweis, T. 1999. Water-yield relations and optimal irrigation scheduling of wheat in the Mediterranean region. *Agricultural Water Management*, 38: 195–211.

Zwarteveen, M. 2008. Men, masculinities and water powers in irrigation. *Water Alternatives*, 1(1): 111–130.

4
WATER GOVERNANCE FOR FSN

The contested nature of water governance

Governance refers to the rules, processes of rule making and exercises of power by both state and non-state actors. How power is exercised and influences decisions is of particular importance for achieving FSN, where those experiencing the worst food insecurity are also those with the least access to power. The governance of water includes the political, social, economic and administrative systems that directly or indirectly affect the use, development and management of water resources and the delivery of water services at different levels of society (Water Governance Facility, 2012). It includes decisions and processes on how water is used and allocated, how needs are interpreted and how these are to be met, and by whom – in short, it deals with the needs, rights and responsibilities of different actors in society around water (see Movik, 2012). As we demonstrate, water governance is polycentric, covering a range of institutional arrangements from local to global, with constant negotiations across different domains of power. Water governance sets the rules, access rights and (largely economic) tools and accountability mechanisms for all actors involved in the management and use of water; it determines how water is allocated across sectors, regions, countries; which decisions are taken (or not) regarding infrastructure and water development, ecosystem regeneration; as well as the alignment (or not) between water, energy, food, trade and wider environmental policies (e.g. forests, biodiversity) etc. Marginalized communities rely on the commons, such as forests, water and biodiversity, for their livelihoods and food security. As a result, governance of the commons, especially in the context of food and nutrition security, requires specific strategies to ensure legal recognition, respect and protection of the informal and/or tenure rights of these rights holders (FAO, 2016).

This chapter focuses on the local and national dimensions of water governance for FSN. The global level, including human rights frameworks, is the focus of the next chapter. In this chapter, we engage with the messy and complex nature of water governance which is often accompanied by high levels of contestation. This is because water is a multifaceted and contested resource, meaning different things to different social actors. However, as illustrated in this chapter, dominant policy frameworks tend to focus on economic use values rather than on the socio-cultural meanings and practices that water has in everyday life and customary arrangements. The nature of water makes it more readily available, both physically and administratively, to those with access to land, resources and entitlements and more difficult to access for the marginalized and poor. While land is highly, and food is largely, location-specific, water moves across geographical, jurisdictional and administrative boundaries, complicating water governance.

There is no one-size-fits-all 'best practice' system of governance of water for FSN. First, as discussed earlier in this book, water resource endowments can vary both over time and across and within countries, as can the nature and intensity of competition for water. Second, FSN situations may be similarly varied over time and across geographic spaces. Third, the actors involved can likewise vary, as different users' situations evolve and change, their access to information and technical and financial resources ebbs or flows, and their political influence on decision making waxes or wanes. Meanwhile, water governance systems are embedded in administrative and legal structures and are immersed in overlapping informal and formal tenure systems. Wider political, economic, social, cultural and even ethical contexts, as well as formal and informal rules of power, shape and condition any water governance system (see Groenfeldt and Schmidt, 2013; Water Governance Facility, 2012).

The critical issue in relation to water for FSN is who gets to use how much water, of what quality and for what purpose. This begs the following questions: what are the methods and approaches used to allocate water between countries, between sectors and between users; what are the institutional arrangements (both formal and informal/customary) that underpin water allocation decisions; and how do these arrangements serve, or not serve, the water requirements of the food insecure. The first question is informed by the policy and legislative frameworks for water management and regulation as well as food security, and the tools used to achieve water allocation such as transboundary agreements, catchment/basin allocation plans, permit systems and water markets/trading. The second question is informed by choices pertaining to centralized or decentralized management, the capacity to manage complex systems, including human capacity, information and data, and roles, responsibilities and power relations, whether public or private, including the degree of participation in decision making by the most vulnerable.

The policy environment also matters. A range of policies impact on water and FSN through a suite of government agencies at the national, sub-national and local levels. Importantly, policy coordination is often fragmented, e.g. domestic water vs irrigation; or agriculture vs environment. In countries where water management is devolved to state or provincial levels, there is a need for both horizontal and vertical integration in decision making. In terms of allocation, when water is distributed to agriculture, it is often diverted to large irrigation schemes or industrial users, not to small-holders. At the local level, land, food and water are tightly linked and of particular relevance to local people's livelihoods and survival strategies. However, formal and national governance systems have developed separately and are often out of sync with local water and land regimes, resulting in ambiguities and possible exclusions for vulnerable communities. Similarly, while integration across water, food and agricultural sectors tends to be a mantra at the global level, at the national, provincial and district levels there are many contradictions and trade-offs concerning water allocation and food security, making integration a key challenge with policies and programmes often disconnected from the needs and interests of poor and marginalized people.

These issues are unpacked in more detail in this chapter. We begin with the politics of water allocation and the range of policies, tools and institutional arrangements that govern water. We then demonstrate how access to water is highly contested and linked to social, power and gender relations. A significant focus is given to the challenges of developing systems that recognize customary water use practices and the needs of marginalized small-scale users in rural areas. We then turn to dominant paradigms and controversies in the water sector such as Integrated Water Resources Management, the nexus, large dams, water privatization as well as water and land grabs, with a particular focus on the impacts on informal and marginalized users of water. Finally, we examine challenges concerning integrating water for FSN concerns with other competing uses of water at the national and global scales.

The politics of allocation

In most countries, the distribution and availability of water – in relation to quantity, quality, seasonality or reliability – make it difficult to share water equitably amongst competing users. Allocation, thus, is the mechanism for determining who can take how much water, where, when and for what purpose. Water is allocated through a variety of mechanisms, influenced by existing institutional and legal frameworks, the infrastructure available as well as traditional water use patterns and customary rights.

In the face of increasing competition for water between countries, between sectors and within sectors, the allocation and regulation of water use become increasingly important. When the impacts of climate change are overlaid on the growing competition for water, optimal allocation and effective regulation of water use become even more important. Climate change is already affecting rainfall regimes around the world, changing the timing, intensity and amount of rainfall, with knock-on effects in terms of both surface and groundwater availability and the occurrence and severity of extreme events (see Chapters 2 and 3). In this context of increasing competition, allocation spans a range of levels, from international (between countries in shared river basins, see Chapter 5) through the national (at the basin or catchment levels); and the sub-catchment level; between catchments, which may include transboundary allocations; to different sectors; and to individual water users, whether enterprises or individuals.

As noted in Chapter 2, water allocation is mediated through institutions, gender, social and power relations, property rights, identity and culture. The structure of any system of water allocation is influenced by the statutory institutional and legal frameworks, the water resources infrastructure as well as traditional water use patterns and customary rights to existing water resources. The three key allocation mechanisms are (1) government or public allocation; (2) user-based allocation; and (3) market allocation (Meinzen-Dick and Mendoza, 1996). While any combination of these three allocation mechanisms can accompany new infrastructure development, the role of the state is particularly strong in intersectoral allocation, as the state is often the only institution that has jurisdiction over all sectors of water use. User-based allocation requires collective action institutions with authority to make decisions on water rights, including localized customary institutions and practices. Market-based allocation refers to an exchange of water-use rights. Most water allocation situations represent a mix of these three allocation mechanisms. Under growing water scarcity, the combination of appropriate mechanisms might well change, requiring a supportive enabling framework that allows flexible incorporation of elements of these three approaches (Rosegrant et al., 2009), as well as that of traditional or customary water uses (Varghese, 2013).

In areas where water demand equals or exceeds supply, the re-allocation of water between sectors tends to increase, moving water from lower to higher value water uses – generally from agriculture to cities, industry and power generation. This not only reduces the potential to produce food, but can also result in local conflicts over water. The re-allocation of water can be done through administrative, market-based or collective negotiation processes. In administrative re-allocation, the state re-allocates water, often in the name of 'public purpose' to support certain national policy priorities. Water re-allocation can have negative effects on food production, rural livelihoods and on food prices. When decisions are made without consultation with affected users or without offering adequate compensation to those losing their water entitlements, it becomes particularly problematic from a governance perspective. The focus of re-allocation is often toward meeting the needs of more powerful water users such as cities and industry, with marginal and 'invisible' rural users (i.e. fishers, small-scale farmers and homestead gardeners) losing out (Meinzen-Dick and Ringler, 2008; Rosegrant and Ringler, 2000). In formal and informal market-based transfers, such as in the western United States, or the Southern Murray Darling Basin in

Australia, water is sold or leased. In the third option, water is re-allocated based on collective negotiations between users and the state or between old and new users. Illegal re-allocation of water between users is also common (Meinzen-Dick and Ringler, 2008).

> **BOX 4.1 WATER ALLOCATION AND REGULATION IN MAHARASHTRA**
>
> In 2005, the state of Maharashtra (India) embarked upon an ambitious water pricing reform strategy by allocating water entitlements for various categories of uses. The central principle of this reform package was to ensure cost recovery in a loss-incurring water sector through issuing entitlements (and associated fees) that would be overseen by an independent regulatory authority. Entitlements were defined as use rights over water and not as ownership rights (Government of Maharashtra, 2005). This development was intended to support the creation of formal water trading (both intra- as well as inter-sectoral) thus leading to improved water use efficiency in this water-stressed Indian state. Introducing entitlements in western Maharashtra, which lies at the heart of the sugarcane economy, faced multiple challenges: (1) resistance on the part of head-end farmers who had previously benefitted from an earlier regime of property rights called the block system and the under-pricing of water; (2) measuring devices established for the calculation of entitlements were destroyed by farmers due to poor system performance; and (3) the top-down character of the water user associations did not allow for participation and equity in decision making, thus creating information asymmetry. Growing a water-intensive crop such as sugarcane in a drought-prone area produced differentiated access to water and situations of socially induced scarcity whereby water demands in the tail-end for staple crops, such as sorghum and household needs, often competed with the politically powerful and rich sugarcane farmers at the head of irrigation systems (see Srivastava, 2015).
>
> In a rapidly urbanizing and industrializing state such as Maharashtra, determining water allocations between different uses and users contributed to prioritizing water for industry over water for agriculture. In reality conflicts abound between water for industry vs water for agriculture; water for agriculture vs drinking water and water for sugarcane vs water for sorghum and livelihoods. This highlights how decision making around water allocation needs to be embedded in a wider democratic process and how water regulation and allocation processes need to bear in mind the diverse patterns of water use and values that people associate with water (see Srivastava, 2015).

Water, FSN and situations of conflict and displacement

Water allocation is as much about power as it is a technical matter, and power asymmetries arise in most situations, including those of conflict. Situations of conflict can threaten access to water for vulnerable communities and affect their FSN. It is not only direct conflicts that impact on poor communities, but also the diversion of state attention from water management functions and the destruction of water infrastructure in both urban and rural areas, often resulting in increased hunger and water-borne diseases. Conflict has also contributed to the salinization of irrigated land where drainage systems were either destroyed or fell into disrepair (ICARDA, 2014). Conflict situations have resulted in long-term changes to water allocations, allowing for corruption and unequal access (Thomas and Ahmad, 2009). Water insecurities arising from conflict situations may be exacerbated in situations of occupation where restricted water withdrawals, combined with discriminatory practices in water sharing, can create new inequalities or exacerbate existing ones. These can affect local communities that require water to produce food for household consumption and for income generation, even in conditions of water abundance (see, for example, Box 4.2 on Palestine). The result can be reduced food production, both commercial and subsistence, and reduced access to water for food preparation and hygiene, as well as reduced access to food itself. Furthermore, lack of water infrastructure during and post-conflict can threaten peace (UNEP, 2013). Indeed, access to water and food is particularly at risk in areas experiencing protracted conflict in different parts of the world.

BOX 4.2 WATER AND CONFLICT: PALESTINIAN WATER INSECURITIES

A water cooperation agreement among Israel, Jordan and the Palestinian Authority initiated a Red Sea–Dead Sea water project, which aimed to desalinate Red Sea water for use in southern Israel and southern Jordan and to replenish the Dead Sea (Kershner, 2013). It also included an agreement that Israel would provide additional freshwater resources to Jordon and that Palestinians could purchase up to 8 billion gallons of fresh water from Israel (ibid.). However, tensions remain regarding water use and availability in the region. Although the Occupied Palestinian Territories are water rich, unequal distribution means that Palestinians face water shortages (Elver, 2014). Palestinians' water consumption is approximately 73 litres per capita per day compared with an average Israeli consumption of approximately 300 litres per capita per day (Gasteyer et al., 2012: 461). Since the occupation of Palestine and the growth of Israeli settlements, strict military orders have been put in place restricting water withdrawals and access to the Jordan River and the Dead Sea by Palestinians. As a result, Palestinians can only access about 10% of the entire annual recharge capacity of the West Bank water system (Gasteyer et al., 2012).

The Israeli–Palestinian Joint Water Committee (JWC) perpetuates this unequal water access. Although the JWC has been lauded as an example of cooperation in the midst of conflict, it also demonstrates how cooperation and conflict can coexist (Zeitoun, 2007). The highly politicized nature of water in the region alongside the committee's licensing procedures and structure as well as power asymmetries on the committee have resulted in highly restricted water access for Palestinians. Moreover, Israel vetoes applications for new wells and generally approves only small local water network projects (Selby, 2013). Additionally, Israel only approves applications for improved Palestinian water supplies if approval is also given for water facilities for its West Bank settlements (ibid.). Such unequal access has led some Palestinians to argue that they are 'systematically denied rights to water, so that there is adequate water to serve Israel's agricultural, industrial and domestic needs' (Gasteyer *et al.*, 2012: 462).

The messy nature of access to water: gender, social difference and policy biases

Water allocation on its own is not sufficient to ensure access to water. Water has symbolic, cultural as well as material dimensions and water allocation regimes are shaped by a mix of politics, power and discourse realms (Cleaver, 2000; Derman and Hellum, 2005; Mehta, 2005; Mosse, 2003; Movik, 2012). Moreover, it is mediated through relevant institutions, gender, social and power relations, property rights, identity and culture. Many smallholder cultivators, mostly women and pastoralists, have use rights in customary arrangements that are largely invisible to policymakers that play a critical role in ensuring their food and livelihood security. Water requires appropriate infrastructure to ensure that it can be accessed and made available where and when it is needed, to meet local water needs. In addition, the water also needs to be of a quality suitable for the purposes required, such as irrigation or for livestock, domestic use or for small-scale 'informal' food production, including that of street food vendors. Poor water quality may make the water unsuitable for use – in other words, amounting to a *de facto* lack of access to water. An example is Flint in the United States where race and class contributed to a major water crisis in one of the richest countries of the world (see Box 4.3; Buncombe, 2018).

BOX 4.3 RACE, CLASS AND WATER CONTAMINATION IN FLINT, USA

The tragic case of Flint is a cautionary tale of how governance failures intersect with systemic race and class biases. Flint has a population of around 100,000 and is 57% African American, with at least 41% living below the federal poverty level. The Safe Water Drinking Act passed in 1974 was one of the earliest initiatives to ensure the purity of the drinking water supply in the United States. Yet, by the summer of 2014, Flint residents were drinking lead-laden water. During the second half of the 20th century, Flint's economy was closely tied to jobs in the auto industry, but the flight of manufacturing, combined with corrupt leadership, saw the city becoming one of the poorest in the country over the last two decades. When Michigan's new Governor assumed office in 2011, he signed into law a series of acts (some of which were repealed) giving him the authority to intervene in local affairs by appointing emergency managers with powers to break or modify agreements with workers and to take financial control of struggling cities such as Flint. Such laws can subvert democracy as they strip local elected officials of power. Emergency Managers are not answerable to criticism; yet, they are granted immense power to rewrite a city's contracts and to liquidate city assets to help pay off debts, regardless of how residents feel about these actions. And residents have limited or no power to question the law itself. In 2014 Flint, under Emergency Management, changed its drinking water supply from the Detroit system to the Flint River, to save money. Inadequate treatment and quality control and a highly polluted source caused significant water quality and health issues for Flint residents and contributed to 12 deaths.

According to the then mayor of the city, the fatal decision to switch the water supply was largely due to the city's race and class composition (Buncombe, 2018). The Michigan Civil Rights Commission also concluded that a combination of historical and structural factors as well as racist and other biases led to actions that would not have been allowed to take place in predominantly white communities (ibid.). Due to their lack of voice and clout, Flint residents were unable to enforce or make use of the provisions under the Safe Drinking Water Act. The Act places the primary '*responsibility for enforcement and supervision*' of public drinking water supply systems and sources of drinking water upon the State as a safeguard. But this assumes a vibrant democracy, with public officials and local authorities being accountable to all, regardless of their class or race. In the case of Flint, the state of Michigan failed in both fulfilling its primary responsibility of providing safe water and the application of safeguards (Buncombe, 2018; Varghese, 2016). The United States is, incidentally, one of the few countries that does not recognize the human right to water.

Even when appropriate infrastructure is in place, societal challenges such as stigma and discrimination that are based on ethnicity, gender or conditions such as homelessness can deter an individual or her community from accessing water or food in a dignified manner. Stigma and discrimination exist in all societies, and particularly in a multicultural context. Alongside assertions of power over marginalized groups, they can be an impediment to the realization of water and food security for all. For example, the caste system in India continues to dominate water management practices on the ground and subverts intended equity in water harvesting schemes and watershed management (see Mehta, 2005).

As discussed earlier in this book, the issue of gender is particularly critical in access to water and land and therefore food security. Norms based on traditional socio-cultural traditions may restrict women's access to land and natural resources, although customary laws often support limited access by women even if they do not permit women's ownership (FAO Gender, Equity and Rural Employment Division, 2012). These norms may persist even after laws change to allow equal access and ownership, and new laws may similarly restrict women's access (ibid.). Allocation and water use authorization systems often allocate water and/or land to the adult male in the household, even where women are the primary farmers (see Box 4.4). For instance, in the Dominican Republic, the deeply rooted patriarchal culture has influenced agrarian reform law that limits female ownership of land by establishing men as the administrators of estates (FAO Gender, Equity and Rural Employment Division, 2012). Given women's role in agricultural production, this gender gap in access to land and water has significant negative impacts on food security, particularly since women are key producers of food consumed in the household (FAO, 2012).

BOX 4.4 GENDER DISCRIMINATION IN AFRICAN WATER MANAGEMENT

Policies on water, land and food security in sub-Saharan Africa still reflect discriminatory colonial gender conceptions. Colonial rulers often promoted the notion of the unitary household, headed by men as the single breadwinner, entitled to exclusive individual control over all productive resources such as land, water and infrastructure as well as their wives' labour. Women were made out to be non-earning housewives (Rogers, 1981). Until today, public support for ploughs, power tillers, fertilizers, irrigation pumps and financing facilities are primarily allocated to men as the supposed representative of all household members (World Bank, FAO and IFAD, 2009). Resource entitlements, irrigated land and membership of Water User Associations are also largely vested in men, and only by exception to female-headed households (van Koppen, 2002). Women are, at best, the target group of domestic water services (van Wijk-Sijbesma, 2002).

This conception continues to clash with rural and peri-urban realities in most of agrarian sub-Saharan Africa. Here, kinship and household relations and land and water tenure are essentially dynamic collective arrangements. Both women and men have resource use rights that ensure the tiller's control over the produce, while protecting communal interests (Dey, 1984; van Koppen, 2009). Under matrilineal land tenure, women's stronger land rights further strengthen women's bargaining powers to maintain control over the benefits of their labour (Peters, 2010). Matrilineal tenure, however, remains largely ignored, even though it is widespread in countries such as Ghana, Malawi, Mozambique, Tanzania and Zambia. Land, water and food security projects tend to follow male-biased targeting strategies eroding women's resource rights and, hence, interest and motivation to provide labour. In contrast, when projects vest resources in the tillers, often women, public resources are well used. This needs to be recognized in water rights allocation systems.

In Burkina Faso, the EU supported project 'Opération Riz' aimed at improving the agronomic practices and water management in rice valleys. With some variation along ethnic lines, rice was mainly cultivated by women, who also had strong land rights and managed water infrastructure. Yet, in the first schemes, the project re-allocated the improved land to 'male household heads who would also take care of the cultural, intra-household affairs'. The women refused to provide labour on men's fields, and the men were more interested in their traditional upland activities. Hence the schemes collapsed. In later schemes, the improved plots were given back to the original women cultivators and other volunteers (mainly women). With control over the output, production increased, and women farmers also ensured regular canal maintenance (van Koppen, 2009).

Finally, agricultural water management projects can and should serve the integration of the extreme, or ultra, poor. Important categories of extreme poor are people with disabilities, and the elderly. The United Nations Convention on the Rights of Persons with Disabilities (UNCRPD) asks for special attention for disabled people, given that poverty and disability are connected. Poor people have a higher exposure to the risks that cause disability, be it from diseases or accidents. By having less access to labour, people with disabilities and the elderly are among the most vulnerable. Moreover, the elderly and people with disability are overrepresented in rural areas. It is thus important for policies to promote the enablement and integration of people with disabilities and the elderly, either through reducing the exposure to disabling (water-borne) diseases and occupational risks, positioning the elderly and people with disabilities in special services through trading and training or functions (supervision) in the operation of agricultural water management programmes, or through using safety net programmes to provide extra assistance in situations of vulnerability (MetaMeta and Enablement, n.d.). Unequal access to and control of water are also complicated by the overlapping nature of water rights to which we now turn.

The fluid nature of water rights

Due to the fluid nature of water, water rights, as distinct from the right to water,[1] are usually competing and overlapping and entail a mixture of formal and informal arrangements (Meinzen-Dick and Bruns, 1999). Attention to water rights emphasizes the importance of institutions in water management (Roth et al., 2005). Common Property Resources (CPR) analyses have made important contributions in focusing attention on the importance of informal institutions in natural resource management (Ostrom, 1990). However, these approaches have looked at purposive institutions, indeed frequently assuming that institutions emerge (are crafted, in Ostrom's terminology) specifically to perform certain water resources management functions. This contrasts with other approaches which look at the complex matrix of institutions in which people live their lives, and in which water management is located. As approaches concerning 'bricolage' highlight (cf. Cleaver, 2012), it is wrong to presuppose a non-interactive divide between formal and informal institutions that fails to capture empirical realities in which interrelationships and overlaps link various institutional domains. In this 'messy middle', institutional arrangements may be highly contested, and beset by ambiguity and openness to divergent interpretations (ibid.; Mehta et al., 2012).

In many parts of the global South, there are plural, overlapping and competing formal and informal legal and customary systems, and most countries in sub-Saharan Africa are characterized by primarily informal water users' practices (Shah and van Koppen, 2005). There are a large number of customary and traditional water users such as pastoralists, those engaged in freshwater fisheries or in traditional agricultural practices and there are informal and formal arrangements of water use, some of them serving multiple functions. Such multiple use of water services (MUS) currently provide the more vulnerable users with low cost services for domestic water, water for agriculture (irrigation, rainfed), homestead, garden, water for cattle, habitats for fish and other aquatic resources and rural enterprise water supplies (van Koppen et al., 2014; see also Box 5.4 in Chapter 5). The study of legal pluralism especially in the water domain (Derman and Hellum, 2007; Spiertz, 2000; von Benda-Beckmann, 2001) highlights how newly crafted water rights and institutions coexist with a range of (often invisible) pre-existing customary arrangements and how diverse institutions and property regimes create different sets of cultural practices and discourses. While different legal and institutional arrangements can create uncertainty and ambiguity, they usually offer routes to livelihood security, enable multiple uses of water, as well as lead to multiple outcomes and compromises in complex settings, as shown for example in studies of legal pluralism (Chimhowu and Woodhouse, 2006; van Koppen et al., 2005; von Benda-Beckmann, 1981). Later in this chapter we highlight how the legally complex situation around water tenure can be challenging in the context of water trading, water markets and new land acquisitions (so called 'grabs') taking place around the world. This is because new commercial users usually coexist with existing non-registered users who are invisible. This legal pluralism can be both enabling and disabling but largely it is difficult for local users to defend their claims.

Land and water use rights

Access to water may be conditioned by access to land whether through legislated systems or customary law. Water use rights often depend on having access to land, making land tenure systems a key determinant of access to water. In India, land and water use rights tend to go hand in hand, resulting in the over-extraction of groundwater and the denial of water use rights to landless populations (Srivastava, 2015). Land tenure systems that discriminate against women, or the poor, also generally discriminate against them in access to water.

Apart from the common pool and customary rights, discussed above, water use rights may be categorized as follows: (1) riparian or prior appropriation, or (2) licensing or permit systems. Riparian rights allow landholders reasonable water use from a water resource on or adjacent to a property, as long as it does not affect the reasonable water use of adjacent riparian landholders. Prior appropriation (first in time, first in right), which first emerged in the western United States in the 1850s, recognizes the water rights of the first person ('senior appropriator') to claim the water, provided it is put to 'beneficial use' (a clause that primarily covered commercial, agricultural, domestic or industrial use).

Under riparian law, water rights are attached to a land right and obtaining a water allocation is conditional on the transfer of land. By contrast, in a prior appropriation system, the water right can either be transferred along with the land or it can be sold or leased separately if the transfer does not impinge upon the rights of other appropriators. The latter thus 'decouples' water from land. This created an enabling environment which led to the development of a water market in the western United States. Riparian law states, on the other hand, have seen specific 'uses', such as extracting and selling or diverting water out of a watershed being allowed as long as it did not affect the balance of other water uses in the watershed (Varghese, 2013). Such diversions can impact both water needs of ecosystems and water for food security and nutrition. This model, based on the settler economy of the western United States, has influenced various water sector reforms around the world. Several countries, including Australia, Chile, China and South Africa, have explored decoupling water use rights from land use rights and enabling tradable water permits to facilitate the reallocation of water in the face of water scarcity, partly in response to the increasing scarcity of water (Saleth and Dinar, 2000). The introduction of formal water use rights can create security for water users, promoting efficiency of use, and opening opportunities for water markets (see Briscoe et al., 1998).

At the same time, the use of tradable permits for water allocation (and for pollution control) has raised concerns. The attachment of significant monetary value to water can undermine equitable distribution (OECD, 2000). A further concern relates to impacts on ecosystems and other parties affected by the transfer of water use entitlements and the possible externalization of costs. For example, the diversion of water towards higher value crops or non-food crops such as cut flowers can have negative impacts on national and local food security and nutrition, particularly for vulnerable communities, as well as on indigenous peoples' way of life (Jackson and Altman, 2009; Varghese, 2013). Evidence from Chile and elsewhere suggests that introducing formal entitlements and permit systems may not always and everywhere be the best legal device to address the challenges of water scarcity (Bauer, 2004; van Koppen, 2007). Challenges encountered in the implementation of tradable permit systems suggest the prior need for clearly structured and recorded water use rights and an effective administration system (Borghesi, 2014). The physical geography of water and lack of conducive infrastructure can also limit the scope for water markets. For example, water can often only be traded downstream, while it may be too costly to move water from one location to another. The Australian model of water markets and water trading is the most developed in terms of separation of the water access rights from land titles (Australian Government, 2014). While it has been effective in driving the economically efficient use of water, it has often failed to address environmental concerns and the perspectives of indigenous groups (Box 4.5).

BOX 4.5 AUSTRALIAN WATER GOVERNANCE REGIME

Australia, the driest continent, has pursued far-reaching water governance reform since the mid-1990s. Climate extremes, such as droughts, floods and fires, competing claims over water and over-allocation in Australia's greatest system of rivers and aquifers, the Murray-Darling Basin, led to an extensive reform of water governance (see Australian Government, 2007).

The Australian model has been extensively studied. On the positive side, Bjornlund and Rossini (2010) report that Australian water markets have allowed irrigators to achieve the highest possible return from their declining seasonal water allocation while reducing the economic hardships associated with the decline. In South Australia, for example, 90% of the additional water purchases were used to expand horticultural production. Fargher (n.d.) reports that the water trading during the recent drought has been indicative of significant economic efficiency gains while providing cash flow to individual farm businesses that sell their water allocations. In the Australian context where allocation is not accompanied by mandatory return flows to the environment, water saving measures have often had negative environmental implications leading to the assertion that 'flawed water trading systems are choking [Australia's] mighty rivers to death' (Young, 2012). The now abolished National Water Commission of Australia recorded concerns that the voices of indigenous peoples have not been adequately heard in these debates (NWC, 2012). There are many catchments where significant efficiencies of scale cannot be achieved. Moreover, the trade-off between water extractions and water essential to the long-term ecological function of river systems, especially in the wake of increasing climate variability, has often been neglected (Grafton et al., 2014).

Several attempts have been made to replicate the Australian experience across the global South (Saleth and Dinar, 2000), with mixed results. As demonstrated in Box 4.1, in Maharashtra, the first state in India to experiment with tradable water entitlements, poor regulatory capacity, political opposition to market-based reforms and the prevalence of small landholdings prevented the uptake of water trading (Srivastava, 2015). Similarly, Movik (2012) in her study on the South African water allocation reform notes the impermeability of the idea of formal water markets. Both cases, influenced by the Australian experience, raise questions regarding wider replicability especially in Africa and Asia where customary systems abound, the financial, institutional, metering and remote sensing capacity required for such reforms is low and the state has poor regulatory capacity (Meinzen-Dick, 2007).

At the same time, informal water markets thrive, in particular those that rely on groundwater extraction. As an example, Bell *et al.* (2015) find for Bangladesh that plots managed by farmers who obtain irrigation water from renting pumps or obtaining water from pump owners fare no worse, and in some cases outperform farmers who own equipment and thus have preferred access to irrigation water. They suggest that informal markets in groundwater irrigation improve access and equity in a context of relatively ample groundwater access. Meinzen-Dick (1996) found, on the other hand, that while informal groundwater markets in Pakistan's Indus Basin Irrigation System increased overall agricultural productivity in the system, there was, however, a gap in productivity with those purchasing groundwater from well and pump owners not achieving the same level of output per unit of input as those selling the extracted water. The politics of water allocation and access have also shaped the outcome of several global water reform processes to which we now turn.

Water reform processes

From New Delhi to Dublin

Water management and governance have evolved considerably from the 'hydraulic imperatives' and supply-driven approaches that dominated in the 1950s–1970s, when the focus was largely on getting the technical solutions right and on building infrastructure (i.e. large dams). The supply-dominated paradigm was dominant until the UN 'Water Decade' (1981–1990) which aimed at achieving universal coverage to drinking water and sanitation by 1990. At the end of the decade the target remained far off. To assess what had happened and to identify future pathways for collective action, the UN held a global consultation in New Delhi in 1990 hosted by the Indian Government (see Nicol *et al.*, 2012).[2]

The New Delhi Statement, with its focus on equity and universality, was, however, rapidly overshadowed by the 'Dublin Statement' of 1992 which was an important turning point in the discourse on water governance. The statement emerged from the International Conference on Water and the Environment

(ICWE) held in Dublin in January 1992. It was organized by water experts and held under the auspices of the World Meteorological Organization. The conference culminated in the formulation of the Dublin Principles which recognized (1) the finite nature of water and its key role in sustaining life, development and the environment; (2) the importance of participatory approaches in water development and management; (3) the central role played by women in the provision, management and safeguarding of water and (4) the economic and competing values of water and the need to recognize water as an economic good (International Conference on Water and the Environment, 1992). It is this fourth principle that has made Dublin a focus of policy differences and global fault lines ever since. Declaring water an 'economic good' in Dublin remains to this day deeply controversial. Some argue that it also provides a solid building block for a global discourse that prioritizes the economic use of water over its other, less tangible, values. The formulation appears to prioritize commercial agriculture, industry, manufacturing, mining, hydropower and other capital intensive activities over smallholder agriculture, community drinking water, traditional fisheries and female headed agriculture (see Franco et al., 2013; HLPE, 2013). While the economic value of water is important, there are many water needs and uses that are challenging to attribute economic values to, including social, cultural and symbolic uses of water.

Integrated Water Resources Management (IWRM)

The elaboration of the 1992 Dublin principles has led to a series of (often donor led) water reform processes around the world. One key concept in such reform processes has been the widespread promotion of the Integrated Water Resource Management (IWRM) approach and governance framework. Its most frequently used definition comes from the Global Water Partnership which calls IWRM 'a process which promotes the coordinated development and management of water, land and related resources, in order to maximize the resultant economic and social welfare in an equitable manner without compromising the sustainability of vital ecosystems' (GWP, 2000).

The IWRM paradigm is the most influential policy model currently being implemented in basins around the world, including in Africa. According to Cherlet (2012), 80% of countries around the world have IWRM principles in their water law or policies and two-thirds have developed IWRM plans. Moreover, IWRM was explicitly added into the Sustainable Development Goals as SDG 6.5 ('By 2030, implement integrated water resources management at all levels, including through transboundary cooperation as appropriate'). While IWRM has created some space for intersectoral collaboration, including with the food and agricultural sectors, there have been significant challenges in implementation especially in the global South, not least due to the political nature of water management and allocation (see Anderson et al., 2008; Bolding et al., 2000; Conca, 2006; Mehta et al., 2016; Molle, 2008). It also presupposes the existence of sufficient water infrastructure, an assumption that is not borne out in many contexts, especially in sub-Saharan Africa (see also van Koppen and Schreiner, 2014). The concept is highly abstract and difficult to implement, not least because the complexity introduced in the IWRM paradigm easily leads to paralysis in water governance, particularly in countries with limited state resources.

Permit licensing systems are an integral part of IWRM. These have been drawn up in many countries to help formalize water use and abstraction. Contemporary statutory water law in many parts of Africa and Latin America has its roots in European civil law, including its administration-based permit systems. In sub-Saharan Africa the introduction of permit systems served, above all, to formally vest ownership of the continents' water resources in the overseas colonial rulers, declaring that only permitted water uses were lawful. At independence, ownership shifted to the new governments but the laws remained largely dormant until permit systems were revived under IWRM. van Koppen (2007) shows how formal administration-based water rights systems in sub-Saharan Africa have tended to dispossess the informal majority by design, as 'permit systems boil down to the formal dispossession of rural informal water users who manage their water under community-based arrangements' (p. 48). Water rights that had historically been arranged locally were now declared subject to formalization under national law. Existing rights were cancelled out with the promise to include them in new laws. In practice, many of these rights were not (and often could not be) included in the registrations leading to a weakening of the position of historical smallholder uses. Complicated and expensive licence registration procedures have ensured that water permits 'favour the administration-proficient' (van Koppen, 2007: 46). However, small-scale water use, mostly for drinking water, but sometimes also including small productive use, was excluded from licensing in many systems, granting it a status of priority use, or setting it aside as a sort of common pool resource (Hodgson, 2004). In practice, this creates pluralistic legal systems in which traditional legal systems are left to govern the thousands of smallholders that are deemed uncontrollable under the registration system (Meinzen-Dick and Nkonya, 2005). In South Africa this is part of the *reserve* or in *general authorizations* (van Koppen *et al.*, 2009), in Mozambique it is called *uso común*, or common use (Veldwisch *et al.*, 2013), elsewhere it is sometimes referred to as 'primary uses' or in Islamic law as 'rights to thirst' (Meinzen-Dick and Nkonya, 2005).

It is questionable whether these *de minimis* rights provide any security in practical terms, as this type of 'entitlement cannot lawfully prevent anyone else from also using the resource even if that use affects his own prior use/entitlement' (Hodgson, 2004: 92). Formal permits with state backing create first-class rights in comparison to any other right (van Koppen, 2007). The exemption from a need for a permit keeps small-scale users from being registered as users, which makes it easier to overlook them in planning and allocation procedures (see Borras et al., 2012; Veldwisch et al., 2013). As an example, in Kenya, nomadic livestock keepers and fisher folk without formal water licences were dispossessed of their traditional rights when large-scale investors started developing the Tana River Delta (Duvail et al., 2012). Williams et al. (2012) demonstrate for three cases in Ghana that smallholders were not even aware that their historic agricultural water rights were not recognized in national legal frameworks and that this favours commercial and large-scale users of land and water. In the context of limited registration of smallholder water use, poor hydrological knowledge, and/or weak enforcement, permits provide an 'easy way in' for newcomers, while giving them the formal backing of the state (van Koppen, 2007).

A recent study of five countries in Africa (van Koppen and Schreiner, 2018), Kenya, Malawi, Uganda, South Africa and Zimbabwe, revealed that implementation of the permit system is very partial in all of the countries, and that small-scale users do not have water use permits, and in most cases are not aware that they are required to have water permits. Their water use has, therefore, been criminalized by the formal water law. And yet, the relevant government departments or authorities do not have the capacity to implement the permit system across a large number of scattered small-scale users. In practice, those who lack formal water entitlements are also generally the food insecure (Molden et al., 2007). Burchi has argued that customary law could coexist alongside statutory water law, but that this would be untenable in practice as 'the two systems are bound to intersect and interact, in space and time' (FAO, 2005: 6). He argues, rather, that pre-existing customary rights should be recognized in the new statutory law. The reality, however, is that the statutory law in many countries fails to recognize these customary rights, leaving small users without legal protection of their water rights in many instances, particularly in sub-Saharan Africa. In other areas and systems, however, customary practice still dominates, without requirement for alignment with statutory law. In spate irrigation systems in Pakistan, for example, flood waters are divided according to customary rules, which have been codified in some areas, but not others. As traditional authority has weakened in power over time, while the weak state failed to step into the gap, and as pressure on limited water resources has increased, there have been increasing cases of conflict over spate water rights (Nawaz and van Steenbergen, n.d.).

In South Africa's National Water Resources Strategy, the ranking of priorities in water allocation gives a high priority to water used for poverty eradication and redress of inequities from the past. However, this has little meaning as long as a permit system exists. This also declares small-scale informal water uses that are vital for food security as unlawful by lack of a permit, while the legal status of micro-uses that are exempted from an obligation to apply for a permit, is weak (van Koppen and Schreiner, 2014). To address this, Merrey (2008) advocates moving from the do-everything approach of IWRM to an expedient water management approach, based on identifying the key water management goals in a particular setting, and developing a management response to achieving those goals. Molle et al. (2007) stress that such an approach must have a strong developmental element to it, particularly in developing countries with high levels of poverty and insufficient water access by the poor. In South Africa, the National Water Resources Strategy II (RSA, 2013) reinterprets IWRM in the context of a developmental state, coining the concept of Developmental Water Management (DWM) which is specifically aimed at achieving the developmental objectives of the state, including poverty eradication. DWM 'takes, as a central premise, the fact that water plays a critical role in equitable social and economic development, and that the developmental state has a critical role in ensuring that this takes place' (RSA, 2013: 14).

The water–energy–food (WEF) nexus

More recently, the concept of IWRM has been extended to look at the notion of the water–energy–food nexus (WEF) (see Allouche *et al.*, 2019; Hoff, 2011; WEF, 2011). Several studies have demonstrated how the world's food, water and energy resources are under stress (Bazilian *et al.*, 2011; Ringler *et al.*, 2013; WEF, 2011) and how demand for these resources will continue to increase in the coming decades, while climate change will impact particularly on issues of water availability and reliability of supply. The nexus approach is based on the recognition of the competing demands for the same resources between the water, energy and food sectors and, much like IWRM, attempts to find an integrated approach to managing all three resources in a manner that reduces negative trade-offs and improves synergies.

The nexus approach imposes further complexities into the already complex arena of water management, and effective implementation guidelines or tools to support implementation in resource-constrained developing countries are largely lacking. In addition, most of the WEF nexus literature fails to adequately address issues of distribution of benefits, power and who takes decisions and for whom (Lele *et al.*, 2013). Allouche *et al.* (2019) highlight that if poverty reduction goals are to be attained, the nexus literature needs to pay specific attention to the issue of whose food, water and energy security is being addressed and how the needs of the marginalized will be prioritized. They also argue that the entire concept of the nexus needs to be reconceptualized, from being a technical solution to natural resource scarcity, which is apolitical in origin and intent, towards a clear and articulated political choice about allocation and trade-offs between resources and the imagining of the future of water–food–energy systems and their interlinkages.

Amongst people living in poverty, at the household and community level, WEF trade-offs are a daily occurrence, not due to a theoretical conceptualization, but due to necessity. At times their innovations in crop production practices are such that they simultaneously conserve water, reduce energy use, and enhance nutrition security through crop diversification, such as in the case of those practising agroecological approaches (Varghese and Hansen-Kuhn, 2013).

Implementation of this approach at the landscape level is more complex and more work is needed to develop and test practical tools for implementation. The discourse on the WEF nexus does not sufficiently address the barriers to an integrated approach and how to address these barriers, and fails to examine under what conditions cross-sector coordination and collaboration do exist (Weitz et al., 2017). Finally, it insufficiently addresses power dynamics that are key in influencing decision making. In sum, while the concept provides an opportunity to improve coherence in the management of these different resources (Weitz et al., 2017), it still remains fundamentally disconnected from the realities of decision making. In addition, while the IWRM and WEF approaches seek to develop an approach that looks beyond water aspects alone – to other linked competitive or synergistic elements in the landscape – the linkage between land and water is insufficiently addressed from a pro-poor perspective in current governance practice. Changes in land ownership and tenure in one location can have impacts on water access rights locally but also downstream or elsewhere in the same aquifer. The implications of the failure to sufficiently address land and water linkages in the interests of the rural poor are particularly relevant in relation to land and water grabbing which is discussed below.

Both the IWRM and WEF approaches tend to focus on the use of raw water, leaving issues of potable water supply to be dealt with under the paradigm of water, sanitation and hygiene (WASH). At the community level, this separation is artificial as water, when available, whether treated or untreated, is used to meet a range of domestic and productive needs. Thus, water provided for domestic purposes may also be used for subsistence gardening and livestock, and is crucial for ensuring food security (see Langford in Woodhouse and Langford, 2009). In addition, research shows that when communities invest in building their own infrastructure, they build multi-purpose infrastructure to serve a range of water uses that contribute to FSN, either in relation to the preparation of food, hygiene practices, the production of food, or in relation to economic activities that allow for the purchasing of food (see van Koppen et al., 2014). We turn to these issues when we look at national policy domains and also in Chapter 5 which focuses on the need to link the domestic and productive uses of water, as well as the human rights to water and food.

From centralization to decentralization

In some regions, IWRM-induced water reform has led to the devolution of water resource institutions to transfer rights and responsibilities to local user groups (Hooja et al., 2002; Meinzen-Dick, 1997) resulting in community-based organizations replacing state agencies in governing their own resources. While decentralized systems have often been highly successful in managing water resources locally, they have not necessarily promoted social and gender equity or participation. They have also often ignored the fact that local communities are made of various interest groups and often ridden with conflicts (Mehta and

Movik, 2014; Mosse, 2005). In the water sector, decentralization in practice means the re-organization of water from administrative units (regions, provinces, districts) to hydrographical boundaries: watersheds, catchments or basins. This provides an opportunity to deal with the dislocated effects of water use (pollution, downstream reduced or peak flows, timing peak uses and releases) but at the same time cuts water management somewhat loose from other processes of governance.

Decentralization policies and approaches often involve the setting up of Water Users Associations (WUAs), Catchment Management Platforms (CMPs) and/or River Basin Organizations (RBOs) which are now important exemplary 'models' in the water sector (Molle, 2006). A large body of literature highlights the mixed experiences with user involvement in water management at all levels of governance (e.g. Boelens, 2008; Wester et al., 2003). It is important to stress that the involvement of local users in water management does not prevent strong actors from capturing unfair shares of water while excluding others from access to the resource. Rather, the setting of user participation often becomes the forum through which the resource capture takes shape, often facilitated by excluding informal, legally not-recognized water users (Warner et al., 2008) as detailed earlier in this chapter. Kemerink et al. (2013) analyse in detail a case in South Africa where, despite the best of intentions, a policy of user participation in water management through the establishment of a WUA was used by the most powerful actors in the catchment to maintain the *status quo* of a highly unequal water distribution pattern established in the Apartheid era. In sum, powerful actors and interests tend to dominate decentralized processes and institutions, unless care is taken to ensure that the interests of the marginalized and powerless are prioritized. The next section further develops some key fault lines and controversies in the water sector that similarly promote the interests of more powerful actors. These largely arise due to dominant economic forms of valuation which downplay water's cultural, ecological and social aspects.

Contestations around water

The question of storage and hydropower

If there is one issue that has deeply divided the water sector, it is the issue of large dams and the role they play in enhancing water and food security. Until a few decades ago, large dams[3] were universally considered as a panacea for water and food security. The proponents of large dams focus on the benefits of hydropower and irrigation and downplay their social and environmental costs. These views have been contested by academics, scientists and members of voluntary agencies who have highlighted the problems of forced displacement and environmental damage due to large dams and have contested their water and food security benefits. At the turn of the century, in response to this controversy and to social movements fighting for the rights of displaced groups, a unique multi-stakeholder process, the

World Commission on Dams was constituted by the World Bank, social movements representing displaced people and several international NGOs to investigate the myriad aspects of dams concerning economic growth, equity, food security, environmental conservation and participation. It found that 40–80 million people had been displaced by dam projects, often forcibly and without adequate compensation. It concluded that while dams have made a considerable contribution to human development, in too many cases unacceptable costs were borne in social and environmental terms. The Commission also argued that water and energy needs could often be met through alternative solutions that would fare better than large dams on equity and environmental grounds (WCD, 2000). Unfortunately, these conclusions have not been picked up or implemented in most countries. This is because powerful players such as the World Bank rejected its conclusions, alongside key dam-building nations such as China, India and Turkey, as well as the International Commission on Large Dams and the International Commission on Irrigation and Drainage.

In the years following the publication of the WCD report, dams have made a comeback (see Molle *et al.*, 2009). The World Bank (re)argued that investment in dams is necessary for economic growth (Calderon and Servén, 2004). In the wake of climate change, hydropower is also seen to be a clean and renewable source of energy (World Bank, 2009). In sub-Saharan Africa, dam construction is favoured to increase the low per capita storage capacity amid very rapid population growth and to address the large seasonal and inter-annual rainfall variability, including multi-year droughts. But controversies remain around the world. As an example, many studies on the proliferation of dams on the Mekong River highlight their adverse impact on artisanal fishing communities and associated livelihoods and nutrition security in that region. If all of the 88 dams planned for the Mekong river basin were to be constructed, fish stocks are estimated to drop by 40% by 2030 (China Dialogue, 2012). This loss of fish stocks would necessitate a switch to (industrial) livestock rearing, counteracting claims that these hydropower projects would reduce carbon emissions (Eyler, 2013). A study by Ansar *et al.* (2014) draws upon cost statistics for 245 large dams built between 1934 and 2007. Without taking into account social and environmental impacts, the study finds that 'the actual construction costs of large dams are too high to yield a positive return' (Ansar *et al.*, 2014: 44). This study also found that dam construction costs were on average more than 90% higher than initial budgets, while 8 out of 10 dams suffered a schedule over-run, thus seriously questioning their economic/financial viability (ibid.). The controversial Sardar Sarovar (Narmada) project in Gujarat India was justified in the name of the drought prone areas of Kutch and Saurashtra (Mehta, 2005). However, dam waters have been allocated to more powerful industrial and urban areas, instead of the intended use – of addressing food security issues amongst marginal farmers in these drought-prone areas (Counterview, 2014). The extensive planned canal network has not been completed and many farmers that were supposed to benefit from the project in the command area are still waiting for the water. Much of the water has been diverted to benefit industries, water parks as well as wealthy urban centres (Desai and Sangomla, 2017). Thousands are still to receive compensation and fair resettlement even after nearly 40 years (Mohanty, 2017).

What is often missing from the dam debates is the need to focus on a '*continuum*', of water storage options that include natural wetlands; enhanced soil moisture; groundwater aquifers; ponds and tanks; and large or small dams/reservoirs (see McCartney and Smakhtin, 2010; see also Chapter 2). Each has a role to play in contributing to food security and water security. However, for prestige and power reasons, large options such as the Sardar Sarovar Dam, the Grand Ethiopian Renaissance Dam or the Three Gorges Dam, are generally prioritized in planning and assessment purposes instead of alternative storage options that have fewer social and environmental costs.

The role of the private sector and growing corporate involvement in water management

Over recent decades there has been significant and heated discussion on the role of the private sector, particularly in relation to the provision of potable water supply. In the early 1990s the solution to the failure in the universal delivery of water services by the public sector was seen to be an increased role for the private sector (World Bank, 1994). Increased involvement of the private sector across a spectrum from contractual arrangements to full privatisation was expected to increase competition and accountability, and remove political interference, resulting in the more efficient delivery of services (ibid.). A number of Europe-based transnational water corporations played a significant role in the attempted privatisation of water services provision and management, with variable results. The promotion of private sector involvement often accompanied structural adjustment programmes imposed on debt-ridden countries by the Bretton Woods institutions (Varghese, 2013). Privatisation proponents have emphasized poor people's willingness to pay for water (Altaf *et al.*, 1992) and, relatively speaking, poor people pay far more than the rich for water. The UNDP's Human Development Report in 2006 notes that

> the poorest 20% of households in Argentina, El Salvador, Jamaica and Nicaragua allocate more than 10% of their spending to water. In Uganda water payments represent as much as 22% of the average income of urban households in the poorest 20% of the income distribution.
>
> *(UNDP, 2006: 51)*

Power relations within the household mean that women cannot always make their own decisions about whether to buy water, which may force them into a daily trudge (taking precious time) for cheaper or free, untreated water, which is likely to result in health problems or increased poverty and destitution (Mehta, 2013).

With failures in regulation, in some privatization cases prices rose beyond contractually agreed levels, resulting in cut-offs for those unable to pay. Popular resistance to water privatization has been widespread. Several transnational water corporation contracts have failed, leading to a retreat of the private sector in some areas with a re-municipalisation of water services (Lobina et al., 2014; Pigeon et al., 2012), primarily in the global North, but also in the global South (Lobina et al., 2014), or to public–public partnerships.

There are a number of models for private sector involvement in water, including management contracts for service delivery, infrastructure design and construction, and build, operate and transfer arrangements. In addition to these business opportunities for the private sector in the delivery of water, increasingly, business risks as a result of uncertain or limited water access come to the forefront in private-sector operations. In response to this, in 2007, the UN Secretary General launched the CEO Water Mandate as a private–public initiative focused on the role of business and water (UN, 2010). As of 2017, the Mandate included 12,000 corporate participants and stakeholders from more than 140 countries. The Water Resources Group, launched at the World Economic Forum by a group of multinational companies concerned about water availability, seeks to promote water governance with a focus on economic efficiency in water use in target countries (Varghese, 2012). As the case of bottled water and beverages (see below) highlights, this is largely to secure their own water interests and needs.

An extremely contested issue pertaining to the private sector in water is in the bottling and selling of water (as water or in soft drinks). The production and bottling of beverage products has been linked to reduced water quantity and quality, through depleting groundwater sources or through polluting the environment with toxic effluents such as heavy metals (IATP, 2010; Upadhyaya, 2013). In India, after significant protest which spread internationally, Coca Cola began requiring that its bottling plants conduct assessments of local water source vulnerability and develop sustainability plans as part of a water resources stewardship programme (Hwang and Stewart, 2008). Clearly, large corporations such as Coca Cola are playing a growing role in water management issues globally (see Box 4.6).

While there is a role for the private sector, whether in the design and construction of infrastructure, as consultants, or even in the contracted management of water supply, in many countries of the global South there is insufficient regulatory capacity to ensure that private sector management and provision of water is pro-poor, and true to the concept of water as a human right and its contribution to the achievement of the human right to food (see Chapter 5). Effective regulation is required to control the drive of the private sector to make profit out of what is a human right and a social good, to counteract the monopolistic nature of the water provision sector, and to ensure that the private sector provides adequate services in poor urban and rural areas (see Bayliss, 2014; Finger and Allouche, 2002). These debates echo the controversies around the 1992

Dublin declaration which tended to highlight water as an economic good over and above its cultural and symbolic characteristics. In many countries of the global South, there is a lack of effective legal and institutional frameworks to protect the rights and interests of poor and marginalized communities, many of whom in rural areas access water under un-protected customary practices. In such cases, the introduction of the private sector in the management of water may reduce local control over water sources and undermine the access of local communities to the human right to water (Cullet, 2014) and to sufficient water to meet their own food needs.

BOX 4.6 CONTRADICTORY POSITIONS AND ACTIONS TAKEN BY COCA-COLA GLOBALLY

Coca-Cola is sub-Saharan Africa's largest non-oil private sector employer (Cotton and Ramachandran, 2006) and Coca-Cola is sold widely across the continent in urban and rural areas. Globally, it has initiated a water stewardship programme and each bottling plant has to conduct a local source vulnerability assessment and the development of a locally relevant water resources sustainability plan addressing challenges at the watershed level, from hydrological challenges to local government capacity (Hwang and Stewart, 2008). These programmes often involve partnerships with local government, communities and NGOs and Coca-Cola has a major partnership with the World Wide Fund for Nature. The company states it is water neutral.

This approach was likely driven by the challenges that it faced in India from 2000 onwards. Their bottling plant in Plachimada, Kerala, India, was forced to close in 2004 due to ongoing protests from communities concerned about the decline of groundwater levels in some areas and pollution of their drinking water sources (due to groundwater pollution) in areas adjacent to the factory (IATP, 2010). A BBC report stated that dangerous levels of known carcinogen Cadmium and other toxic metals in the waste products had been distributed as fertilizer to local communities by the factory.[4] Coca-Cola pointed to an independent report undertaken in 2008 by The Energy and Resources Institute (TERI) which assessed its practices in six plants out of 49 that were operating in India at the time. While this report found the six plants to be complying with government regulations, it asserted that Coca-Cola must take into account the community's water needs when deciding its location, since excessive bacteria and other pollutants were found at some plants. The TERI report also said that Coca-Cola India had exploited the groundwater resources by giving precedence to its company's business over the rights of farmers. The legal battle by Coca-Cola to get its plant to re-open was finally resolved in 2017, when HCCB, the Indian bottling entity of the Coca-Cola Company stated in the

Supreme Court that it did not intend to restart its operations in Plachimada (Konikkara, 2019).

Mexico is currently the number one Coca-Cola consuming nation in the world. The beverage has attained religious significance in places like San Juan Chamula in the state of Chiapas, replacing traditional beverages used in religious ceremonies and as dowry payment for marriage (Rovira, 2000). A key reason for its large consumption may be the lack of potable water. Since it is cheaper than milk (and water), it has been reported that in some situations indigenous Chamula women even nurse their babies with Coca-Cola (Ewing, 2004). Adults and children can be physiologically and psychologically dependent on caffeinated drinks, and withdrawal can lead to headaches and lethargy (ibid.), not to speak of problems of poor nutrition and obesity.

Vicente Fox, Mexico's former president, was the President of the Coca-Cola Corporation of Mexico before coming to power and during his mandate the company started to bottle water from water-rich Chiapas. The drink is often handed out for free during local elections. Since 2000, the company has been allowed to extract water from 19 aquifers and 15 rivers. In 2003 the company paid $20,000 to compensate for over-extracting water while the profits of one bottling plant alone reached $40,000.

Sources: Bellon, 2006; Bokaie, 2007; Faheem, 2009; Rovira, 2000; Shiva, 2006; Wooters, 2008, BBC News, 2003, Konikkara, 2019.

In the agricultural sector, water pricing policies can improve the efficiency and sustainability of water use when combined with appropriate supporting policies (Rosegrant *et al.*, 2002). But there are significant barriers to water pricing, especially in countries of the global South, mainly due to administrative requirements and the challenges of developing a billing system that effectively balances issues such as affordability, cost recovery, and targeted subsidies. Poorly constructed pricing regimes can result in subsidies not being available to those who need them most. Adding to the difficulty of pricing reform, often long-standing practices and cultural and religious beliefs have treated water as a valuable, but free, good (see Chapter 3).

Appropriate pricing systems can also provide incentives for improved water use efficiency. Implementing polluter-pays regulations can generate revenues to better manage water quality. But pricing remains controversial in terms of affordability criteria, and especially regarding its impacts on the poor. In practice, it is not always effective. In public surface systems, such as the Indus Basin Irrigation System, for example, farmers have little (if any) control over when and how much water arrives at their field intake (Akram, 2013), and thus little motivation to pay for a service that is not provided on-demand. In many cases, prices high enough to induce significant changes in water allocation (or to recover capital costs) can severely reduce farm income, and price irrigators out of business (de Fraiture and Perry, 2007). It is important to note that domestic and industrial sources and irrigation usually get bulk water deliveries, whereas mining and fracking generally directly take water out of streams or groundwater. The latter is rarely metered, measured or priced, especially when there is no bulk supplier. How to combine the use of taxes, tariffs and transfers to cover the costs of water provision in a manner that supports the meeting of food security and nutrition is a key challenge. The HLPE report on investing in smallholders (HLPE, 2013) provides guidance to governments in developing the appropriate combination of taxes, tariffs and transfers for ensuring access to water for smallholder production systems.

Land and water grabbing

In the last decade, attention was raised on the rapid growth of large-scale land deals around the world (see Borras and Franco, 2010; Cotula *et al.*, 2009; Deininger, 2011; De Schutter, 2011; von Braun and Meinzen-Dick, 2009; World Bank, 2010). The rush to acquire land as sources of alternative energy, crops and environmental services has led to the phenomenon popularly known as 'land grabbing' which has made global headlines and contributed to skyrocketing global food prices in 2008. It is important to note that not all see these land deals as 'grabs' but instead as business transactions or financial investments, involving *bona fide* negotiations and agreements between private corporate actors and governments and/or local communities (or their representatives). The World Bank and others argue that large-scale investment is often desperately needed in rural areas to deliver social and environmental benefits and to help reduce rural poverty (cf. Deininger, 2011; World Bank, 2010).

Various studies have made the linkage between land acquisitions for agriculture (for food, feed, fuel and raw material for industrial use) and associated water access or acquisitions (ibid.; Franco *et al.*, 2013; Mehta *et al.*, 2012; Woodhouse, 2012). This is because in many parts of sub-Saharan Africa rainfall is too erratic for large investment into agricultural production without securing access to reliable water. This is one of the reasons why land deals for agriculture almost per definition include water dimensions and acquisitions, even when not explicitly specified in the land deals (HLPE, 2011; Skinner and Cortula, 2011). Globally, most agricultural production is based purely on rainwater that has locally infiltrated the soil (so called 'green water'), but diverted surface water and pumped-up groundwater (the so-called 'blue water') is a far more reliable source for commercial agricultural production (Hoekstra *et al.*, 2012); hence, the proliferation of political narratives such as 'unexploited and underutilized' land and water resources, and how they 'need' new and large-scale investment to 'unlock' their potential and to awaken Africa's 'sleeping giant' and promote a blue revolution in Africa (see Mehta *et al.*, 2012). Even when investment plans do not specify requirements for water beyond rain, experience shows that additional water will have to be mobilized for the crops to do well and this may typically be in the most water-scarce period and in competition with existing and/or potential future uses.

The rise in land and water grabs in the global South has also raised issues of the protection of the water rights of the rural poor. Land and water grabs can be seen as a new colonialism, dispossessing small farmers and indigenous people of land and water in the interest of foreign and national investors, driven by a perceived scarcity of food and biofuels, and enabled by global financial instruments and commodity speculation (Gasteyer et al., 2012). According to De Schutter (2011), there are questions about the capacity of the governments in countries targeted for land grabs to ensure that they contribute to rural development and poverty alleviation. Authors working on the issue have demonstrated how water grabbing has led to a significant re-appropriation of water resources and water tenure relations leading to violations of human rights with implications for local water and food security (see Mehta et al., 2012). In Ghana, Williams et al. (2012) observe how companies initially leased large-scale lands to grow Jatropha, which is less water demanding, but then diversified into other crops that require full or supplemental irrigation for optimal yields. Houdret (2012) for Morocco describes how deep drilling by agricultural investors may intensify water conflicts and increase the marginalisation of small farmers as shallower wells used by local communities may dry up. Furthermore, farmers were not compensated adequately for the land acquired for the new water pipeline. Bues and Theesfeld (2012) describe how water rights have changed both directly and indirectly on foreign horticulture farms in Ethiopia. Direct changes include new associations reshaping formal agreements and indirect changes to water access and withdrawal rights which are directly tied to land rights. The re-appropriation of resources described is only possible due to sharp power inequalities between resource-poor smallholders and government-based investors and companies.

Of course, water control is as old as the hills and what we now call water grabs are often a mere continuation of a long history of control of water and land, having implications for food and water insecurities. In Colombia, already marginalized Afro-descendant communities lost their access to the Cauca river (a powerful symbol of life) which provided transportation, riverine gold mining, fishing, and recreation. This also radically affected their traditional culture, which depends on the river (Vélez Torres, 2012). Another historical case of water grabbing, that of Palestine, also highlights significant injustices in terms of water rights. Since the occupation of Palestine and the growth of Israeli settlements, strict military orders restrict water withdrawals and access to the Jordan river and the Dead Sea by Palestinians with Palestinians having access to only about 10% of the entire annual recharge capacity of the West Bank water system (Gasteyer et al., 2012). While land and water are interconnected, a focus on the grabbing of water resources helps to bring out an additional, distinct set of issues that are linked to the materiality of water. As already discussed in this book, water availability fluctuates across time and space, flows within watershed boundaries and often has pronounced dislocated (downstream) effects, in terms of quantities and qualities. It is very difficult to pinpoint (the effects of) reallocations, amongst others, due to surface water/groundwater interactions and inter-annual variability, which in some settings has important 'spillover' implications for water and food security as well as policy and political action (see Franco *et al.*, 2013). This calls for more integration across land and water governance, and also across the rights to water and food, the focus of the next chapter. Integration is also required across policies and programmes at the national level, to which we now turn.

National policies and processes that affect water for food security

At the national level, critical choices are often made concerning industrial, agricultural and environmental issues which all affect water for FSN. In this section, we highlight some of the competing trade-offs and also how these are often out of sync with the local complexities discussed earlier in this chapter. The most critical policy interface for water and FSN relates to the issue of water allocation between and within economic sectors and how this relates to food policy. This is particularly true where there are constraints on water availability, and choices must be made whether to allocate water to agriculture, or to other water use sectors such as the industrial, power generation or municipal sectors. In Tanzania, for example, there are policy tensions arising from competing uses for water. Food security as a national priority has led to a national irrigation plan and the recent National Irrigation Act, but the energy policy emphasizes hydropower development, thus setting up competing water demands (Lein and Tasgeth, 2009). While the 2002 National Water Policy notes the need for consideration of 'water for food security, energy production and other economic activities' (Ministry of Water and Livestock Development, 2002: 14), integration of decision making in this regard has been weak. Similarly, there are tensions arising from growing interest in biofuel production and its demands on water (Sosovele, 2010). In Ecuador, on the other hand, constitutional reform in 2008 clearly outlined the order of priorities for water allocation: '(1) water for domestic use (2) irrigation for food sovereignty (3) ecological flows and, lastly (4) productive activities' (Harris and Roa-García, 2013: 24). Fully implementing these reforms remains a challenge, however (ibid.).

Where water is allocated to agriculture, the choice must be made whether it is allocated to large irrigation schemes, or to small holders. For example, if the national policy is to grow sufficient food for at least a large portion, if not all, of the national food security requirements, then the allocation of water must take this into account, particularly where irrigation plays an important role in ensuring food security. But sometimes both large and small farmers lose out to industry when it comes to water allocation at state and national levels (see HLPE, 2015). In Tanzania, the *Kilimo Kwanza* policy of 2008, also known as the 'Agriculture First' vision, calls for a greater role for the private sector and commercial agricultural development. Even though the government owns all land and water, water extraction is fee-based and requires a permit (Lein and Tasgeth, 2009). The 2009 Water Management Act regulates use for 'sustainable management and development of water resources' (Tanzania Parliament, 2012). Although customary rights are recognized (but require conversion to permits), the tension of recognizing them alongside formal rights has meant poor treatment of customary users of land and water (Vorley et al., 2012). Legislation favours 'the estate sector, formal irrigation and hydropower over farmer-managed irrigation' (Lein and Tasgeth, 2009: 210) despite the fact that smallholders produce most of the food in the country (Vorley et al., 2012), and farmer and community water management play key roles in local farming systems (Lein and Tasgeth, 2009). Despite smallholders' livelihoods being protected on paper by two Land Acts, loopholes in the law have led to vast tracts of 'Village Land' being transferred to 'General Land' for investors, and there have been cases of water permits granted to companies to grow sugarcane for ethanol production without sufficient water being available for such operations. This water grabbing has caused conflicts between farmers and pastoralists and displacements from local land and water resources as well as livelihoods (van Eeden et al., 2016).

In Bangladesh, poor national water management policies have received some criticism due to current problems with arsenic-contaminated groundwater, which are partially caused by overexploitation of groundwater resources (Alauddin and Quiggin, 2008; UN, 2003). This overexploitation points to a trade-off between water security and food security at the national policy level. Historically, water management in Bangladesh focused on agriculture and flood control in order to achieve food security and support rural agrarian livelihoods (Ahmad, 2003; Das Gupta et al., 2005; Pal et al., 2011). However, while Bangladesh's successful use of groundwater resources through shallow and deep tube wells for irrigation has allowed it to achieve cereal-based food security (Pal et al., 2011), since groundwater supplies 95% of domestic and industrial use and 70% of irrigation water (Das Gupta et al., 2011), policymakers are now concerned that overreliance on groundwater for agriculture 'is pre-empting the possibility of environmental replenishment and balance' (Government of the People's Republic of Bangladesh, 2008: 68), illustrating one of many relationships between national policies that must be addressed with regard to water security and FSN.

While the water implications of such decisions are specifically considered in some countries, in others there is a lack of integration in decision making, with decisions on irrigation, industrial or power generation development being taken in different departments with little consideration for the cumulative impacts on water demand or water quality. It should be remembered that water quality impacts derive not only from waste discharge by a particular user, but also as a result of reduced river flows and hence reduced dilution of existing waste discharge (see also HLPE, 2015). In Jordan, for example, water policy has focused on managing water for efficient use (Wardam, 2004), focusing on mega-projects such as desalination, micromanaging supplies, and exploiting available resources, particularly through wastewater reclamation for agriculture (Alqadi and Kumar, 2014). Use of wastewater for agriculture has been increasing, which has significantly reduced agriculture's use of freshwater (Alfarra et al., 2011). However, even with strict controls, concerns regarding food security remain. In particular, since Jordan imports 90% of its food, the population is vulnerable to global price shifts (Alqadi and Kumar, 2014). Additionally, the increasing population and large number of refugees resulting from regional tensions mean that Jordan continues to face a water crisis that requires further work to maintain water and food security (ibid.).

The case of China highlights how success in achieving irrigation and food security water meets with challenges and competing demands. China's food security policy is that 95% of food should be produced internally. China feeds 20% of the world's population on 10% of the world's farmland and using 6% of the world's freshwater (Doczi et al., 2014). China's economic growth and poverty reduction in the 1990s were driven in part by expanding agricultural production, which increased by over 130% (measured as value added per worker). The total irrigated area also increased, although agricultural water-use intensity has declined. The food security policy and a focus on developing the rural areas have led to high levels of public investment in agriculture and water sectors. Despite these successes there are several challenges. These include clashes between economic and environmental targets, with economic targets tending to take priority. Widespread social inequalities make balancing water efficiency and equity difficult. Increasing competition for water is being driven by 49 coal-fired power plants that are being built in some water-stressed areas and increasing consumption of meat (ibid.).

In sum, at the national level there are many trade-offs and competing policies concerning water, agriculture and food security, as well as trade. Integration remains a key challenge and more often than most, policies and planning remain disconnected from the needs and interests of poor and marginalized people. Finally, while many national policies around food, water and the environment are informed by international frameworks that implicitly or explicitly recognize gender concerns, formal policies and programmes around water, land and agriculture, as we have outlined in this chapter, often tend to be gender blind. Women's participation has too often translated into tokenism or co-optation. There is also a need to challenge and re-work the discourses, cultures, practices, biases and gender stereotypes that beset policy institutions and organizations across scales (e.g. the notion that women cannot own land and are not productive users of water).

Implications for food governance and conclusions

As discussed in this chapter, water tenure and access to water are informed by a mixture of formal legislation, continuing customary practices, the fluid nature of water rights, self-supply and state-driven processes, and a range of players either directly or indirectly influencing decisions on water use. In addition, the governance of water is complicated by the need to manage issues of availability and reliability, issues of water quality – both for raw water and treated water –

and issues of ecosystem protection. Water for food security is hence embedded in this complex web of challenges and institutional arrangements. It is thus important that future water reform and allocation must recognize the range of customary rights and rights holders that are often ignored when new infrastructures and water allocation mechanisms are developed. Similarly, we have demonstrated the growing role of corporate actors in water supply and management and their contradictory outcomes on the ground, in terms of local users' water and food security.

At the local level, land, food and water are tightly linked and of particular relevance to local people's livelihoods and survival strategies. But local water and land governance regimes have often developed separately from formal, national systems, resulting in ambiguities and possible exclusions for vulnerable communities. Access to land and water, and the benefits derived from them (e.g. goods, services or access to nutritious food) is determined by a range of socio-economic considerations as well as racial/caste/ethnic and gender considerations. As a result, water governance at local, national and international levels must address the specific needs of marginalized communities, how power relations play out in access to water, and therefore how water and power affect the FSN of these communities. Achieving global FSN is, after all, partly dependent on the effective governance of water, across a range of scales from local to global, in both public and private arenas.

Food security governance is equally complex. Apart from the four dimensions of food security – availability, access, utilization and stability – that were presented in Chapter 2, it is also important to look at issues concerning adequacy – nutritious, safe food that supports health, and is produced in an environmentally sustainable manner; acceptability – culturally acceptable food that is produced and obtained in ways that protect people's dignity, self-respect and human rights; and agency – policies and processes that enable the achievement of food security. The term 'agency' refers to the need for stakeholders to 'own' and deliver food security (Rocha, 2008). According to Lang and Barling (2012), the traditional productionist paradigm for FSN was based primarily around the issues of food prices, and reducing the price of food was the main focus. And yet, the issue of access to food is fundamentally an issue of power, and a social, not a production challenge. According to McKeon (2014), there are currently more people in the world suffering from obesity and diabetes than hunger – an issue that highlights issues of unequal distribution and access to food as well as the nutritional value of many contemporary diets. Where power issues are addressed at the policy level, it generally relates to the issue of trade relations between the global North and global South (Lang and Barling, 2012). And yet, as the literature recognizes, the food insecure lack power – evidenced both in lack of purchasing power and lack of access to land and water. This begs the question as to whether the need is to produce more food or to improve the distribution of existing food resources, and balance the current over-consumption in some areas and the under-consumption in others – an issue that impacts directly on the issue of distribution in access to water use. Addressing issues of equity in access to land and water, and therefore issues of power, cannot be avoided in addressing the governance arrangements for water and FSN, including the roles and responsibilities of the public sector, and the private sector, both large and small.

As expressed, inter alia, by the global food sovereignty movement (see Chapter 5), a limited number of large corporations control much of the production, processing, distribution, marketing and retailing of food. In essence, they also control large volumes of water in this process. While these corporations are responsible for producing large amounts of food, this food is not always available to the rural and urban poor, either due to failures in distribution systems, or cost, nor is this food necessarily healthy. Such corporations are in direct competition with small land owners and water users for limited natural resources, and, due to their access to decision makers, are able to protect their interests, potentially contributing to food and water insecurity for the rural poor in these areas. McKeon (2014) argues that regulatory responsibility for food and nutrition security is increasingly being left to the same private sector that profits out of food production and distribution, with the market being assumed to be a neutral arbiter, despite considerable evidence to the contrary.

To break the concentration of global food systems in the hands of a small number of transnational corporations, the international food sovereignty movement has developed six defining principles which encompass focusing on food for people not food as a commodity, valuing food providers whether smallholder farmers or agricultural workers, localizing food systems and providing for local needs before exporting food, localizing the control of land, grazing, water, seeds, livestock and fish populations, building knowledge and skills through appropriate research systems and avoiding energy-intensive industrial methods that damage the environment" (Global Justice Now, 2019). These principles have implications for water governance, including ensuring that local food providers have access to water for food production, ensuring that water use for food production is environmentally sustainable, preventing the commodification of water and ensuring that water is used first to meet the food needs of communities before it is used for generating profit. These principles link to the social justice and human rights aspects of water and food which is the focus of Chapter 5 to which we now turn.

Notes

1 See Chapter 5 for a detailed discussion on the Right to Water, which is protected under international human rights law, that several countries have now incorporated into a national legal framework.
2 Under the slogan, 'Some for all rather than all for some', the New Delhi Statement stressed (1) Protection of the environment and safeguarding of health through the integrated management of water resources and liquid and solid wastes (2) Institutional reforms promoting an integrated approach (3) Community management of services, backed by measures to strengthen local institutions and (4) Sound financial practices, achieved through better management of existing assets, and widespread use of appropriate technologies (see Nicol et al., 2012).

3 According to the World Commission on Dams, there are over 800,000 dams in the world of which 45,000 are large. A large dam has a wall height of more than 15 metres (WCD, 2000).
4 http://news.bbc.co.uk/2/hi/south_asia/3096893.stm (accessed May 2019).

References

Ahmad, Q.K. 2003. Towards poverty alleviation: The water sector perspectives. *International Journal of Water Resources Development*, 19(2): 263–277.

Akram, A.A. 2013. Is a surface-water market physically feasible in Pakistan's Indus basin irrigation system? *Water International*, 38(5): 552–570.

Alauddin, M. and Quiggin, J. 2008. Agricultural intensification, irrigation and the environment in South Asia: Issues and policy options. *Ecological Economics*, 65(2008): 111–124.

Alfarra, A., Kemp-Benedict, E., Hötzl, H., Sader, N. and Sonneveld, B. 2011. A framework for wastewater reuse in Jordan: Utilizing a modified wastewater reuse index. *Water Resource Management*, 25(4): 1153–1167.

Allouche, J., Middleton, C. and Gyawali, D. 2019. *The Water–Food–Energy Nexus: Power, Politics and Justice*. London: Routledge.

Alqadi, K. and Kumar, L. 2014. Water policy in Jordan. *International Journal of Water Resources Development*, 30(2): 322–334.

Altaf, A., Jamal, H. and Whittington, D. 1992. *Willingness to Pay for Water in Rural Punjab, Pakistan*. Washington, DC: UNDP-World Bank Water and Sanitation Program.

Anderson, A., Karar, E. and Farolfi, S. 2008. Synthesis: IWRM lessons for implementation. *Water SA*, 34(6): 665–669.

Ansar, A., Flyvbjerg, B., Budzier, A. and Lunn, D. 2014. Should we build more dams? The actual costs of hydropower megaproject development. *Energy Policy*, 69: 43–56.

Australian Government. 2007. *Water Act 2007*. Canberra: Department of Environment.

Australian Government. 2014. *About the Water Market*. Canberra: Australian Government National Water Market.

Bauer, C.J. 2004. *Siren Song: Chilean Water Law as a Model for International Reform*. Washington, DC: Resources for the Future.

Bayliss, K. 2014. The financialization of water. *Review of Radical Political Economics*, 46(3): 292–307.

Bazilian, M., Rogner, H., Howells, M., Hermann, S., Arent, D., Gielen, D., Steduto, P., Meuller, A., Komor, P., Tol, R.S.J. and Yumkella, K.K. 2011. Considering the energy, water and food nexus: Towards an integrated modelling approach. *Energy Policy*, 39(12): 7896–7906.

BBC News. 2003. Coca-Cola's 'toxic' India fertiliser. Available at: http://news.bbc.co.uk/go/pr/fr/-/2/hi/south_asia/3096893.stm.

Bell, A.R., Bryan, E., Ringler, C. and Ahmad, A. 2015. Rice productivity in Bangladesh: What are the benefits of irrigation? *Land Use Policy*, 48(November): 1–12.

Bellon, M.R. 2006. Crop research to benefit poor farmers in marginal areas of the developing world: A review of technical challenges and tools. *CAB Reviews: Perspectives in Agriculture, Veterinary Science, Nutrition and Natural Resources*, 1. doi:10.1079/PAVSNNR20061070

Bjornlund, H. and Rossini, P. 2010. *Climate Change, Water Scarcity and Water Markets – Implications for Farmers' Wealth and Farm Succession*, 16th Pacific Rim Real Estate Society Conference, Wellington, New Zealand.

Boelens, R. 2008. Water rights arenas in the Andes: Upscaling networks to strengthen local water control. *Water Alternatives*, 1(1): 48–65.

Bokaie, J. 2007. News analysis: Coke must prove it really cares. Available at: www.questia.com/magazine/1G1-164868273/news-analysis-coke-must-prove-it-really-cares. Accessed May 2019.

Bolding, A., Mollinga, P.P. and Zwarteveen, M. 2000. *Interdisciplinarity in Research on Integrated Water Resource Management: Pitfalls and Challenges*, paper presented at the UNESCO-Wotro international working conference on 'Water for Society', Delft, the Netherlands, 8–10 November.

Borghesi, S. 2014. Water tradable permits: A review of theoretical and case studies. *Journal of Environmental Planning and Management*, 57(9): 1305–1332.

Borras Jr., S. and Franco, J. 2010. From threat to opportunity? Problems with the idea of a 'code of conduct' for land-grabbing. *Yale Human Rights and Development Law Journal*, 13(2): 507–523.

Borras Jr., S., Franco, J., Gomez, S., Kay, C. and Spoor, M. 2012. Land grabbing in Latin America and the Caribbean. *Journal of Peasant Studies*, 39(3–4): 845–872.

Briscoe, J., Anguita Salas, P. and Peña, T.H. 1998. *Managing Water as an Economic Resource: Reflections on the Chilean Experience*. Environment Department Working Paper No. 62, Environmental Economic Series. Washington, DC: World Bank.

Bues, A. and Theesfeld, I. 2012. Water grabbing and the role of power: Shifting water governance in the light of agricultural foreign direct investment. *Water Alternatives*, 5(2): 266–283.

Buncombe, A. 2018. Flint water crisis: Race 'was factor' in authorities' slow and misleading response, say city's black major. *The Independent*, May 2018. Available at: www.independent.co.uk/news/world/americas/flint-water-crisis-michigan-racism-city-mayor-karen-weaver-police-a8369981.html. Accessed May 2019.

Calderon, C. and Servén, L. 2004. *The Effects of Infrastructure Development on Growth and Income Distribution*. World Bank Policy Research Working Paper 3400. Washington, DC: World Bank.

Cherlet, J. 2012. *Tracing the Emergence and Deployment of the 'Integrated Water Resources Management' Paradigm*, Proceedings of the 12th EASA Biennial Conference Belgium, Ghent University.

Chimhowu, A. and Woodhouse, P. 2006. Customary vs private property rights? Dynamics and trajectories of vernacular land markets in sub-Saharan Africa. *Journal of Agrarian Change*, 6(3): 346–371.

China Dialogue. 2012. Laos forges ahead with controversial Mekong dam, 18 October. Available at: www.chinadialogue.net/blog/5222–Laos-forges-ahead-with-controversial-Mekong-dam-/en. Accessed 11 May 2019.

Cleaver, F. 2012. *Development through Bricolage: Rethinking Institutions for Natural Resource Management*. London: Earthscan.

Conca, K. 2006. *Governing Water: Contentious Transnational Politics and Global Institution Building (Global Environmental Accord: Strategies for Sustainability and Institutional Innovation)*. Cambridge, MA: MIT Press.

Cotton, L. and Ramachandran, V. 2006. Governance and the private sector. In N. Van de Walle, N. Bell and V. Ramachandran, eds. *Beyond Structural Adjustment: The Institutional Context of African Development*. Basingstoke, UK: Palgrave Macmillan.

Cotula, L., Vermeulen, S., Leonard, R. and Keeley, J. 2009. *Land Grab or Development Opportunity? Agricultural Investment and International Land Deals in Africa*. London/Rome: IIED (International Institution for Environment and Development)/FAO (Food and

Agriculture Organisation of the United Nations)/IFAD (International Fund for Agricultural Development).

Counterview. 2014. 30 lakh liters of Narmada water to Cola: Why waste water in Gujarat, Maharashtra and MP, asks Patkar. 11 September. Available at: www.counterview.net/2014/09/30-lakh-liters-of-narmada-water-to-cola.html. Accessed 11 May 2019.

Cullet, P. 2014. Groundwater law in India: Towards a framework ensuring equitable access and aquifer protection. *Journal of Environmental Law*, 26(1): 55–81.

Das Gupta, A., Babel, M.S., Albert, X. and Mark, O. 2005. Water sector of Bangladesh in the context of integrated water resources management: A review. *International Journal of Water Resources Development*, 21(2): 385–398.

de Fraiture, C. and Perry, C. 2007. Why is agricultural water demand irresponsive at low price ranges? In F. Molle and J. Berkhoff, eds. *Irrigation Water Pricing: The Gap between Theory and Practice*. Wallingford, UK and Colombo: CABI Publishing and International Water Management Institute.

De Schutter, O. 2011. How not to think of land-grabbing: Three critiques of large-scale investments in farmland. *Journal of Peasant Studies*, 38(2): 249–279.

Deininger, K. 2011. Challenges posed by the new wave of farmland investment. *Journal of Peasant Studies*, 38(2): 217–247.

Derman, B. and Hellum, A. 2005. *Observations on the Intersections of Human Rights and Custom: A Livelihood Perspective on Water*, paper presented at the International Workshop on 'African Water Laws: Plural Legislative Frameworks for Rural Water Management in Africa', 26–28 January 2005, Johannesburg, South Africa.

Derman, B. and Hellum, A. 2007. Livelihood rights perspective on water reform: Reflections on rural Zimbabwe. *Land Use Policy*, 24(4): 664–673.

Desai, D. and Sangomla, A. 2017. Sardar Sarovar Project faces its toughest challenge. *DownToEarth*, 24 October. Available at: www.downtoearth.org.in/news/water/sardar-sarovar-s-ta-nker-trail-58912. Accessed 11 May 2019.

Dey, J. 1984. *Women in Rice Farming Systems. Focus: Sub-Saharan Africa. Women in Agriculture 2. Women in Agricultural Production and Rural Development Service*. Rome: FAO.

Doczi, J., Calow, R. and d'Alançon, V. 2014. *Growing More with Less: China's Progress in Agricultural Water Management and Reallocation; Case Study Summary*. London: ODI.

Duvail, S., Médard, C., Hamerlynck, O. and Nyingi, D.W. 2012. Land and water grabbing in an East African coastal wetland: The case of the Tana Delta. *Water Alternatives*, 5(2): 322–343.

Elver, H. 2014. Celebrating water cooperation: Red Sea to Dead Sea. *Aljazeera*, 24 January. Available at: www.aljazeera.com/indepth/opinion/2014/01/celebrating-water-cooperation-r-201412072619203800.html. Accessed 11 May 2019.

Ewing, R. 2004. Cola consumption and the Chamula Indians. Available at: http://robinewing.com/2013/09/22/cola-consumption-and-the-chamula-indians/. Accessed May 2019.

Eyler, B. 2013. China needs to change its energy strategy in the Mekong region. *China Dialogue*, 16 July. Available at: www.chinadialogue.net/article/show/single/en/6208-China-needs-to-change-its-energy-strategy-in-the-Mekong-region. Accessed 11 May 2019.

Faheem, H. 2009. *Coca-Cola India's Corporate Social Responsibility Strategy*. Available at: https://oikos-international.org/wp-content/uploads/2013/10/oikos_Cases_2009_Coca_Cola_India.pdf. Accessed 11 May 2019.

FAO. 2005. *The Interface between Customary and Statutory Water Rights: A Statutory Perspective*. Rome: FAO.

FAO. 2012. *Coping with Water Scarcity: An Action Framework for Agriculture and Food Security*. FAO Water Reports 38. Rome: FAO.

FAO. 2016. *Governing the Security of the Commons: A Guide to Support the Implementation of the Voluntary Guidelines on the Responsible Governance of Tenure of Land, Fisheries and Forests in the Context of National Food Security*. Rome: FAO.

FAO Gender, Equity and Rural Employment Division. 2012. *Improving Gender Equality in Territorial Issues*. Land and Water Division Working Paper 3. Rome: FAO.

Fargher, W. n.d. *Responding to Scarcity: Lessons from Australian Water Markets in Supporting Agricultural Productivity during Drought*. Paris: OECD.

Finger, M. and Allouche, J. 2002. *Water Privatisation: Trans-National Corporations and the Re-Regulation of the Water Industry*. London and New York: Spon Press.

Franco, J., Mehta, L. and Veldwisch, G.J. 2013. The global politics of water grabbing. *Third World Quarterly*, 34(9): 1651–1675.

Gasteyer, S., Isaac, J., Hillal, J. and Walsh, S. 2012. Water-grabbing in colonial perspective: Land and water in Israel/Palestine. *Water Alternatives*, 5(2): 450–468.

Global Justice Now. 2019. *The Six Pillars of Food Sovereignty*. Available at: www.globaljustice.org.uk/six-pillars-food-sovereignty. Accessed 11 May 2019.

Global Water Partnership (GWP). 2000. *Integrated Water Resources Management*. TAC Background Papers No. 4. Stockholm: GWP.

Government of Maharashtra. 2005. *Maharashtra Water Sector Improvement Project: Project Implementation Plan (Executive Summary)*. Mumbai: Water Resources Department.

Government of the People's Republic of Bangladesh. 2008. *National Strategy for Poverty Reduction II*. Dhaka: General Economics Division, Planning Commission Government of the People's Republic of Bangladesh.

Grafton, R.Q., Pittock, J., Williams, J., Jiang, Q., Possingham, H. and Quiggin, J. 2014. Water planning and hydro-climatic change in the Murray-Darling Basin, Australia. *AMBIO*, 43(8): 1082–1092.

Groenfeldt, D. and Schmidt, J.J. 2013. Ethics and water governance. *Ecology and Society*, 18 (1): 14.

Harris, L.M. and Roa-García, M.C. 2013. Recent waves of water governance: Constitutional reform and resistance to neoliberalization in Latin America (1990–2012). *Geoforum*, 50: 20–30.

HLPE. 2011. *Land Tenure and International Investments in Agriculture*. A report by the High Level Panel of Experts on Food Security and Nutrition of the Committee on World Food Security. Rome: HLPE.

HLPE. 2013. *Investing in Smallholder Agriculture for Food Security*. A report by the High Level Panel of Experts on Food Security and Nutrition of the Committee on World Food Security. Rome: HLPE.

HLPE. 2015. *Water for Food Security and Nutrition*. A report by the High Level Panel of Experts on Food Security and Nutrition of the Committee on World Food Security. Rome: HLPE.

Hodgson, S. 2004. *Land and Water: The Rights Interface*. Rome: FAO.

Hoekstra, A., Mekonnen, M., Chapagain, A., Mathews, R. and Richter, B. 2012. Global monthly water scarcity: Blue water footprints versus blue water availability. *PloS ONE*, 7(2): e32688.

Hoff, H. 2011. *Understanding the nexus*. Background paper for the Bonn 2011 Nexus Conference: The Water, Energy and Food Security Nexus, Stockholm: Stockholm Environment Institute.

Hooja, R., Pangare, G. and Raju, K.V. 2002. *Users in Water Management: The Andhra Model and Its Replicability in India*. New Delhi: Rawat Publications.

Houdret, A. 2012. The water connection: Irrigation, water grabbing and politics in southern Morocco. *Water Alternatives*, 5(2): 284–303.

Hwang, L. and Stewart, E. 2008. Drinking it in: The evolution of a Global Water Stewardship Program at the Coca-Cola Company. *Business for Social Responsibility*. Available at: http://business-humanrights.org/en/pdf-drinking-it-in-the-evolution-of-a-global-water-stewardship-program-at-the-coca-cola-company. Accessed 11 May 2019.

IATP. 2010. *Response to Request for Input on Human Rights Obligations in the Context of Private-Sector Participation in the Provision of Water and Sanitation Services*. Geneva: UNHCR.

ICARDA. 2014. *Managing Salinity in Iraq*, Iraq Salinity Assessment, 3rd synthesis report. Amman: ICARDA.

International Conference on Water and the Environment. 1992. *The Dublin Statement on Water and Sustainable Development*. Rio de Janeiro: United Nations Conference on Environment and Development (UNCED).

Jackson, S. and Altman, J. 2009. Indigenous rights and water policy: Perspectives from Tropical Northern Australia. *Australian Indigenous Law Review*, 13(1): 27–48.

Kemerink, J.S., Méndez, L.E., Ahlers, R., Wester, P. and van der Zaag, P. 2013. The question of inclusion and representation in rural South Africa: Challenging the concept of water user associations as a vehicle for transformation. *Water Policy*, 15(2): 243–257.

Kershner, I. 2013. A rare Middle East agreement, on water. *The New York Times*, 9 December. Available at: www.nytimes.com/2013/12/10/world/middleeast/israel-jordan-and-palestinians-sign-water-project-deal.html?_r=0. Accessed 11 May 2019.

Konikkara, A. 2019. Nearly 15 years after Coca Cola plant shut down, Plachimada's fight for Rs 216 crore in compensation continues. *The Caravan*. Available at: https://caravanmagazine.in/communities/coca-cola-plachimada. Accessed May 2019.

Lang, T. and Barling, D. 2012. Food security and food sustainability: Reformulating the debate. *The Geographical Journal*, 178(4): 313–326.

Lein, H. and Tasgeth, M. 2009. Tanzanian water policy reforms: Between principles and practical applications. *Water Policy*, 11(2): 203–220.

Lele, U., Klousia-Marquisb, M. and Goswamic, S. 2013. Good governance for food, water and energy security. *Aquatic Procedia*, 1: 44–63.

Lobina, E., Kishimoto, S. and Petitjean, O. 2014. *Here to Stay: Water Remunicipalisation as a Global Trend*. London: Public Services International Research Unit (PSIRU), Transnational Institute (TNI) and Multinational Observatory.

McCartney, M. and Smakhtin, V. 2010. *Water Storage in an Era of Climate Change: Addressing the Challenge of Increasing Rainfall Variability*. Colombo, Sri Lanka: International Water Management Institute (IWMI).

McKeon, N. 2014. *Food Security Governance: Empowering Communities, Regulating Corporations (Routledge Critical Security Studies)*. London: Routledge.

Mehta, L. 2005. *The Politics and Poetics of Water: The Naturalisation of Scarcity in Western India*. Hyderabad: Orient BlackSwan.

Mehta, L. 2013. *Ensuring Rights to Water and Sanitation for Women and Girls*, Interactive Expert Panel: Challenges and achievements in the implementation of the Millennium Development Goals for women and girls, 4–15 March 2013, New York, United Nations Commission on the Status of Women.

Mehta, L. and Movik, S. 2014. Liquid dynamics: Challenges for sustainability in the water domain. *Wiley Interdisciplinary Reviews: Water*, 1(4): 369–384.

Mehta, L., Movik, S., Bolding, A., Derman, A. and Manzungu, E. 2016. Introduction to the special issue – flows and practices: The politics of Integrated Water Resources Management (IWRM) in Southern Africa. *Water Alternatives*, 9(3): 389–411.

Mehta, L., Veldwisch, J.G. and Franco, J. 2012. Water grabbing? Focus on the (re)appropriation of finite water resources. *Water Alternatives*, 5(2): 193–207.

Meinzen-Dick, R. 1996. Groundwater markets in Pakistan: Participation and productivity. IFPRI Research Report. Washington, DC: IFPRI.

Meinzen-Dick, R. 1997. Valuing the multiple uses of irrigation water. In M. Kay, T. Franks and L. Smith, eds. *Water: Economic, Management and Demand*. London: Spon Press.

Meinzen-Dick, R. 2007. Beyond panaceas in water institutions. *Proceedings of the National Academy of Sciences*, 104(39): 15200–15205.

Meinzen-Dick, R. and Bruns, B. (eds). 1999. *Negotiating Water Rights*. London: ITDG Publications.

Meinzen-Dick, R. and Nkonya, L. 2005. *Understanding Legal Pluralism in Water and Land Rights: Lessons from Africa and Asia*, African Water Laws Workshop: Plural Legislative Frameworks for Rural Water Management in Africa, 26–28 January, Johannesburg, South Africa.

Meinzen-Dick, R. and Pradhan, R. 2001. Implications of legal pluralism for natural resource management. *IDS Bulletin*, 32(4): 10–18.

Meinzen-Dick, R. and Ringler, C. 2008. Water reallocation: Drivers, challenges, threats, and solutions for the poor. *Journal of Human Development*, 9(1): 47–64.

Meinzen-Dick, R.S. and Mendoza, M. 1996. Alternative water allocation mechanisms: Indian and international experiences. *Economic and Political Weekly*, 31(13): A25–230.

Merrey, D.J. 2008. Is normative integrated water resources management implementable? Charting a practical course with lessons from Southern Africa. *Physics and Chemistry of the Earth, Parts A/B/C*, 33(8–13): 899–905.

MetaMeta and Enablement. n.d. Disability inclusive water management & agriculture. *MetaMeta and Enablement*. Available at: mmenable.wix.com/inclusionandwater. Accessed 11 May 2019.

Ministry of Water and Livestock Development. 2002. *National Water Policy – July 2002*. Dar es Salaam: Government of Tanzania.

Mohanty, S. 2017. Indian farmers uprooted by dam win compensation after decades long battle. Available at: www.reuters.com/article/india-landrights-court-idUSL5N1FV1LE. Accessed May 2019.

Molden, D., Oweis, T., Steduto, P., Kijne, J., Hanjra, M. and Bindraban, P. 2007. Pathways for increasing agricultural water productivity. In D. Molden, ed. *Water for Food, Water for Life: A Comprehensive Assessment of Water Management in Agriculture*. London: Earthscan.

Molle, F. 2006. *Planning and Managing Water Resources at the River Basin Level: Emergence of a Concept*. Colombo, Sri Lanka: International Water Management Institute (IWMI).

Molle, F. 2008. Nirvana concepts, narratives and policy models: Insights and the water sector. *Water Alternatives*, 1(1): 131–156.

Molle, F., Mollinga, P. and Wester, P. 2009. Hydraulic bureaucracies and the hydraulic mission: Flows of water, flows of power. *Water Alternatives*, 2(3): 328–349.

Molle, F., Wester, P. and Hirsch, P. 2007. River basin development and management. In D. Molden, ed. *Water for Food, Water for Life: A Comprehensive Assessment of Water Management in Agriculture*. London: Earthscan.

Mosse, D. 2005. *The Rule of Water: Statecraft, Ecology, and Collective Action in South India*. New Delhi: Oxford University Press.

Movik, S. 2012. *Fluid Rights: Water Allocation Reform in South Africa*. Pretoria: Human Sciences Research Council.

Nawaz, K. and van Steenbergen, F. n.d. *Water Rights, Water Distribution Rules and Codification in Spate Irrigation Systems Experience from Pakistan and Other Countries*. Available at: www.thewaterchannel.tv/images/waterrightcodificationpakistanelsewhere.pdf.Accessed 11 May 2019.

Nicol, A., Mehta, L. and Allouche, J. 2012. 'Some for all?' politics and pathways in water and sanitation. *IDS Bulletin*, 43(2): 1–9.

NWC (National Water Commission). 2012. Position statement. Indigenous access to water resources. Australian Government National Water Commission. Available at: www.nwc.gov.au/__data/assets/pdf_file/0009/22869/Indigenous-Position-Statement-June-2012.pdf.

OECD. 2000. *Implementing Domestic Tradable Permits for Environmental Protection (Proceedings)*. Paris: OECD.

Ostrom, E. 1990. *Governing the Commons: The Evolution of Institutions for Collective Action*. New York: Cambridge University Press.

Pal, S.K., Adeloye, A.J., Babel, M.S. and Das Gupta, A. 2011. Evaluation of the effectiveness of water management policies in Bangladesh. *International Journal of Water Resources Development*, 27(2): 401–417.

Peters, P.E. 2010. 'Our daughters inherit our land, but our sons use their wives' fields': Matrilineal–matrilocal land tenure and the New Land Policy in Malawi. *Journal of Eastern African Studies*, 4(1): 179–199.

Pigeon, M., McDonald, D., Hoedeman, O. and Kishimoto, S. 2012. *Remunicipalisation: Putting Water Back into Public Hands*. Amsterdam: Transnational Institute.

Ringler, C., Bhaduri, A. and Lawford, R. 2013. The nexus across Water, Energy, Land and Food (WELF): Potential for improved resource use efficiency? *Current Opinion in Environmental Sustainability*, 5(6): 617–624.

Rocha, C. 2008. *Brazil–Canada Partnership: Building Capacity in Food Security*. Toronto: Center for Studies in Food Security, Ryerson University.

Rogers, B. 1981. *The Domestication of Women: Discrimination in Developing Societies*. New York: Routledge.

Rosegrant, M.W., Cai, X., Cline, S. and Nakagawa, N. 2002. *The Role of Rainfed Agriculture in the Future of Global Food Production*. EPTD Discussion Paper 90. Washington, DC: IFPRI.

Rosegrant, M.W. and Ringler, C. 2000. Impact on food security and rural development of transferring water out of agriculture. *Water Policy*, 1(6): 567–586.

Rosegrant, M.W., Ringler, C. and Zhu, T. 2009. Water for agriculture: Maintaining food security under growing scarcity. *Annual Review of Environment and Resources*, 34: 205–222.

Roth, D., Boelens, R. and Zwarteveen, M. (eds.). 2005. *Liquid Relations: Contested Water Rights and Legal Complexity*. Brunswick, NJ: Rutgers University Press.

Rovira, G. 2000. *Women of Maize*. Mexico: Editorial Era.

RSA. 2013. *National Water Resources Strategy Second Edition*. South Africa: Republic of South Africa.

Saleth, R.M. and Dinar, A. 2000. Institutional changes in global water sector: Trends, patterns, and implications. *Water Policy*, 2: 175–199.

Selby, J. 2013. *Water Cooperation – or Instrument of Control?* Global insights Policy Brief 05. Brighton: University of Sussex.

Shah, T. and Van Koppen, B. 2005. Is India ripe for integrated water resources management? Fitting water policy to national development context. *Economic and Political Weekly*, 41(31): 3413–3421.

Shiva, V. 2006. *Resisting Water Privatisation, Building Water Democracy*. A paper on the occasion of the World Water Forum in Mexico City, March 2006.

Skinner, J. and Cortula, L. 2011. *Are Land Deals Driving 'Water Grabs'?* IIED Briefing 17102IIED. London: IIED.

Sosovele, H. 2010. Policy challenges related to biofuel development in Tanzania. *Africa Spectrum*, 45(1): 117–129.

Spiertz, J.H.L. 2000. Water rights and legal pluralism: Some basics of a legal anthropological approach. In R. Meinzen-Dick and B. Bruns, eds. *Negotiating Water Rights*. London: ITDG Publications.

Srivastava, S. 2015. Rule(s) over regulation: The making of water reforms and regulatory culture(s) in Maharashtra. PhD thesis, Brighton, UK: University of Sussex.

Tanzania Parliament. 2012. *The Water Resources Management Act, 2009*. Dar es Salaam: Tanzania Parliament.

Thomas, V. and Ahmad, M. 2009. *A Historical Perspective on the Mirab System: A Case Study of the Jangharoq Canal, Baghlan*. Kabul: Afghanistan Research and Evaluation Unit.

UN. 2003. *Commission on Human Rights, Sixtieth Session: Economic, Social and Cultural Rights: The Right to Food*. Report by the Special Rapporteur on the right to food, Addendum: Mission to Bangladesh; Jean Ziegler. New York: UN.

UN. 2010. *Guide to Responsible Business Engagement with Water Policy*. CEO Water Mandate, UN Global Compact. New York: UN.

UNDP. 2006. *Beyond Scarcity: Power, Poverty and the Global Crises*. Human Development Report 2006. New York: UNDP.

UNEP (United Nations Environment Programme). 2013. Smallholders, food security and the environment. IFAD and UNEP. Available at: www.unep.org/pdf/SmallholderReport_-WEB.pdf.

Upadhyaya, P. 2013. Depleting groundwater resources and risks to India's water security. In E. Miklian and A. Kolas, eds. *India's Human Security: Lost Debates, Forgotten People, Intractable Challenges*. London: Routledge.

van Eeden, A., Mehta, L. and van Koppen, B. 2016. Whose waters? Large-scale agricultural development and water grabbing in the Wami-Ruvu River Basin, Tanzania. *Water Alternatives*, 9(3): 608–626.

van Koppen, B. 2002. *A Gender Performance Indicator for Irrigation: Concepts, Tools, and Applications*. Research Report 59. Colombo, Sri Lanka: International Water Management Institute (IWMI).

van Koppen, B. 2007. Dispossession at the interface of community-based water law and permit systems. In B. van Koppen and M. Butterworth, eds. *Community-Based Water Law and Water Resource Management Reform in Developing Countries*. Wallingford, UK: CABI Comprehensive Assessment of Water Management in Agriculture Series.

van Koppen, B. 2009. Gender, resource rights, and wetland productivity in Burkina Faso. In J. Kirsten, A. Dorward, C. Poulton and N. Vink, eds. *Institutional Economics Perspectives on African Agricultural Development*. Washington, DC: IFPRI.

van Koppen, B., Butterworth, J. and Juma, I. 2005. *African Water Laws: Plural Legislative Frameworks for Rural Water Management in Africa*, compendium of papers presented at the International Workshop, International Water Management Institute, Johannesburg, 26–28 January.

van Koppen, B. and Schreiner, B. 2014. Priority general authorizations in rights-based water use authorization in South Africa. *Water Policy*, 16(S2): 59–77.

van Koppen, B. and Schreiner, B. 2018. *A Hybrid Approach to Decolonize Formal Water Law in Africa*. IWMI Research Report 173. Colombo, Sri Lanka: International Water Management Institute (IWMI) and Pegasys Institute.

van Koppen, B., Smits, S., Moriarty, P., Penning de Vries, F., Mikhail, M. and Boelee, E. 2009. *Climbing the Water Ladder: Multiple-Use Water Services for Poverty Reduction*. Technical Paper Series 52. Colombo, Sri Lanka: IRC International Water and Sanitation Centre, International Water Management Institute and Challenge Program on Water and Food.

van Koppen, B., Smits, S., Rumbaitis del Rio, C. and Thomas, J. 2014. *Scaling up Multiple Use Water Services: Accountability in the Water Sector*. London: Practical Action.

van Wijk-Sijbesma, C. 2002. *The Best of Two Worlds? Methodology for Participatory Measurement of Sustainability, Use and Gender and Poverty-Sensitive Participation in Community-Managed Domestic Water Services*. Delft: Wageningen University.

Varghese, S. 2012. *Corporatizing Water: India's Draft National Water Policy*. Minneapolis, MN: IATP.

Varghese, S. 2013. *Water Governance in the 21st Century: Lessons from Water Trading in the U.S. and Australia*. Minneapolis, MN: IATP.

Varghese, S. 2016. Drinking water and democracy. Tale of two cities. Available at: www.iatp.org/blog/201602/drinking-water-and-democracy-tale-of-two-cities. Accessed May 2019.

Varghese, S. and Hansen-Kuhn, K. 2013. *Scaling Up Agroecology*. IATP. Available at: www.iatp.org/sites/default/files/2013_10_09_ScalingUpAgroecology_SV_0.pdf.

Veldwisch, G.J., Beekman, W. and Bolding, A. 2013. Smallholder irrigators, water rights and investments in agriculture: Three cases from rural Mozambique. *Water Alternatives*, 6(1): 125–141.

Vélez Torres, I. 2012. Water grabbing in the Cauca Basin: The capitalist exploitation of water and dispossession of afro-descendant communities. *Water Alternatives*, 5(2): 431–449.

von Benda-Beckman, F. (ed.). 1981. *Rechtsantropologie in Nederland, Themanummer Sociologische Gids No. 4*. Meppel: Boom.

von Benda-Beckmann, F. 2001. Legal pluralism and social justice in economic and political development. *IDS Bulletin*, 32(1): 46–57.

von Braun, J. and Meinzen-Dick, R. 2009. *'Land Grabbing' by Foreign Investors in Developing Countries: Risks and Opportunities*. IFPRI Policy Brief No. 13. Washington, DC: IFPRI.

Vorley, B., Cotula, L. and Chan, M. 2012. *Tipping the Balance: Policies to Shape Agricultural Investments and Markets in Favour of Small-Scale Farmers*. Oxford, UK: Oxfam International.

Wardam, B. 2004. *More Politics than Water: Water Rights in Jordan*. Global Issue Paper No. 11. Ramallah: Heinrich Boll Foundation.

Warner, J., Wester, P. and Bolding, A. 2008. Going with the flow: River basins as the natural units for water management? *Water Policy*, 10(S2): 121–138.

Water Governance Facility. 2012. *Human Rights-Based Approaches and Managing Water Resources: Exploring the Potential for Enhancing Development Outcomes*. Water Governance Facility Report No. 1. Stockholm: International Water Institute.

Weitz, N., Strambo, C., Kemp-Benedict, E. and Nilsson, M. 2017. *Governance in the Water-Energy-Food Nexus: Gaps and Future Research Needs*. Working Paper No. 2017-07. Stockholm: Stockholm Environment Institute.

Wester, P., Merrey, D.J. and De Lange, M. 2003. Boundaries of consent: Stakeholder representation in river basin management in Mexico and South Africa. *World Development*, 31(5): 797–812.

Williams, T.O., Gyampoh, B., Kizito, F. and Namara, R. 2012. Water implications of large-scale land acquisitions in Ghana. *Water Alternatives*, 5(2): 243–265.

Woodhouse, M. and Langford, M. 2009. Crossfire: There is no human right to water for livelihoods. *Waterlines*, 28(1): 1–12.

Woodhouse, P. 2012. New investment, old challenges: Land deals and the water constraint in African agriculture. *The Journal of Peasant Studies*, 39(3–4): 777–794.

Wooters, M. 2008. Coca Cola and water resources in Chiapas. *Colectivos de Apoyo, Solidaridad y Acción*. Available at: www.casacollective.org/index.php.

World Bank. 1994. *World Development Report 1994: Infrastructure for Development*. New York: Oxford University Press.

World Bank. 2009. *Directions in Hydropower*. Washington, DC: World Bank.

World Bank. 2010. *Rising Global Interest in Farmland: Can It Yield Sustainable and Equitable Benefits?* Washington, DC: World Bank.

World Bank, FAO and IFAD. 2009. *Gender in Agriculture Sourcebook*. Washington, DC: World Bank.

World Commission on Dams (WCD). 2000. *Dams and Development: A New Framework for Decision-Making*. London: Earthscan.

World Economic Forum. 2011. *Water Security: The Water–Food–Energy–Climate Nexus*. Washington, DC: New Island Press.

Young, M. 2012. Opinion: Australia's rivers traded into trouble. *Australian Geographic*, 9 May. Available at: www.australiangeographic.com.au/topics/science-environment/2012/05/opinion-australias-rivers-traded-into-trouble/. Accessed 12 January 2015.

Zeitoun, M. 2007. The conflict vs. cooperation paradox: Fighting over or sharing of Palestinian–Israeli groundwater? *Water International*, 32(1): 105–120.

5
WATER, FSN AND SOCIAL JUSTICE

Introduction

This chapter focuses on how to advance a social justice perspective on the water and FSN debate through strengthening human rights and global frameworks around water and food security. We build on Chapter 4's discussion of water governance, largely focusing on global governance[1] related to water and food. The chapter begins with a discussion of the global water governance regime, including the Sustainable Development Goals (SDGs) and their commitment to universal access to water and food. We demonstrate how land and food governance are not adequately integrated into major global initiatives around water. At the global level, there is a great deal of institutional ambiguity regarding water and no clear procedures regarding decision making. The chapter then turns to discussing the genesis of and linkages between the rights to food and water. We recognize that there are significant challenges in realizing these rights and that they are routinely violated around the world. We argue that strengthening the interpretations and understandings of underexplored aspects of the right to water (RTW) and of its inter-linkages with the right to food (RTF) are key to ensuring water for FSN.

The RTW as recognized by the UN General Assembly in 2010 largely focuses on drinking water and sanitation services and has not been deployed to look at the productive use of water, despite earlier, broader interpretations in the General Comment No. 15, reinforced in later reports such as United Nations Human Rights Council (UNHRC) (Hall *et al.*, 2013). The RTW and the RTF have close ties because water and sanitation are crucial for health and nutrition and because access to water is indispensable for food producers and the RTF of producers. It is important to note that local water users rarely separate the domestic and productive uses of water or water and food issues. We thus join others such as Hellum *et al.* (2015), Hall *et al.* (2013), and Van Koppen *et al.* (2014) to call for an exploration of how these two rights can be joined up in a meaningful way in order to promote a human rights approach to water governance and water management for FSN that supports achievement of water for FSN. The chapter also focuses on the need to define the extra-territorial obligations of international investors as well as governments of the host country in order to ensure good outcomes for FSN. We conclude by spelling out the book's final conclusions and implications for policy and practice.

The emergence of a global water governance regime for FSN?

As discussed in the previous chapter, the allocation and use of water are fundamentally not technical matters, but are largely driven by political and economic interests. Taking this view, an analysis of the key players and the power relations at the global level becomes a useful tool in understanding the water and FSN debate. While most solutions to water challenges or exploitation of water-based opportunities take place at the local, national or regional levels, there is a complex network of players at the global level that inform the dominant policy discourse. Contemporary water governance at the international level is characterized by a high degree of political contestation, competing regulatory actors and processes, and a great deal of institutional ambiguity with few agreed rules or procedures regarding decision making (Franco *et al.*, 2013).

Since there are few formal agreements, there is no clear-cut global water regime with agreed-upon rules of the game providing normative prescriptions, clear expectations and institutionalized relationships (Conca, 2006). Partly this is because water is not really a global issue or a 'global public good' (cf. Mehta, 2003) but instead highly localized and at best regional in scope. Even though the 'global' nature of water is difficult to capture, there are various competing global discourses, such as the discussion and consensus (reflected in SDG 6 on water) around Integrated Water Resources Management (IWRM) versus the global struggles for water justice. The key global actors include the UN system, intergovernmental organizations and international financing institutions (such as the World Bank and the Global Environmental Facility), international non-governmental organizations (such as the Global Water Partnership (GWP), World Water Council (WWC), World Wide Fund for Nature), and international networks of these organizations (such as the International Union for the Conservation of Nature (IUCN)), global knowledge networks (such as the CGIAR research bodies and programmes), transnational, corporate-led international water initiatives (such as Water Resources Group 2030, UN Global Compact's CEO Water Mandate and Water Futures Partnership), public water employees unions and global networks of social movements.

UN Water is the inter-agency coordination mechanism covering all freshwater- and sanitation-related matters, particularly in relation to the implementation of the SDGs. Its work also covers surface and groundwater resources and estuaries, in terms of quality and quantity issues, infrastructure development and water-related disasters and extreme events in relation to their impact on human security. But it remains a virtual institute with little influence. The World Health Organization, UNICEF and UNEP all have a role to play in the water sector – the first two focus primarily on issues of safe drinking water and sanitation and monitor progress around access to water and sanitation via the Joint Monitoring Programme. The Water Supply and Sanitation Collaborative Council was set up in 1990 following a UN mandate to continue the work of the decade of water supply and sanitation and now primarily focuses on access to basic sanitation.

A number of donor agencies and international financing institutions play a significant role in the water sector through the provision of financing for water management and infrastructure, and through their influence of global and national policies in relation to food and water. These bodies include the World Bank, the International Finance Corporation (IFC) (which provides financing to the private sector), regional financing bodies such as the African Development Bank and the Asian Development Bank, and international co-operation partners such as DFID, USAID, and GIZ. The Chinese government has also become a major player in financing and developing water-related infrastructure, including in Africa. The role of the World Bank has been controversial around both the hydropower and privatization debates (see also Chapter 4). The World Bank also houses the Water Resources Group 2030, an initiative of private companies such as Nestlé, Coca-Cola and Pepsi, some donor organizations, such as the Swiss Development Cooperation, the governments of Hungary and Israel, some development banks, UN organizations and international NGOs, such as IUCN.[2]

Significant research bodies operate in the global water sector, not least the 15 CGIAR centres and their associated multi-centre research programmes. Of these, the International Water Management Institute (IWMI) focuses entirely on water, and largely on water and agriculture. Other CGIAR research programmes also deal with issues of water and food security and this is especially true in the context of climate change, through CGIAR initiatives linked to climate change. The challenge is to ensure that a diversity of perspectives and actors (especially from southern contexts) also drive research and action agendas on water for food. A further challenge is to ensure that research is translated into practice at scale.

Both GWP and WWC were inaugurated in 1996; GWP with the goal to support IWRM in the wake of the establishment of the Dublin Principles in 1992 and a Secretariat in Stockholm; and WWC with the goal to promote awareness, build political commitment and trigger action on critical water issues and headquarters in Marseille, France. WWC, which organizes the tri-annual World Water Forum, was founded by a group that included the International Commission on Irrigation and Drainage, the IUCN, the International Water Association (IWA), Suez Lyonnaise des Eaux, the United Nations agencies UNDP and UNESCO, and the World Bank. Members of the current Board of Governors include four categories: intergovernmental institutions, governments and government authorities, enterprises and facilities, and civil society organizations and water user associations. The latter grouping, however, does not include any groups that represent the interests of marginalized and poor communities in developing countries. It was only at the sixth World Water Forum that some attempts were made to bring grassroots civil society organizations and representatives of social movements into the mainstream, but even then, as before, civil society discussions on water justice concerns were held in a separate venue, distinct, and sometimes at considerable distance, from the main venue. Whether this was driven by civil society, or by the Forum organizers, it represents the top-down nature of the water sector and problems concerning transparency and accountability (Mukhtarov and Gerlak, 2013).

Counter-balancing the private sector discourse, water has been a key focus of social movements around the world. The issues that have mobilized communities have included struggles against bottled water, mining related pollution, the displacement caused by large dams and the privatization of water services, amongst others. The focus has often been to safeguard local livelihoods, food and water security as well as strengthening the capacity of public utilities to fulfil their responsibilities and re-municipalize privatized water systems.

Many struggles focused on food security issues also recognize water as crucial for peasants and small farmers to retain control over the 'commons' necessary for their livelihoods. As an example, La Vía Campesina, the international peasant's movement, is strongly focused on issues of land rights and sustainable agricultural practices. It considers water to be a key resource that needs protection from corporate control (see the Declaration of Nyéléni, 2007), and notes the increasing lack of protection of small-scale producers by the state, under the pretext that they are inefficient, despite the fact that they produce some 70% of global food supplies (ibid.). These social movements are growing in strength, not least due to the power of social media and the internet in linking erstwhile isolated groups. After this brief overview of the global governance arrangements, we review transboundary issues before turning to international frameworks concerning the human rights to water and food.

Transboundary and global approaches to FSN

When dealing with the issue of water for FSN, it is important to recognize that water resources often transcend national boundaries, making their management and use a function of transnational agreements and relationships. There are 263 transboundary river basins in the world, and 46% of the world's land surface falls inside these basins.[3]

Article 2 of Rio Declaration on Environment and Development in 1992 upholds an important principle in this regard affirming that

> the States have, in accordance with the Charter of the United Nations and the principles of international law, the sovereign right to exploit their own

Water, FSN and social justice **169**

resources pursuant to their own environmental and developmental policies, and the responsibility to ensure that activities within their jurisdiction or control do not cause damage to the environment of other States or of areas beyond the limits of national jurisdiction.

(United Nations, 1992)

In 1966, the International Law Association (ILA) adopted the Helsinki Rules on the Uses of the Waters of International Rivers as an international guideline regulating how rivers and their connected groundwaters that cross national boundaries may be used. However, there is no mechanism in place that enforces these Rules. In 1997 the UN adopted the Convention on the Law of Non-Navigational Uses of International Watercourses; the Convention only came into force in August 2014 after a sufficient number of countries had ratified it. It imposes an obligation on UN member states to consider the impact of their actions on other riparian states and sets out the principles of reasonable and equitable use of shared water courses.

BOX 5.1 TRANSBOUNDARY COOPERATION FOR FSN

The Mekong River Commission provides one example of successful transboundary water governance to promote food security. Food security for 73 million people living in the basin requires regional water planning and cooperation, particularly since 85% of the population in the basin depends on agriculture for their livelihoods (Jacobs, 2002) and get 80% of their calories from rice and 15% from aquatic based food (Bach et al., 2012) making their food security highly dependent on water. Although regional cooperation in the basin has a long history, the Mekong River Commission made up of Cambodia, Laos, Thailand and Vietnam, recently shifted the focus of this cooperation to smaller scale programmes that include food security concerns (ibid.). Integrating agreed-upon procedures among these four countries provides opportunities for pro-poor water management approaches with the aims of maintaining sufficient water flows, safeguarding water quality, monitoring water use, ensuring equitable use and exchanging quality data. While implementation of these procedures remains a challenge, the approach is laudable (Bach et al., 2012).

The Nile Basin Initiative, initiated in 1999 (Nile Basin Initiative, 2015), has attempted to establish several regional cooperation projects in a transboundary river-basin context to advance socio-economic development in the basin countries including food security and water productivity. The approach still faces challenges in addressing sustainability and it is hard to avoid state interests being given precedence over regional plans and commitments.

> Finalized in 1960, the Indus Waters Treaty (IWT) was considered path-breaking as it put an end to the post-partition India–Pakistan dispute regarding the use of water from the Indus River system. It not only specifies the rights and privileges regarding the sharing of river waters but also created a conflict resolution mechanism in case of future disputes between India and Pakistan regarding the river and its tributaries. Nonetheless, there remains contestation over water between the two countries, particularly as water scarcity deepens.
>
> Another example of successful coordination is the Mexico–US International Boundary and Water Commission that was established in its current structure by treaty in 1944 and provides for 'minutes,' or binational decisions adjusting water allocation based on local and temporal circumstances (McCarthy, 2011).

The management of transboundary basins is complicated when there are 'different national (sometimes conflicting) interests, power disparities between riparian states, differences in national institutional capacity, limited information exchange and lack of sufficient, basin scale knowledge and institutional capacity to make decisions' (Bach *et al.*, 2012: 15). Additional complexity occurs when attempting to balance local and basin needs (ibid.). However, international water governance and food security at the regional level can be essential building blocks towards regional cooperation and economic integration (see also Box 5.1).

International processes and agreements that affect water for food security

Globally, numerous competing governance mechanisms have emerged around the issue of global capital engaging with local natural resources. High profile governance initiatives addressing land use, management and access in relation to agriculture include, among others: (1) the World Bank led 'Principles of Responsible Agricultural Investment'; (2) the Committee on World Food Security (CFS) endorsed 'Voluntary Guidelines on the Responsible Governance of Tenure of Land, Fisheries and Forests in the Context of National Food Security' (VGGT); (3) the CFS endorsed 'Principles for Responsible Investment in Agriculture and Food Systems' (CFS-RAI) and (4) more recently, the G8's 'Land Transparency Initiative' (G8LTI). These agriculture-oriented governance initiatives, including those endorsed by the CFS, tended to neglect a wide and deep range of issues related to water. The CFS-HLPE report on water for food security and nutrition that we were part of sought to amend this lacuna (HLPE, 2015).

The VGGT warrant special attention since they constitute the most recent site of struggle between competing views and interpretations of natural resources and the way they should be governed (Seufert, 2013; Suárez, 2013, Box 5.3).

Water, FSN and social justice 171

The VGGT mark an important step forward in elaborating a human RTF as they are 'the first international instrument which applies an ESC- [Economic, Social and Cultural] Rights based approach to the governance of land' (Suárez, 2012: 37). Though the understanding of tenure pertaining to natural resources in these guidelines has its problems and contradictions, water remains a serious challenge as a result of being excluded from coverage.[4] During the final negotiations, the effort by civil society to get water into the guidelines ran up against opposition and resistance from other participants who denounced water and water governance as 'too complicated'. This poses a major ambiguity since water is indeed deeply and inextricably interconnected with other natural resources.[5]

Multilateral and bilateral trade and investment agreements and partnerships also warrant attention for the binding nature of these agreements as well as the significant direct impact they have on agricultural and food policies, not only at the national level but also at the local level. Box 5.2 describes the World Trade Organization, the movement toward regional and bilateral agreements and potential implications for water and FSN.

When it comes to water security, the Investor–State Dispute Settlement (ISDS) process – a system through which investors can sue nations for alleged discriminatory practices – which is now part of most multilateral or bilateral investment agreements, needs particular attention. ISDS gives foreign investors the right to demand compensation for environmental, public interest and other laws that undermine their anticipated profits. This provision, initially put in place to protect investors' rights against nationalization or expropriation, has evolved to become a tool for corporations to tie up governments in long and expensive legal cases, with chilling effects on public interest rules around the world. With the number of ISDS cases growing exponentially across the globe over the last two decades, ISDS has become quite controversial globally, especially because of the way it affects food and water security. Some of these cases involve agriculture-related foreign investments as well as land or water grabbing from local communities. In other cases, communities find that their water sources are either depleted or polluted, affecting not only their irrigation water but also their drinking and cooking water. The fallouts are not limited to agriculture-related investments. Investments in other sectors (such as extractive industries) also can directly affect the food and/or water security of impacted communities (Varghese, 2017). Moreover, trade agreements can have indirect impacts on water for FSN as water is diverted for the production of export oriented commodities. There are, however, some examples where the rights of local communities have been protected through legal processes.

The successful struggles of El Salvadorians against the mining giant Pacific Rim (also OceanaGold), that was contaminating their waters and environment, is a case in point. After a decade-long battle, and a case at the International Centre for Settlement of Investment Disputes (ICSID), in mid-October 2016 Pac-Rim's lawsuit against El Salvador was deemed without merit; as a result El

Salvador did not have to pay the company the $250 million that it sought in compensation. Moreover, the company was asked to pay $8 million towards the legal expenses incurred by El Salvador. This decision has implications, not only for the right to drinking water and sanitation, but also for other water dependent fundamental rights such as the right to health and the right to food (see Varghese, 2017), despite the fact that it was not won on the grounds of legal arguments based on human rights violations by the investors.

Investment tribunals rarely examine human rights arguments based on international human rights law against investors' claims. However, for the first time, in a recent case the tribunal award considered the host state's counter claim related to the violation of the human right to water (against the investor's claim regarding breach of 'fair and equitable standard of treatment') (ICSID, 2016). The ICSID award on Urbaser vs. Argentina is the first to provide a detailed discussion of a host state's counterclaim based on international human rights law. It stated:

> It is not disputed that the human right to water and sanitation is recognized today as part of human rights and that this right has as its corresponding obligation the duty of States to provide all persons living under their jurisdiction with safe and clean drinking water and sewage services.
> *(2016: 319–320)*

While this new acknowledgement of the right to water is encouraging, the frequent use of 'fair and equal treatment' in investor–state dispute settlements is evidence of how this vague legal standard can be used by corporations to protect their interests at the cost of public interest.

BOX 5.2 TRADE AND INVESTMENT AGREEMENTS: IMPLICATIONS FOR WATER QUALITY AND WATER AVAILABILITY FOR FOOD SECURITY

The World Trade Organization (WTO) is the multilateral space for trade agreements. However, since there has not been much progress since the Doha Round in 2001, proponents of trade agreements, especially those engaged in international trade, have been urging for developing trade partnerships outside the WTO. Since 2009, several major partnerships have been developed as a result; these include the Comprehensive Economic and Trade Agreement (CETA), the Transatlantic Trade and Investment Partnership (TTIP) and the Trans Pacific Partnership (TPP).

These agreements have been criticized for their lack of transparency, not only to the public but at times even to lawmakers of the countries concerned, be it the US, Canada or the EU. Concerns have also been raised due to potential threats to food safety, public services, health, ecosystems and waters that humans rely on, and the ability of the local and sub-regional governments to make decisions about these issues at the appropriate level (Hansen-Kuhn, 2014; Hansen-Kuhn and Suppan, 2013).

The provisions in the agreements are often geared toward meeting the lowest common denominator which has the potential to drive standards down. As an example, concerns about TTIP caused the United Kingdom Environment Audit Committee (EAC) of the UK parliament to launch an enquiry to examine whether the agreement could weaken national regulations on chemical and pesticide use, oil and gas extraction and genetically modified food (Carrington, 2015).

Another notable development has been the Global Forum for Food and Agriculture Communique of 2017, signed by 83 ministers of agriculture, that agreed to take on increased responsibility for water resource management for the protection and sustainable use and management of water in agriculture (see also Chapter 3).

Sustainable Development Goals

The UN General Assembly adopted the SDGs in September 2015. A wide process of consultation and engagement had been implemented to develop the SDGs, which are successors to the Millennium Development Goals (MDGs) adopted in 2000.

Four of the 17 goals (UNGA, 2015) are most directly relevant for the water and FSN debate:

Goal 1: End poverty in all its forms everywhere;
Goal 2: End hunger, achieve food security and improved nutrition and promote sustainable agriculture;
Goal 5: Achieve gender equality and empower all women and girls;
Goal 6: Ensure availability and sustainable management of water and sanitation for all.

While the MDGs focused on domestic water supply (and sanitation which was added at the World Summit on Sustainable Development (WSSD) in Johannesburg in 2002), Goal 6 of the SDGs is focused on achieving universal access to safe drinking water, sanitation and hygiene; improving the sustainable use and development of water resources; strengthening the sustainable use and development of water resources; reducing pollution and improving water quality and reducing mortality and economic loss from natural and human-induced water-related disasters. In addition, Goal 2 of the proposed SDGs aims to double agricultural productivity of small scale food producers and to ensure sustainable food production systems and implement resilient agricultural practices.

The way these goals, targets and indicators are formulated, how they are measured and implemented will be one of the main drivers shaping the water for food security discussion in the near future. It is a process with substantial challenges. As an example, a report by UN Women (2014) acknowledged that global efforts to integrate gender and sustainable development thus far have been mixed, ranging from complete exclusion to nominal inclusion while goals, targets and implementation remained separate. The SDG discussion offers a possibility for more joined up thinking and efforts. This needs to be complemented by far more inclusion of gender equality concerns and representation of women's interests in ongoing international policy processes around water, land and food.

What is not expanded on in the SDGs is the definition of equitable access to water, particularly in the context of FSN, and whether there is an implication that poor women and men should have access to sufficient water to meet their food needs, or whether it simply refers to sufficient safe water for domestic purposes. Moreover, the SDG focus on water security (along with food and energy security) seems to be a shift away from the rights-based approach to development (Hamm, 2001) that informed the MDGs to one framed by the nexus approach promoted by the World Economic Forum (Allouche *et al.*, 2014). At the same time, international human rights law has moved increasingly toward establishing a broader concept of land, water and associated resources such as fisheries and forests as matters of human rights. This has for instance led to the inclusion of access to land as part of 'the right to feed oneself' (Künnermann and Monsalve Suárez, 2013). Although there is as yet no distinct human right to land, the pressure to establish such a right remains (Borras and Franco, 2010). We now turn to a detailed discussion on the right to water (RTW) and the right to food (RTF).

BOX 5.3 RELEVANT INTERNATIONAL HUMAN RIGHTS INSTRUMENTS, AGREEMENTS AND TEXTS APPLICABLE TO WATER POLICIES AND OTHER MEASURES TO ENHANCE FOOD SECURITY

Human Rights Instruments

The Universal Declaration of Human Rights www.un.org/en/documents/udhr/, in particular Article 25: 'Everyone has the right to a standard of living adequate for the health and well-being of himself and of his family, including food, clothing, housing and medical care'.

The International Covenant on Economic, Social, and Cultural Rights (ICESCR) (UN, 1966) www.ohchr.org/EN/ProfessionalInterest/Pages/cescr.aspx (Article 11 as well as General Comments 12 and 15).

The UN's 2010 binding resolution on the human right to water and sanitation (UN, 2010) http://daccess-dds-ny.un.org/doc/UNDOC/LTD/N10/464/64/PDF/N1046464.pdf?OpenElement, see Section 3.9 for a fuller discussion.

The UN Declaration on the Rights of Indigenous Peoples (UNDRIP) (UN, 2007) www.un.org/esa/socdev/unpfii/documents/DRIPS_en.pdf, in particular Articles 8, 20, 21, 23, 25, 27, 32 stressing the rights of indigenous peoples to have redress from dispossession and their rights to development, subsistence, health, water, sanitation etc.

The UN Declaration on the Rights of Peasants and other People Working in rural Areas (UNHRC, 2018) http://undocs.org/A/C.3/73/L.30. This declaration recognizes the 'special relationship and interaction between peasants and other people working in rural areas and the land, water and nature to which they are attached and on which they depend for their livelihood', affirms the *Voluntary Guidelines on the Responsible Governance of Tenure of Land, Fisheries and Forests in the Context of National Food Security* (adopted by the Committee on World Food Security). See Articles 4, 15, 17, 18, 21, stressing elimination of all forms of gender based discrimination, right to food, right to land, right to conserve and protect their environment, and the right to water for personal and domestic use, farming, fishing and livestock keeping and to securing other water-related livelihoods.

Voluntary Guidelines
The Voluntary Guidelines to support the Progressive Realization of the Right to Adequate Food in the Context of National Food Security (the Right to Food Guidelines) (FAO, 2004) ftp://ftp.fao.org/docrep/fao/meeting/009/y9825e/y9825e.pdf – see discussion to follow. Guideline 8c explicitly acknowledges that access to water in sufficient quantity and quality for all is fundamental for life and health and that states should strive to improve access to, and promote sustainable use of, water resources and their allocation among users giving due regard to efficiency and the satisfaction of basic human needs in an equitable manner.

Voluntary Guidelines on the Responsible Governance of Tenure of Land, Fisheries and Forests in the Context of National Food Security (FAO, 2012) www.fao.org/docrep/016/i2801e/i2801e.pdf This report notes that responsible governance of tenure of land, fisheries and forests is inextricably linked with access to and management of other natural resources, such as water and mineral resources, and the preface of the Tenure Guidelines invites states to take into account the governance of water in the implementation of the Tenure Guidelines (FAO, 2012). Particularly important in this context is the recognition and protection of customary land systems and the commons; and of the rights of indigenous peoples to land and territory and to Free Prior and Informed Consent.

Voluntary Guidelines for Securing Sustainable Small-Scale Fisheries in the Context of Food Security and Poverty Eradication (FAO, 2014). www.fao.org/cofi/23885-09a60857a289b96d28c31433643996c84.pdf This international instrument was adopted in June 2014. Based on the increasing recognition of small-scale fisheries as a principal contributor to poverty alleviation and food security, the report recognizes that the tenure rights to land in the coastal/waterfront area are critical for ensuring and facilitating access to fisheries and for accessory activities. It further suggests that states should adopt specific policy measures to ensure the harmonization of policies affecting the health of marine and inland water-bodies and ecosystems and to ensure that fisheries, agriculture and other natural-resource policies collectively enhance the interrelated livelihoods derived from these sectors.

Voluntary Guidelines on Food Systems and Nutrition (ongoing process of the CFS). The guidelines are expected in 2020 based on the HLPE report on food systems and nutrition (HLPE, 2017)

Conventions and Other Binding or Non-Binding Instruments
The Convention on the Elimination of All Forms of Discrimination against Women (CEDAW) (UN, 1979) www.un.org/womenwatch/daw/cedaw/text/econvention.htm#part1 (see Preamble and Article 14 (on rural women): 'To enjoy adequate living conditions, particularly in relation to housing, sanitation, electricity and water supply, transport and communications'.

The Ecosystem Approach Principles adopted by the Convention on Biological Diversity (CBD, no date (c)) www.cbd.int/doc/meetings/cop/cop-09/media/cop9-press-kit-ea-en.pdf, especially
Principle 1: 'The objectives of management of land, water and living resources are a matter of societal choice'. 'Different sectors of society view ecosystems in terms of their own economic, cultural and societal needs. Indigenous peoples and other local communities living on the land are important stakeholders and their rights and interests should be recognized' … 'Decisions should be based on, and contribute to, inter-sectoral communication and coordination with clear implementation guidelines' (p. 9).
Principle 2: 'Management should be decentralized to the lowest appropriate level' Rationale: decentralized systems 'lead to greater efficiency, effectiveness and equity. Management should involve all stakeholders and balance local interests with the wider public interests'. 'With recognition of the various communities of interest in management'.

The Convention to Combat Desertification (UN, 1994) www.unccd.int/en/about-the-convention/Pages/Text-overview.aspx
Prologue: Mindful that desertification and drought affect sustainable development through their interrelationships with important social problems such as poverty, poor health and nutrition, lack of food security, and those arising from migration, displacement of persons and demographic dynamics, see in particular Articles 4: 1, 5, 10, 17 18, 19, 21 etc.

The UNECE Convention on Access to Information, Public Participation in Decision-making and Access to Justice in Environmental Matters (Aarhus Convention) (UNECE, 1998) www.unece.org/fileadmin/DAM/env/pp/documents/cep43e.pdf

> Ramsar Convention (Convention on Wetlands of International Importance especially as Waterfowl Habitats) (The Ramsar Convention on Wetlands, 1971) www.ramsar.org/cda/en/ramsar-documents-texts-convention-on/main/ramsar/1-31-38%5E20671_4000_0__
>
> UN convention on shared water courses (UN Watercourses Convention, 2014) www.unwatercoursesconvention.org/the-convention/ (especially www.unwatercoursesconvention.org/the-convention/part-ii-general-principles/)
>
> The United Nations Framework Convention on Climate Change (UNFCCC) is an international environmental treaty negotiated at the United Nations Conference on Environment and Development (UNCED) in 1992. Its objective is to 'stabilize greenhouse gas concentrations in the atmosphere at a level that would prevent dangerous anthropogenic interference with the climate system' (UN, 1992).

A human rights approach to water for FSN

The Human Right to Food and the Human Right to Safe Drinking Water and Sanitation are part of the international legal framework pertaining to water for FSN. A human rights approach to water for food security explores the linkages between the rights to food and water. It integrates human rights norms, standards and principles, into plans, policies and developmental processes related to water and food security at all levels. These include accountability, transparency, empowerment, participation, non-discrimination (equality and equity) and attention to vulnerable groups (UNHRC, 2008). Box 5.3 provides an overview of relevant international human rights instruments.

A human rights approach places emphasis on 'substantive' rather than formal equality: that is, all people, regardless of race, class, gender, or other differences should be allowed to enjoy their fundamental human rights, and this may require positive discrimination to favour the most vulnerable. Human rights thus guide states in mobilizing commitments to achieve effective access to and fairer use of a range of resources and in taking steps to empower people, especially the poorest citizens. Human rights are crucial in identifying injustices and, in framing remedies, can also assist in building social consensus and building political legitimacy. The approach offers guidance in formulating policies and programmes that address injustice and therefore are more likely to be accountable, equitable and sustainable, with the potential to eliminate extreme poverty. Indisputable causal links exist between the violation of human rights and the economic, social, cultural and political deprivations which characterize poverty. The realization of all human rights and efforts to eliminate extreme poverty are therefore mutually reinforcing, and human rights norms and principles can guide efforts to reduce, and ultimately eradicate, poverty (Sepúlveda and Nyst, 2012). Amartya Sen's capabilities approach focuses on 'substantive freedoms' – the freedom to choose a life one has reason to value. Human rights for Sen are entitlements to rights to certain specific freedoms, i.e. capabilities (2004) and these include both functioning (i.e. having access), as well as having the opportunity to make use of a good supply of water. This approach would also take a broad view of water (i.e. not just focused on water for survival and domestic purposes) and would link to local agency, and the right to determine and set one's own priorities and strategies regarding water (see Mehta, 2014).

All human rights impose three types of obligations on governments: namely to respect, protect and fulfil human rights in a non-discriminatory, participatory and accountable manner. With reference to water specifically, this means that states must: (i) refrain from interfering with or curtailing the enjoyment of existing rights of access to (enough safe) water; (ii) must protect individuals andgroups against human rights abuses in relation to their access to (enough safe)water; and (iii) must take action to enable people to get access to (enough safe) water for basic human needs (see also de Albuquerque, 2012). As with other economic and social rights, the RTW is to be 'progressively realized'. As such, states are obliged to take targeted steps to realize their human rights commitments in the case of water, despite political, economic and other constraints. Ensuring the accessibility of water, the quality of the water and the availability of the water are all crucial aspects of realizing the RTW.

The right to food (RTF)

The RTF was endorsed in the Universal Declaration of Human Rights (UDHR, 1948) and is also part of the International Covenant on Economic, Social and Cultural Rights (ICESCR, 1966). Writing on the transformative potential of the RTF, the UN special rapporteur on the RTF drew on the General Comment No. 12 on RTF (UNCESCR, 1999) and defines it as the right of every individual, 'alone or in community with others, to have physical and economic access at all times to sufficient, adequate and culturally acceptable food, that is produced and consumed sustainably, preserving access to food for future generations' (UNGA, 2014: 4).

The General Comment on the RTF further states that the right to adequate food imposes on the state parties the obligations to *respect*, to *protect* and to *fulfil*. States' obligation to *respect* existing access to adequate food requires states parties not to take any measures that result in preventing such access (UN CESCR, 1999; E/C.12/1999/5 para 15). Similarly, 'the obligation to *protect* requires measures by the state to ensure that enterprises or individuals do not deprive individuals of their access to adequate food'. Further, the obligation to *fulfil* (*facilitate*) means the state must proactively engage in activities intended to strengthen people's access to and utilization of resources and means to ensure their livelihood, including food security (UN CESCR, 1999 E/C.12/1999/5 para 15). Here too, extrapolating on these obligations to respect, protect and fulfil the means of food-production, it appears that the state parties have an obligation to protect the water resources from being diverted for other purposes, so that there is adequate access to water for subsistence farming and for securing livelihoods.

Especially in the case of indigenous peoples, the realization of the RTF is dependent not only on recognizing their individual rights but also on upholding their collective rights – the right not to be subjected to forced assimilation or destruction of their culture, their right to self-determination (by virtue of which they freely determine their political status and freely pursue their economic, social and cultural development), the rights to their lands, territories and resources, the right to maintain, control, protect and develop their cultural heritage, traditional knowledge and traditional cultural expressions (as well as the manifestations of their sciences, technologies and cultures, including human and genetic resources, seeds, medicines etc.) and their right to non-discrimination (UNGA, 2007). Thus, in the case of communities with distinct cultural traditions – most of them small-scale producers, pastoralists, fisher folks etc. – the call for food as a human right is intrinsically connected to the call for eliminating harmful policies and practices that prevent them from exercising their right to self-determination (FAO, 2009).

Moreover, the RTF also implies that the accessibility of food must be 'in ways that *are sustainable and do not interfere with the enjoyment of other human rights*' [emphasis added] (UN CESCR, 1999 E/C.12/1999/5 para 15). This implies that the activities and processes undertaken towards the realization of the RTF must respect the environmental limits (such as minimum flow requirements), and the carrying capacity of resources must not be at the cost of other human rights such as the RTW (priority for drinking water and sanitation in the community) or right to health (such as protection for agricultural workers from agro-chemicals). The special recognition given in General Comment No. 12 to the term sustainability when it comes to access and availability of food, implies that food should be accessible for both present and future generations (General Comment No. 12, paragraph 7). This could also be relevant for water use in agriculture (see Windfuhr, 2013). For example, if water resources are overexploited, leading to depletion or salinity in soils, food security cannot be sustained.

The General Comment on the RTF states that

> [f]inally, whenever an individual or group is unable, for reasons beyond their control, to enjoy the right to adequate food by the means at their disposal, States have the obligation to *fulfil (provide)* that right directly. This obligation also applies for persons who are victims of natural or other disasters.
>
> *[E/C.12/1999/5 para 15]*

To successfully implement this right, the Voluntary Guidelines on the RTF (VG 14 UN – Doc E/C.12/1999/5) call on states to develop strategies to realize the RTF, especially for vulnerable groups in their societies. No such guidelines exist for the RTW.

The right to water (RTW)

The human right to safe drinking water and sanitation was recognized by the UN General Assembly in 2010.[6] The emergence of this right was the result of a protracted struggle. Unlike other basic rights such as the RTF, the RTW and sanitation was not explicitly acknowledged in the 1948 Universal Declaration of Human Rights. Until the turn of the 21st century, there remained considerable resistance to the RTW on the part of some nations and corporations (see Mehta, 2014; Sultana and Loftus, 2015). It is telling that 41 nations including the USA, Canada and Australia abstained from recognizing water as a human right in 2010 (and these three countries have abstained up to now). Box 4.4 describing the risks of poor, black residents in parts of Flint, Michigan, demonstrated some of the challenges that might occur or be magnified if the RTW and sanitation is not recognized. Despite the long-overdue global recognition, the RTW remains conceptually ambiguous. For example, there have been heated debates about whether the RTW is compatible or not with parallel global trends of water commodification and privatization (see Sultana and Loftus, 2015). It is also still unclear what constitutes the RTW, i.e. in terms of the actual amount but also whether its narrow scope should be expanded to also look at wider livelihood and survival needs beyond domestic issues.

We focus on the latter issue and explore a broader definition and scope of the RTW. We respond to growing calls to elaborate a human rights perspective to water and food/land that encompasses the productive uses of water and is more interconnected than the current RTW (see Franco et al., 2013). While the water sector has traditionally separated water services from water resources or water for domestic and productive purposes (e.g. UNDP, 2006), many have argued that such distinctions are unhelpful (see also Mehta and Movik, 2014). By drawing on practices on the ground, the capabilities and other approaches as well as a range of legal provisions, we seek to break down such distinctions. We argue that such a broader conceptualization is more representative of how water is understood and embedded in the daily lives of local women and men around the world. In doing so, we build on calls from other authors, such as Van Koppen et al. (2017) and Hellum et al. (2015) who have argued for a broader conceptualization of the RTW. Work on multiple use services of water (MUS, see Box 5.4) also highlights the multiple linkages between water for food and production and livelihoods as they are manifest in the everyday contexts of communities around the world.

BOX 5.4 MULTIPLE WATER USE SERVICES

Research on multiple water user services (MUS) shows that when communities invest in infrastructure, they are more likely to build cost-effective multi-purpose infrastructure in order to enable a broad range of uses for multiple dimensions of well-being, which all directly and indirectly contribute to food security. Moreover, communities efficiently use and re-use multiple water

> sources. They manage these sources in conjunction, thus mitigating water variability. In contrast, the fragmented set-up of the public water sector implies that the different departments, divisions and programs operate in parallel as top-down silos, focusing on one single use only, either for water services for domestic uses and sanitation, or for irrigation, or for fisheries etc. The domestic sector seeks to reach everybody, in line with the human RTW for domestic uses and sanitation of 2010. However, the productive sectors have little ambition to meet at least everybody's basic productive water needs for basic food security. Food insecure women and men remain hidden behind the discourse of monolithic, homogenous sectors especially interested in aggregate production figures. Thus, there is no public 'owner' taking responsibility for water development to contribute to the human RTF and an adequate standard of living (Van Koppen et al., 2014). One solution is to 'climb the multiple use water ladder'. Instead of providing only 20 or 50 litres per capita per day, supposedly only for domestic uses, up to 50 or 100 litres per capita per day are provided to promote homestead-based productive uses. The incremental investments in such expansion can be repaid from the incremental income in half a year to three years (Renwick et al., 2007). This builds on what people in practice had already started doing with water provided ostensibly for domestic uses only. Hall et al. (2013) found in Colombia, Kenya and Senegal that between 71% and 75% of households were engaged in productive activities. Piped water supplies were a more important source than other water sources: between 54% and 61% of households used piped water for these productive activities. In Senegal and Kenya, this happened even though households only used a median of 23 and 31 litres per capita per day, respectively, barely more than the 20 litres per capita per day that are globally seen as the minimum for domestic uses only. This underscores the importance of small-scale productive uses for food security.

Mehta (2014) and Anand (2007) draw on Amartya Sen's capabilities approach to promote a holistic view regarding the RTW and its links with wider survival issues and livelihoods to highlight that the one cannot be guaranteed without the other. Capabilities refer to the 'actual living that people manage to achieve' (Sen, 1999: 730). This approach focuses on 'substantive freedoms – the capabilities – to choose a life one has reason to value' (1985, 1993, 1999: 74). Thus, at the heart of this approach one must look at the freedoms that an individual can enjoy. In his capabilities approach the focus is not on the quantity of the bundles of entitlements but instead on the principle of equality and capability to do and to be.

Sen has suggested the notion of basic capabilities which are a subset of all capabilities and encompass the freedom to do 'basic' things. As Sen says, basic capabilities help in 'deciding on a cut-off point for the purpose of assessing poverty and deprivation' (Sen, 1987: 109). They provide a kind of threshold or the minimum standard required for basic functioning and are useful for poverty/ wellbeing analysis. When translated to water, this would mean that a basic amount of water is required for basic human functioning (drinking, cooking, washing and to be free of disease) and it has been argued that this minimum requirement for human functioning should also capture livelihood and subsistence purpose (see Mehta, 2014).

The capabilities approach refrains from outlining what exactly this minimum threshold should be and evidence from the water sector in setting up standards around what constitutes a 'basic water requirement' highlights the variations by country and by institution. Basic water requirements have been suggested by various donor agencies and they range from 20 to 50 litres a day, regardless of culture, climate or technology. However, culture, climate, livelihoods and location (whether urban or rural) do matter. The WHO prescribes between 20 and 100 litres a day (WHO, 2003) and recognizes that below 50 litres can only reach a 'low' level of impact and that 100 litres is the minimum required for basic food and personal hygiene, though this amount excludes water for productive or survival activities such as growing food (Mehta, 2014). Clearly, the low-end provision takes a very narrow view of the water needs of the poor, inimical to the capability approaches' focus on human flourishing and freedoms which should also take into account livelihood and subsistence needs. Moreover, men's and women's ability to function on the basis of the same allocation of any one resource varies dramatically. People ultimately need different basic amounts of water to enjoy the same standard in terms of capability. Take the case of South Africa which was one of the first countries that explicitly recognized the RTW (see Box 5.5).

BOX 5.5 THE RIGHT TO WATER IN SOUTH AFRICA

South Africa was one of the first countries that explicitly recognized the RTW, and its Free Basic Water policy provided a minimum of 25 litres per capita per day based on a household size of eight people free (see McDonald and Ruiters, 2005). (It is now only provided to indigent families.) Implementing the RTW in South Africa has been fraught with difficulties and there are huge debates regarding whether it has had a significant impact on improving the well-being of poor South African citizens and how equitable it is (ibid., see also Flynn and Chirwa, 2005). First, there have been heated debates about whether the RTW is compatible or not with parallel trends of water privatization which have resulted in pre-paid meters, cut-offs and disconnections. These have been interpreted by many to run contradictory to citizens' basic RTW whilst also creating new forms of poverty and ill-being (see Flynn and Chirwa, 2005; Loftus, 2005; McDonald and Ruiters, 2005). There have also been debates concerning the sufficiency of 25 litres per day per person, especially if the number of household members is large. In rural

> areas, this has not been deemed to be sufficient for poor people to successfully maintain their livelihoods and escape the trap of poverty and HIV/AIDS. Others have argued that most poor households in South Africa do not enjoy a 'healthy environment' on the basis of the 25 litres provided. Instead, more like 80–100 litres are required per person for basic personal and food hygiene and this does not even take into account water for subsistence, which is crucial for poverty reduction and survival (see Flynn and Chirwa, 2005). South Africa, the first country to recognize RTW in its constitution, is also the only country that recognizes RTW for ecosystems to maintain a minimum flow (Ziganshina, 2008) through its unique concept of the ecological reserve.

Insights from General Comment No. 15

On November 27, 2002 the UNCESCR adopted the General Comment No. 15 on the RTW.[7] The Committee stressed the state's legal responsibility in fulfilling the right and defined water as a social and cultural good and not solely as an economic commodity. In July 2010 access to clean water and sanitation was recognized by the General Assembly of the United Nations as a human right. In September the UN Human Rights Council affirmed by consensus that the RTW and sanitation is derived from the right to an adequate standard of living, which is contained in several international human rights treaties and that is both justiciable and enforceable (UN, 2010).

It is important to note that, like the RTF, the RTW does not mean that water will be available for free to all. Instead, it implies obligations to respect, protect and fulfil the RTW. But it does mean that market-based mechanisms such as pricing tools should not harm people's basic rights to water. In water debates, the declaration of water as a human right was a key discursive shift. During the two preceding decades, water was framed around the so-called Dublin Principles, which largely stressed water as an economic good, amongst other principles concerning participation, sustainability and gender (see Nicol *et al.*, 2012). The long road in explicitly recognizing water as a human right has been attributed to a lack of political will and resources in this area when compared to investment in other sectors (UNDP, 2006).

> Since the poor – who suffer the most from a lack of access to improved water and sanitation services – tend to have a limited voice in political arenas, as is often argued, their claims for these services can be more easily ignored if the human RTW and sanitation is not explicit.
>
> *(Hall et al., 2014a: 852)*

Through the establishment of water as a human right, states have been obliged 'as duty bearers to ensure that every citizen has affordable access to water infrastructure services for drinking, personal and other domestic uses and sanitation' (Van Koppen et al., 2017: 130). The human rights emphasis also highlights the weaknesses of mainstream notions of efficiency that promote profit maximization and disregard associated social costs (Lobina, 2018).

As elaborated in the General Comment on the human right to drinking water and sanitation, everyone is entitled to sufficient, safe, acceptable, physically accessible and affordable water for basic personal and domestic use (UNCESCR 2002; E/C.12/2002/11 para 1). Further, the normative content of the RTW includes the right to maintain access to existing water supplies necessary for the RTW, the right to be free from interference, such as arbitrary disconnections or contamination of water supplies, as well as the right to a system of water supply and management that provides equality of opportunity to enjoy the RTW (E/C.12/2002/11 para 10). It is stressed that water should be treated as a social and cultural good, and not primarily as an economic good. Moreover, the realization of the RTW must be done in a sustainable manner, ensuring that the right can be realized for present and future generations.

While the development of the human right to safe drinking water and sanitation has been indeed largely focused so far on domestic water, the CESCR's General Comment No. 15 (GC 15) on the RTW has already identified other aspects of the RTW which have remained under-explored and under-developed. These include:

- The clear recognition that 'water is required for a range of different purposes, besides personal and domestic uses, to realize many of the Covenant rights. For instance, water is necessary to produce food (right to adequate food) and ensure environmental hygiene (right to health). Water is essential for securing livelihoods (right to gain a living by work) and enjoying certain cultural practices (right to take part in cultural life)' (GC 15, paragraph 6).
- The inextricable linkages of the RTW to the right to the highest attainable standard of health and the rights to adequate housing and adequate food. This understanding of the RTW calls to see it in conjunction with other rights enshrined in the International Bill of Human Rights, foremost amongst them the right to life and human dignity (GC 15, paragraph 3), and the rights enshrined in the Convention on the Elimination of All Forms of Discrimination Against Women and in the Convention on the Rights of the Child (GC 15, paragraph 4).
- The development of criteria to give priority in the allocation of water resources to the RTW for personal and domestic uses, and to the RTW in connection with the RTF and health to prevent starvation and disease as well as to meet the core obligations of each of the Covenant rights (GC 15, paragraph 6).
- The importance of ensuring sustainable access to water resources for agriculture to realize the right to adequate food, giving particular attention 'to

ensuring that disadvantaged and marginalized farmers, including women farmers, have equitable access to water and water management systems, including sustainable rain harvesting and irrigation technology' (GC 15, paragraph 7).
- The importance of taking note of the duty in article 1(2), paragraph 2, of the Covenant, which provides that a person may not 'be deprived of its means of subsistence. States parties should ensure that there is adequate access to water for subsistence farming and for securing the livelihoods of indigenous peoples' (GC 15, paragraph 7).
- Reference to the 'Statement of Understanding accompanying the United Nations Convention on the Law of Non-Navigational Uses of Watercourses' (A/51/869 of April 11, 1997), which declared that, in determining vital human needs in the event of conflicts over the use of watercourses 'special attention is to be paid to providing sufficient water to sustain human life, including both drinking water and water required for production of food in order to prevent starvation'.
- The importance of protecting natural water resources from contamination by harmful substances and pathogenic microbes, and the need to take steps on a non-discriminatory basis to prevent threats to health from unsafe and toxic water conditions (GC 15, paragraph 8).

A draft version of GC15 had a section which stated that '[t]he right to adequate food entitles an individual or group to secure the water necessary for the production of food' (in Winkler, 2017: 121). However, the two resolutions on the RTW by the UN General Assembly and the UN Human Rights Commission, as well as the final GC15 by the CESCR, decided on a rather narrow focus on safe drinking water, personal and other domestic uses and sanitation. This represents a political prioritization which does not adequately pay attention to other uses of water, for example by subsistence farmers. Hall *et al.* present three further possible explanations why the RTW for productive use has not been operationalized: i) 'water is just one input in productive activities, so benefits are more indirect'; ii) 'productive water uses vary and depend on highly diverse hydrological, technical, institutional, and socio-economic contexts' and iii) 'water use norms and practices tend to be overlooked in developing and operationalizing human rights law' (2014: 857–858).

Even though the Committee dropped the above-cited sentence for its final version, it still maintained a section on other uses of water such as water for subsistence farming. They directly linked this to the right of food, highlighting that efforts should be directed towards ensuring 'that disadvantaged and marginalized farmers, including women farmers, have equitable access to water and water management systems, including sustainable rain harvesting and irrigation technology' (CESCR, 2002, para. 7) (in Langford, 2005: 276). There is thus much scope to strengthen the interpretation and understanding of different aspects of the RTW, and of its inter-linkages with the RTF. A positive step in this direction was taken in 2018 when the UN General Assembly passed the resolution on the Rights of Indigenous Peasants and other People Working in Rural Areas (UN, 2018). It recognized the rights 'of peasants and other people working in rural areas' to water for personal and domestic use, farming, fishing and livestock keeping and to securing other water-related livelihoods, ensuring the conservation, restoration and sustainable use of water.

Convergences and conflicts

Both the General Comments on the RTW and the RTF converge in the prioritizing of the RTW, including sufficient water to produce food. For example, the General Comment No. 15 highlights how the RTW is inextricably related to the RTF and stresses that priority should be given to water resources required to prevent starvation and disease (see UNHRC, 2003 – E. CN.4/2003/54). The General Comment No. 12 notes the importance of ensuring sustainable access to water resources for agriculture to realize the right to adequate food. Both rights are also governed by humanitarian law and it is acknowledged that the destruction of water resources and distribution points during conflict situations can kill more people than actual weapons (see UNHRC, 2003). International water course law also clearly states that in the event of conflicts, human needs must be prioritized and attention should be paid to providing sufficient water to sustain human life (i.e. both for drinking water and water required for producing food to prevent starvation, ibid.). This is critical because more than 250 rivers on earth cross international boundaries and provide water for 40% of the world's population. Both rights also suggest that state parties should ensure that there is adequate access to water for subsistence farming and for securing livelihood needs of indigenous peoples, and that water should not be diverted for other needs at the cost of these communities.

In addition, human rights standards maintain that the costs of securing water and sanitation should not undermine a person's ability to acquire other essential goods and services such as food, housing, health services and education (COHRE, AAAS, SDC and UN-HABITAT, 2007). There is a tension present between such a reading and the international focus on environmental sustainability and protection of ecosystems where the setting aside of sufficient water to maintain aquatic ecosystem functioning may be seen to be in conflict with the right to sufficient water to grow food. Should this indeed be the case, the state is obliged to ensure that the RTF is met through other means.

Often difficult choices have to be made at the individual or household level when water is scarce. For example, in rural areas women often have to decide how much time to spend on water collection (RTW) vs food production or fuel gathering (RTF); or whether a girl child should help collect water (RTW) or go to school (right to education); similarly, in urban slums poor families have to apportion the money for meeting their food requirements vs. their water needs. Here, these rights are not in conflict with each other; rather each of these rights is being violated simultaneously.

Importantly, at the community or society level these rights sometimes conflict with each other. At times, especially under water-scarce conditions, when states attempt to fulfil RTW obligations of urban communities, the RTF and RTW of rural communities can be violated. With increasing urban migration and related urban development, water is often diverted away from rural areas and agriculture, including subsistence production systems, to meet urban water needs (Rosegrant and Ringler, 2000). In fact, many communities find both their RTW and the RTF violated as states pursue policies that protect the interests of their more powerful stakeholders or try to fulfil the right to development of some citizens (24/7 water, energy, infrastructure) over others who need to give up their lands and water resources in this process. Finally, as discussed elsewhere in this book investments in agriculture to ensure access to food and to realize the RTF can also affect some people's RTW or damage ecosystems.

These are competing trade-offs and pathways with different outcomes for different social groups. According to Windfuhr (2013), decision making needs to be determined by taking into account the priorities of vulnerable groups and their basic human needs. While domestic needs (i.e. water for drinking, bathing and hygiene) are usually given the highest priority, it is also important to prevent starvation. Accordingly, water for agriculture should first and foremost be allocated to disadvantaged and marginalized groups (something which is rarely the case in reality).

Another point that needs to be stressed is that the mandate of the Special Rapporteur on the RTF also includes tracking violations and this has been a powerful tool to counteract food-related injustices. The Special Rapporteur for food can respond to allegations with respect to violations and can also write to relevant governments to ask them to take action to ensure redress and accountability (UNHRC, 2003). The Special Rapporteur for water lacks this explicit mandate and thus far has largely focused on 'best practices'. This is probably due to the controversial nature of the RTW, the initial resistance to its existence on the part of many powerful (corporate) players and their ongoing convening power in the sector. Largely, the human RTW has not been deployed to focus explicitly on water management issues or the water implications of land and water grabs because of the limitation of its scope to domestic uses of water. This is in sharp contrast to the Special Rapporteur on the RTF who has in recent years frequently commented on land acquisitions and grabs and their impacts on local people's food security (see Franco et al., 2013).

One explanation could be that the office of the Special Rapporteur on the RTF was created in 2000 and had the mandate to help enhance food security in the world. The UN Food and Agricultural Organization contributed resources to help explain the normative content, state obligations and implications of the RTF and disseminated the information through its publications.[8] By contrast, UN Water, the inter-agency mechanism responsible for coordinated policy development in the area of water, has not been active in developing similar materials in the case of the RTW. The office of the Special Rapporteur on the RTW, created in 2008, thus needed to spend time defining the contours and implications of the work. The water Special Rapporteurs have also tended to take a narrower interpretation of the right, focusing largely on water services and domestic uses, and not necessarily forming alliances with civil society as the Special Rapporteurs on food have, for instance on the issue of land grabbing.

It is perhaps also fair to say that food discourses tend to be more political than water ones. Take for example the concept of food sovereignty which was developed and presented to the public in 1996 by La Vía Campesina, an international peasant organization: the Declaration on Food Sovereignty (La Vía Campesina, 1996).[9] The idea of food sovereignty exposes wider issues of social control and power in food systems (Patel, 2009) and stresses the role of the state as the guarantor of rights as well as the sovereignty of people and their agency in managing and creating local food systems and their claim-making capacities (see Mann, 2017). The notion of food sovereignty also acknowledges the socially constructed nature of scarcities to land, water and food and the importance of the rights of vulnerable food producers, especially rural women (ibid.).

Bridging the rights

There are early examples bringing together the rights to water and food that pre-date the official UN discourses. In 2010, Ziganshina asserted that 'the human RTW should be the basis for states' obligations to supply water not only for drinking and sanitation but also for the water-dependent livelihood needs of their residents' (Ziganshina, 2008: 117). This and similar assertions are backed up by those of already existing legal bodies, such as Article 14 of CEDAW which challenges the sharp distinction between water for domestic and for productive purposes (Hellum, Ikdahl and Kameri-Mbote, 2015). As Van Koppen et al. (2017) argue, even if the current prioritization of domestic water use persists, this still does not exclude the possibility for a rights-based approach regarding other uses of water (Van Koppen et al., 2017). They also claim that GC15 'implies a right to water for livelihoods with core minimum service levels for water to homesteads that meet both domestic and small-scale productive uses' (Van Koppen et al., 2017: 130). This has been taken up by some NGOs such as Bread for the World (Gorsboth, 2017) and as discussed earlier, most recently, it is also reflected in the UN Declaration on the Rights of Peasants and Other People Working in the Rural Area (United Nations, 2018). Its article 21.2 states that 'peasants and other people working in rural areas have the right to water for farming, fishing and livestock keeping and to securing other water-related livelihoods'.[10]

The Voluntary Guidelines on the Right to Food by the FAO mention in guideline 8 that 'States should facilitate sustainable, non-discriminatory and secure access and utilization of resources' (FAO, 2005: 16), listing water as an example. The High Level Panel of Experts on Food Security and Nutrition (HLPE)'s report on water for food security and nutrition (HLPE, 2015) calls on the Human Rights Council and its Special Rapporteurs (especially those concerning water, sanitation and food) to strengthen the realization of the RTW and to explore the implications of the linkages between water and food security and nutrition on the realization of human rights.

While discussing water as a human right in the Middle East and North Africa (MENA), Brooks (2007) argues that this concept is very old in MENA and goes back at least to the Code of Hammurabi in Babylon. The UN focus on the household and domestic uses of water is not very useful in a region characterized by sharp competition where average annual supply for the region is well under 1500 cubic metres per capita. Thus, he advocates consideration of the RTW to grow food and the RTW for a liveable environment (that is, water to support the ecosystem) (ibid.). Water's greatest use is for growing food and he argues that everybody should have a right to a sufficient quantity of water of decent quality 'to enable the growing of enough nutritious food for a healthy life' (Brooks, 2007: 233).

Some countries have already walked the talk. Bolivia combines the RTW and food in one article in its 2009 Constitution: 'Artículo 16. I. Toda persona tiene derecho al agua y a la alimentación'.[11] Ecuador states in its constitution that energy production cannot be promoted in opposition to the RTF and RTW.[12] In a comment on the RTW in Ecuador, the Ombudsman Office writes:

> The human right to water, due to its transversal nature in regards to other rights, especially the right to an adequate life, is directly linked to food, as human beings need water and food to survive and to guarantee adequate health. In this sense, there is a direct relationship between land tenure and access to water – understood as factors of production – since both are indispensable to a right to food.[13]

Hellum et al. (2015) list further countries that have joined the rights in their constitutions.

> By grouping of the RTW together with other social and economic rights (most importantly the RTF and health), the ICESR, the Maputo Protocol, and the Kenyan, South African and Zimbabwean constitutions imply a right to affordable and available water for personal, domestic and livelihood uses. All these international, regional, and national instruments recognize the indivisibility of human dignity, social justice, equality, and non-discrimination and protection of the poor and marginalized as basic principles.
>
> *(Hellum et al., 2015: 18–19)*

In Switzerland too, the RTW is considered a precondition to the enjoyment of the RTF.[14]

Despite this constitutional recognition, in reality, tensions between water for agriculture, urban use, mining and industry abound and often get in the way of ensuring the water and food security of indigenous and poorer populations (for Ecuador see Mena-Vásconez et al., 2017). Still, this human rights perspective to water, land and food can allow for legal claims and local struggles that can slowly help realize the RTW for livelihoods/subsistence (see Clark, 2017; Mehta and Ntshona, 2004). The history of human rights reveals that there is often a huge gap between rights talk and rights practice and that rights can only be realized through struggle and mobilization.

Rights under threat

While there have been several international initiatives to protect the interests of investors under the binding agreements such as those on trade and investment, there appears to be a lacuna in international agreements or covenants that protect communities affected by such international investments. In the context of increasing international investments and associated human rights violations, as well as other impacts on the lives and livelihoods of local communities, defining the extra-territorial obligations of the investors/home states is becoming important.[15]

In addition, with increasing globalization, the RTF of many communities is constantly under threat not only by the actions of national actors but also actors accountable to other states. Thus there is a need to look at the human rights obligations of states towards persons outside their territories, including the extra territorial private sector impacts.

ETO Consortium is an international network working on extra-territorial human rights obligations of states (ETO Consortium, no date). The terms of reference are based on the Maastricht Principles on Extraterritorial Obligations in the Area of Economic, Social and Cultural Rights, an international expert opinion (issued in 2011) which can serve as a source of international law according to article 38 of the Statutes on the International Court of Justice. The Maastricht Principles on ETOs lay down the states obligations to respect, protect and fulfil ESCRs extra-territorially. Several principles are especially relevant in the context of the RTF and RTW: 'States have the obligation to protect individuals ESCRs by regulating non-state actors (Principles 23–27). States are obliged to regulate and/or influence the business sector in order to protect those affected by them outside their territory'.

In the context of human rights violations associated with IFI investments, states parties have asserted in their submissions that

> the right to life not only emanates from specific international human rights treaties but that it now constitutes a general principle of international law. On account of this, the rights bind the entire international community and not just States Parties to human rights treaties.
>
> *(Gibney and Vandenhole, 2013: 209)*

Extending this argument would imply that extra-territorial obligations need to be assessed not only in the context of agriculture related investments but also other investments including through development cooperation or international trade when they impact the rights (RTF, RTW, right to life) of local communities. The land acquisitions on the part of foreign investors around the world are a good case in point. In some cases, there can be violations of both the RTF and the RTW (see also Chapter 1). The HLPE (2011) report on land tenure and international investments in agriculture states:

> As with land deals in general, little evidence exists which document the rights gained by investors over water. But the evidence which exists indicates that small-scale farmers may suffer greatly. As a result, awareness of water issues is paramount and because acquiring water rights is such a key issue in investment projects, they will invariably impact on water management for many inhabitants both up and downstream.
>
> (p. 22)[16]

Discussion and conclusions

This chapter has focused on exploring synergies between the rights to water and food. A core argument has been that a broader conceptualization of the right to water is more true to how water is understood and embedded in the daily lives of local women and men around the world. Local communities rarely distinguish between water for domestic and subsistence purposes. We have asked whether the right to water could be expanded to incorporate water for meeting individual and household food and nutrition requirements, with a focus on meeting the rights of the poor as a priority. Adopting this approach to the right to water as a conduit to achieving the right to food would fundamentally shift the current global discourse on water allocation in which water for economic purposes is given greater weight and priority than water for the self-provision of food for the poor. It would provide a substantial impetus towards the strong recognition of water as a social good and on the objective of first meeting the basic food and water needs of the poor. This presents an important opportunity to revisit how the right to water is conceptualized so that it intersects with and supports the right to food in ways that are sustainable, equitable and that respond to changing climatic conditions. The current definitions of the right to water are clearest on the need for potable water and water for sanitation, but there are emerging discussions on expanding the scope to address the importance of adequate water for ecosystem sustenance and subsistence agriculture. The alignment of the rights to food and water would prioritize the right to water for food production over water use for other uses, at whatever scale.

Food debates have been broader and more political and inclusive than water debates which have tended to be somewhat apolitical and which have not pushed for these wider interpretations. This includes the work so far of the Special Rapporteurs of water that have tended to promote a more narrow focus of the RTW. It is important for states to focus on productive uses of water and how these are key for the well-being and survival of vulnerable communities, and to protect them against dispossession through land and water grabs. We have shown how some countries and legal provisions are already embracing this broader scope. There are, of course, many tensions and competing trade-offs and pathways around broadening the scope that we have also highlighted in this chapter.

We are now nearly at the end of this book and it is worth revisiting some of the core discussions and arguments. This book has argued that without water there can be no food security and nutrition. Water is life. Water of sufficient quantity and quality is an essential input to agricultural production as well as to the consumption, preparation and processing of food. Safe drinking water and sanitation are fundamental to the nutrition, health and dignity of all. Water is what brings life to ecosystems, such as forests, lakes or wetlands that provide poor people with nutrition, and is fundamental for all other productive sectors, including energy and manufacturing. Millions of people around the world lack access to safe drinking water and adequate sanitation facilities, affecting their nutritional and health status. Even though accessible freshwater resources are adequate at global levels to meet the water needs of the world, these resources are unevenly distributed across the globe. From local to global, there is vast inequality in access to water, determined by socio-economic, political, gender and power relations that also affect food security and nutrition.

In Chapters 2 and 3 we argued that without improvements in agricultural water productivity, the world will need to substantially increase water withdrawals to produce more food. However, this is not inevitable and world food demands can be satisfied with available water and land resources by increasing water and land productivities through upgrading rainfed and irrigated systems; improving water use efficiency along food value chains; reducing waste; optimizing virtual water flows (trade) between countries based on comparative advantages; changing dietary patterns, and improving the efficiency of food processing and distribution.

To produce more food with less water, a paradigm change is needed in the way water is used in agriculture. It is not only technological advancements that are required but also national policies; they need to shift toward the maximization of agricultural water productivity while protecting the fundamental rights of communities, and institutions that are enabled for such a change. Agro-ecological approaches can help ensure that such a shift in focus is sustainable. Addressing water in agriculture at scale would allow for more water productive, equitable and efficient use. To address the negative impacts from climate change on water and agriculture requires interventions in both adaptation and mitigation. Research is still needed to address the impacts of increased water requirements, drought, intensive precipitation, soil erosion, and reduced soil water storage. Available technologies need to be better aligned with projected climatic changes, building on local knowledge and experience. A multi-scalar approach is required that allows for embracing both hydrological and social complexities while also taking into account local users' needs and perspectives. This will help ensure that water management practices are sustainable.

Substantial food security is achieved through trading virtual water. Especially in water scarce regions, importing food may be more efficient than producing locally and can reserve available water resources for more pressing needs and better options. This strategy however, may fail to ensure food security under certain conditions. During the food price crisis of 2007/08, prices spiralled out of control, reducing access to basic staples for countries relying on food imports. Unilateral and even international sanctions can affect the trade of food and the needed investment in water development for agriculture. Under those conditions, people, and especially the rural poor, have to rely on subsistence farming to survive. The ability and capacity of people to produce their food locally requires that water is available and that institutions are geared to respond. This is not to underestimate the importance of trading virtual water but to provide the alternative options for poor communities when politics pressure their livelihoods.

Problems and solutions around water for FSN are often conceptualized and framed in ways that neglect the needs and interests of poor, food insecure and marginalized women and men, including and especially children, and efforts across sectors are rarely joined up. Poor or vulnerable women's and men's capabilities and entitlements to water and food are neglected, together with their ability to ensure that the water and food needs of their children are met. It is important to address current inequalities in water and food supply, consumption and related distributional processes at global, national and local levels and focus on enhancing equity, gender and social justice around water for FSN.

Smallholder farmers produce more than 70% of the world's food but often lack recognition of their land and water rights in formal legal systems; women and girls often spend several hours a day collecting water but lack decision-making power when it comes to water management; indigenous peoples are often displaced from their lands and rivers as a result of large infrastructure projects; and the interests of fisher folk and pastoralists are rarely advanced in national policies. This is why mechanisms to allocate water need to give adequate priority to water for local food production as well as for the basic needs of the poorest populations and those pushed to the edges of society.

As demands on water increase, there is increasing corporate interest in protecting their interests from undue risk, as well as increasing pressure for available land and water in developing contexts. In such processes and transactions, states have a binding obligation to ensure that private and public sector investments, whether national or international, respect the human rights to water, sanitation and food of poor and marginalized communities.

Other emerging trends that interact with and affect the highly dynamic water–FSN linkages include the growing competition between food and energy over water resources, changing consumption and production patterns, and the potential and challenges around addressing food loss and waste. How each of these play out going forward could substantially improve – or reduce – food and water security of the poor.

In Chapter 4 we argued that effective water governance is crucial to ensure equitable and gender-just decision making and allocation processes around water. In reality, though, water governance processes tend to be highly political and are often fragmented. The politics of allocation are often biased by the ability of powerful actors to influence decision-making processes, making water grabbing an increasingly key issue to be addressed. Water, food and land governance regimes tend to be highly disconnected, often doubly disadvantaging marginal land and water users. While approaches such as IWRM and the nexus are intended to break down existing silos, they are often executed in a top-down manner and are difficult to implement, leaving the poor still marginalized. Water reform processes have often not served to enhance the water and food security of poor or vulnerable people – indeed, it can be argued that some water reform processes have further marginalized the water use of the rural poor. In addition, large-scale land acquisitions that have been taking place in recent years have often tended to displace local populations from their lands and water resources and increased local level conflicts.

There is a critical role for public sector funded research and development in the area of water for FSN, conducting research including into evidence-based policy improvements, integrated and adaptive management systems that incorporate indirect environmental externalities and are based on policy coherence across sectors, gender disaggregated data and monitoring systems and, critically, on the alignment of the RTW and the RTF. Of equal importance is that the research knowledge is translated into action in the implementation of water for FSN, which requires that the research outputs are appropriate to the needs of and accessible to end users, whether governments, water managers, private sector, or water users including small-scale farmers, especially in southern contexts. This requires the recognition by governments of the importance of research and development in this regard and the investment of public funds into the research sector. It is also important that this research is driven by context-specific (i.e. regional and local, rather than donor-driven) agendas and that national and local expertise is drawn on and built in the process.

The lack of integration in major global and national initiatives around water, land and food governance is also true of the human rights to water and food. We explored the relationship between the globally endorsed human right to safe drinking water and sanitation and the right to food, and spelt out key convergences and potential conflicts. We have pushed for an expansion of the RTW which would be more attuned to on-the-ground realities where local people tend not to separate water for domestic and productive purposes.

An early draft that we wrote for the HLPE report on water for food security and nutrition recommended exploring the synergies between the rights to water and food. We had proposed an expansion of the right to drinking water to include productive uses and possibly water for conserving ecosystem functions. This was widely criticized by key donors and also actors in the UN system, including the advisors on water and sanitation of the then Secretary General and the former Special Rapporteur of the Human Right to Safe Drinking Water and Sanitation. The argument was that many countries in the global South are currently struggling to realize the basic right to drinking water due to funding constraints, and an expansion of this right or indeed the existence of another right that focuses on water for livelihood or productive uses would impede the progressive realization of the RTW and create confusion and shift priorities and financial resources. We find this to be a weak argument. While financial constraints are often mentioned as the key reason that impedes the realization of basic rights, we believe the main problem lies in the lack of political will and accountability as well as the ability of powerful actors to violate vulnerable people's basic rights with impunity. We recall the initial resistance to the RTW in the 1990s and around the turn of the century which began to change slowly after the General Comment No. 15 emerged explicitly providing an authoritative interpretation of the RTW. But by 2010, water was declared as a fundamental human right by the UN General Assembly. This shows that ideas often rejected as utopian and impractical are realized when the time is ripe. Whether the RTW can be expanded to look at subsistence and productive uses while conserving ecosystem functions or whether there is a need for a separate human right for water for livelihood/subsistence purposes still needs to be worked out. However, we end this book in the hope that the key global players such as the World Committee on Food Security, the Human Rights Council and also the Special Rapporteurs on water, food and health will seriously explore pushing the linkages and synergies between the rights to water and food in order to ensure healthy and productive lives for all, for now and in the future.

Notes

1 Some of the ideas discussed in this chapter are also covered in Mehta and Langmeier (2019). The rights to water and food: Exploring the synergies. In Farhana Sultana and Alex Loftus (Eds.) *Water: Governance, Justice and the Right to Water.*
2 See www.globalresearch.ca/water-life/5633171 (accessed May 2019). www.indiaenvironmentportal.org.in/files/file/Corporatizing%20Water.pdf
3 See www.unwater.org/water-facts/transboundary-waters/ (accessed May 2019).
4 No mention of water is made beyond a single reference to the governance of water and other 'associated natural resources', such as for instance fisheries, by national states on basis of their own 'different models and systems of governance' (FAO, 2012: iv).
5 This leaves small-scale fishers vulnerable to other governance initiatives, which have the potential to facilitate 'ocean-grabbing' (see World Forum of Fisher Peoples (WFFP) and World Forum of Fish Harvesters and Fish Workers (WFF), 2013).

6 The RTW and to sanitation were jointly recognized by the 2010 UN General Assembly. In effect they are two different rights following the position of the Special Rapporteur on the Human Right to Safe Drinking Water and Sanitation (de Albuquerque, 2012: 27). In this chapter, we largely focus on the human RTW and not on sanitation issues.
7 General Comment No. 15, The right to water (arts. 11 and 12 of the International Covenant on Economic, Social and Cultural Rights), U.N. Doc. E/C.12/2002/11 (Twenty-ninth session, 2002)
8 www.fao.org/3/ap554e/ap554e.pdf
9 https://nyeleni.org/spip.php?article290
10 https://documents-dds-ny.un.org/doc/UNDOC/GEN/G18/038/14/PDF/G1803814.pdf?OpenElement Page12
11 'Article 16. I. Everyone has a right to water and food'. www.mindef.gob.bo/mindef/sites/default/files/nueva_cpe_abi.pdf
12 Art. 15. www.oas.org/juridico/pdfs/mesicic4_ecu_const.pdf
13 Translation by Daniel Langmeier http://repositorio.dpe.gob.ec/bitstream/39000/119/1/IT-005-EL%20AGUA%20COMO%20UN%20DERECHO%20HUMANO.pdf page 39.
14 www.eda.admin.ch/dam/deza/en/documents/themen/staats-wirtschaftsreformen/170500-human-rights-approach-water-sanitation_EN.pdf
15 This section is based on the work of the ETO consortium, especially their work on RTF. www.etoconsortium.org/en/about-us/eto-consortium/
16 In 2011, participants from 25 countries from four continents raised the issues of human rights violations taking place through land deals around the world and asked of governments to fulfil their obligations under the Universal Declaration of Human Rights, UN ESCR and UN CPR as well as raised the issue of extra-territorial obligations (see Wicht, 2011).

References

Allouche, J., Middleton, C. and Gyawal, D. 2014. Nexus Nirvana or Nexus Nullity? A dynamic approach to security and sustainability in the water-energy-food nexus. *STEPS Working Paper 63*. Brighton: STEPS Centre.

Anand, P. 2007. Right to water and access to water: An assessment. *Journal of International Development*, 19(4): 511–526.

Bach, H., Bird, J., Clausen, T.J., Jensen, K.M., Lange, R.B., Taylor, R., Viriyasakultorn, V. and Wolf, A. 2012. *Transboundary River Basin Management: Addressing Water, Energy and Food Security*. Lao PRD: Mekong River Commission.

Borras, Jr., S. and Franco, J. 2010. From threat to opportunity? Problems with the idea of a 'code of conduct' for land-grabbing. *Yale Human Rights and Development Law Journal*, 13(2): 507–523.

Brooks, D. 2007. Human rights to water in North Africa and the Middle East: What is new and what is not; what is important and what is not. *International Journal of Water Resources Development*, 23(2): 227–241.

Carrington, D. 2015. MPs to investigate TTIP trade deal's impact on environmental protections guardan. *The Guardian*. Available at: www.theguardian.com/environment/2015/jan/09/mps-investigate-ttip-trade-deals-impact-on-environmental-protections.

Clark, C. 2017. Of what use is a deradicalized human right to water? *Human Rights Law Review*, 17(2): 231–260.

COHRE, AAAS, SDC and UN-HABITAT. 2007. *Manual on the Right to Water and Sanitation*.

Conca, K. (eds). 2006. *Governing Water: Contentious Transnational Politics and Global Institution Building.* Global Environmental Accord: Strategies for Sustainability and Institutional Innovation. Cambridge, MA: MIT Press.

de Albuquerque, C. 2012. *On the Right Track: Good Practices in Realising the Rights to Water and Sanitation.* Available at: www.worldwatercouncil.org/sites/default/files/Thematics/On_The_Right_Track_Book.pdf.

Declaration of Nyéléni. 2007: Declaration from the Nyeleni Forum for Food Sovereignty held in Mali in 2007. Available at: https://nyeleni.org/DOWNLOADS/Nyelni_EN.pdf.

FAO. 2004. *Voluntary Guidelines to Support the Progressive Realization of the Right to Adequate Food in the Context of National Food Security.* Rome: FAO. Available at: ftp://ftp.fao.org/docrep/fao/meeting/009/y9825e/y9825e.pdf.

FAO. 2005. *Voluntary Guidelines to Support the Progressive Realization of the Right to Adequate Food in the Context of National Food Security.* Rome: FAO.

FAO. 2009. *The Right to Adequate Food and Indigenous Peoples: How Can the Right to Food Benefit Indigenous Peoples?* Rome: FAO. Available at: www.fao.org/3/a-ap552e.pdf.

FAO. 2012. *Voluntary Guidelines on the Responsible Governance of Tenure of Land, Fisheries and Forests in the Context of National Food Security.* Rome: FAO.

FAO. 2014. *Agriculture's Greenhouse Gas Emissions on the Rise.* Rome: FAO. Available at: www.fao.org/news/story/en/item/216137/icode/.

Flynn, S. and Chirwa, D.M. 2005. The constitutional implications of commercialising water in South Africa. In D. McDonald and G. Ruiters, eds. *The Age of Commodity: Water Privatization in Southern Africa*, pp. 59–96. London: Earthscan.

Franco, J.C., Mehta, L. and Veldwisch, G.J. 2013. The global politics of water grabbing. *Third World Quarterly*, 34(9): 1651–1675.

Gibney, M. and Vandenhole, W. (eds.). 2013. *Litigating Transnational Human Rights Obligations: Alternative Judgments*, 1 edition. Milton Park, Abingdon, Oxon: Routledge.

Gorsboth, M. 2017. *Wasserreport: Die Welt im Wasserstress – Wie Wasserknappheit die Ernährungssicherheit bedroht (Water Report: The World Suffers from Water Stress – How Water Scarcity Threatens Food Security).* Berlin: Brot für die Welt.

Hall, R.P., Van Koppen, B. and Van Houweling, E. 2013. The human right to water: The importance of domestic and productive water rights. *Science and Engineering Ethics*, 20(4): 849–868.

Hall, R.P., Van Koppen, B. and Van Houweling, E. 2014a. The human right to water: The importance of domestic and productive water rights. *Science and Engineering Ethics*, 20(4): 849–868.

Hall, R.P., Vance, E. and van Houweling, E. 2014b. The productive use of rural piped water in Senegal. *Water Alternatives*, 7(3): 480–498.

Hamm, B. 2001. A human rights approach to development. *Human Rights Quarterly*, 23(4): 1005–1031.

Hansen-Kuhn, K. May 2014. Trading away localization in TTIP. IATP. Available at: www.iatp.org/documents/trading-away-localization-in-ttip. Accessed 12 May 2019.

Hansen-Kuhn, K. and Suppan, S. October 2013. Promises and Perils of the TTIP: Negotiating a transatlantic agricultural market. IATP. Available at: www.iatp.org/sites/default/files/2013_10_25_TTIP_KHK.pdf. Accessed 12 May 2019.

Hellum, A., Ikdahl, I. and Kameri-Mbote, P. 2015. Against the current: Engendering the human right to water and sanitation. In A. Hellum, M. Kameri and B. van Koppen, eds.

Water is Life: Women's Human Rights in National and Local Water Governance in Southern and Eastern Africa. Harare: Weaver Press.

Hellum, A., Kameri-Mbote, P. and Van Koppen, B. (eds). 2015. *Water Is Life: Women's Human Rights in National and Local Water Governance in Southern and Eastern Africa*. Harare: Weaver Press.

HLPE. 2011. *Land Tenure and International Investments in Agriculture*. A report by the High Level Panel of Experts on Food Security and Nutrition of the Committee on World Food Security. Rome: FAO.

HLPE. 2015. *Water for Food Security and Nutrition. A Report by the High Level Panel of Experts on Food Security and Nutrition of the Committee on World Food Security*. Rome: FAO.

HLPE. 2017. *Nutrition and Food Systems*. A report by the High Level Panel of Experts on Food Security and Nutrition of the Committee on World Food Security. Rome: FAO.

ICESCR. 1966. UN General Assembly, 16 December 1966, United Nations, Treaty Series, *International Covenant on Economic, Social and Cultural Rights*, vol. 993, p. 3. Available at: www.refworld.org/docid/3ae6b36c0.html. Accessed 17 July 2019.

ICSID. 2016. Proceeding between Urbaser S.A. and Consorcio de Aguas Bilbao Bizkaia, Bilbao Biskaia Ur Partzuergoa (Claimants) and The Argentine Republic (Respondent) ICSID Case No. ARB/07/26 December 2016. pp. 308–310; pp. 316–322. Available at: www.italaw.com/sites/default/files/case-documents/italaw8136_1.pdf.

Jacobs, J. 2002. The Mekong River Commission: Transboundary water resources planning and regional security. *The Geographical Journal*, 168(4): 354–364.

Künnermann, R. and Monsalve Suárez, S. 2013. International human rights and governing land grabbing: A view from global civil society. *Globalizations*, 10(1): 123–139.

La Vía Campesina. 1996. The right to produce and access to land – Food sovereignty: A future without hunger. Available at: www.acordinternational.org/silo/files/decfoodsov1996.pdf. Accessed 12 March 2018.

Langford, M. 2005. The United Nations concept of water as a human right: A new paradigm for old problems? *International Journal of Water Resources Development*, 21(2): 273–282.

Lobina, E. 2018. Commentary on the European Commission's "Study on water services in selected member states". Technical Report. European Federation of Public Service Unions (EPSU).

Loftus, A. 2005. Free water as a commodity: The paradoxes of Durban's water service transformation. In D. McDonald and G. Ruiters, eds. *The Age of Commodity: Water Privatization in Southern Africa*, pp. 189–203. London: Earthscan.

Mann, A. 2017. Food sovereignty and the politics of food scarcity. In M.C. Dawson, C. Rosin and N. Wald, eds. *Global Resource Scarcity: Catalyst for Conflict or Cooperation?*, Chapter 8. Oxon, UK and New York: Routledge.

McCarthy, R. 2011. Executive authority, adaptive treaty interpretation, and the international boundary and water commission, U.S.–Mexico. *University of Denver Water Law Review*, 14(2): 197–299.

McDonald, D. and Ruiters, G. (eds). 2005. *The Age of Commodity: Water Privatization in Southern Africa*. London: Earthscan.

Mehta, L. 2003. Problems of publicness and access rights: Perspectives from the water domain. In I. Kaul, P. Conceição, K. Le Goulven and R.U. Mendoza, eds. *Providing Global Public Goods: Managing Globalization*, pp. 556–570. Oxford, UK: Oxford University Press.

Mehta, L. 2014. Water and human development. *World Development*, 59: 59–69.

Mehta, L. and Movik, S. 2014. Liquid dynamics: Challenges for sustainability in the water domain. *Wiley Interdisciplinary Reviews: Water*, 1(4): 369–384.

Mehta, L. and Ntshona, Z. 2004. Dancing to two tunes? Rights and market-based approaches in South Africa's water domain. *Sustainable Livelihoods in Southern Africa Research Paper Series*, no 17.

Mena-Vásconez, P., Vincent, L., Vos, J. and Boelens, R. 2017. Fighting over water values: Diverse framings of flower and food production with communal irrigation in the Ecuadorian Andes. *Water International*, 42(4): 443–461.

Mukhtarov, F. and Gerlak, A. 2013. Epistemic forms of integrated water resources management: Towards knowledge versatility. *Policy Sciences*, 2014, 47(2): 101–120.

Nicol, A., Mehta, L. and Allouche, J. 2012. Introduction: Some for all rather than more for some? Contested pathways and politics since the 1990 New Delhi statement. *IDS Bulletin*, 43(2): 1–9.

Nile Basin Initiative. 2015. *Nile Basin Initiative: About Us*. Nile Basin Initiative. [online] Available at: www.nilebasin.org/index.php/about-us/nile-basin-initiative.

Patel, R. 2009. Food sovereignty. *Journal of Peasant Studies*, 36(3): 663–706.

Ramsar. 1971. Convention on wetlands of international importance especially as Waterfowl Habitat. Available at: www.ramsar.org/sites/default/files/documents/library/curren t_convention_text_e.pdf.

Renwick, M., Joshi, D., Huang, M., Kong, S., Petrova, S., Bennett, G. and Bingham, R. 2007. *Multiple Use Water Services for the Poor: Assessing the State of Knowledge*. Arlington, VA: Winrock International.

Rosegrant, M.W. and Ringler, C. 2000. Impact on food security and rural development of transferring water out of agriculture. *Water Policy*, 1(6): 567–586.

Sen, A. 1985. Well-being, agency and freedom: The Dewey Lectures 1984. *The Journal of Philosophy*, 82(4), 169–221.

Sen, A. 1987. *On Ethics and Economics*. Oxford, UK: Basil Blackwell.

Sen, A. 1993. Capability and well-being. In M. Nussbaum and A. Sen, eds. *The Quality of Life*. Oxford, UK: Clarendon Press.

Sen, A. 1999. *Development as Freedom*. Oxford, UK: Oxford University Press.

Sen, A. 2004. Elements of a theory of human rights. *Philosophy and Public Affairs*, 32(4): 315–356.

Sepúlveda, M. and Nyst, C. 2012. The human rights approach to social protection. Ministry of foreign affairs: Finland. Available at: www.ohchr.org/Documents/Issues/EPov erty/HumanRightsApproachToSocialProtection.pdf. Accessed May 2019.

Seufert, P. 2013. The FAO voluntary guidelines on the responsible governance of tenure of land, fisheries and forests. *Globalizations*, 10(1): 181–186.

Suárez, S.M. 2012. The recently adopted guidelines on the responsible governance of tenure of land, fisheries and forests: A turning point in the governance of natural resources? In *Right to Food and Nutrition Watch: Who Decides About Global Food and Nutrition? Strategies to Regain Control*. Bread for the World, FIAN International, and Interchurch Organization for Development Cooperation (ICCO). Heidelberg, Germany: FIAN International, pp. 37–42.

Suárez, S.M. 2013. The human rights framework in contemporary Agrarian struggles. *Journal of Peasant Studies*, 40(1): 239–290.

Sultana, F. and Loftus, A. 2015. The human right to water: Critiques and condition of possibility. *Wiley Interdisciplinary Reviews: Water*, 2(2): 97–105.

UN. 1948. *The Universal Declaration of Human Rights* (UDHR). [online] Available at: www .un.org/en/documents/udhr/.

UN. 1979. *Convention on the Elimination of All Forms of Discrimination against Women*. UN Women. [online] Available at: www.un.org/womenwatch/daw/cedaw/text/econvention .htm.

UN. 1992. *Report of the United Nations Conference on Environment and Development*. Rio de Janeiro, 3–14 June 1992. Available at: www.un.org/documents/ga/conf151/aconf15126-4.htm. Accessed May 2019.

UN. 1994.UNCCD United Nations Convention to Combat Desertification in those Countries Experiencing Serious Drought and/or Desertification, Particularly in Africa, Paris, 14 October 1994.

UN. 2010. *General Assembly Adopts Resolution Recognizing Access to Clean Water, Sanitation as Human Right, by Recorded Vote of 122 in Favour, None against, 41 Abstentions*. [online] Available at: www.un.org/press/en/2010/ga10967.doc.htm. Accessed 12 March 2018.

UN 2018: United Nations Declaration on the Rights of Peasants and Other People Working in Rural Areas: resolution / adopted by the Human Rights Council on 28 September 2018. Available at: https://digitallibrary.un.org/record/1650694/files/A_HRC_RES_39_12-EN.pdf.

UN CESCR. 1999. *General Comment No. 12: The Right to Adequate Food (Art. 11)*, E/C.12/1999/5.

UN CESCR. 2002. *General Comment No. 15: The Right to Water (Arts. 11 and 12 of the Covenant)*, E/C.12/2002/11.

UN convention on the law of the non-navigational uses of international watercourses A/51/869 of 11 April 1997. Available at: www.un.org/law/cod/watere.htm. Accessed 12 May 2019, E/CN.4/2003/54.

UN General Assembly. 2007. *Resolution Adopted by the General Assembly on 13 September 2007-61/295*. United Nations Declaration on the Rights of Indigenous Peoples, A/RES/61/295.

UN General Assembly. 2014. *Report of the Special Rapporteur on the Right to Food, Olivier De Schutter – Final report: The transformative potential of the right to food*, A/HRC/25/57.

UN General Assembly. 16 December 1966. *International Covenant on Economic, Social and Cultural Rights*. United Nations. Treaty Series, vol. 993, p. 3. Available at: www.ohchr.org/en/professionalinterest/pages/cescr.aspx. Accessed 12 May 2019.

UN Women. 2014. *The World Survey on the Role of Women in Development 2014: Gender Equality and Sustainable Development*. New York: United Nations.

UNCCD. 2012. *Text of the Convention Including All Annexes*. [online] Available at: www.unccd.int/en/about-the-convention/Pages/Text-overview.aspx.

UNDP. 2006. *Beyond Scarcity: Power, Poverty and the Global Water Crisis*. Basingstoke, UK: Palgrave Macmillan.

UNECE. 1998. *Convention on Access to Information, Public Participation in Decision-Making and Access to Justice in Environmental Matters*. [online] Available at: www.unece.org/fileadmin/DAM/env/pp/documents/cep43e.pdf.

UNGA (United Nations General Assembly). 2015. Transforming our world: The 2030 agenda for sustainable development. Available at: www.un.org/ga/search/view_doc.asp?symbol=A/RES/70/1&Lang=E.

UNHRC. 2003. General Comment No. 15: The Right to Water (Arts. 11 and 12 of the Convenant). Adopted at the 29th Session of the Committee on Economic, Social and Cultural Rights on 20 January 2003.

UNHRC. 2008. *Building Resilience: A Human Rights Framework for World Food and Nutrition*. Promotion and protection of all human rights, civil, political, economic, social and cultural rights, including the right to development. Report of the Special Rapporteur on the right to food, Jean Ziegler. [online] Available at: www2.ohchr.org/english/issues/food/docs/A.HRC.9.23.pdf.

UNHRC. 2018. *Draft United Nations Declaration on the Rights of Peasants and Other People Working in Rural Areas*: Resolution / adopted by the Human Rights Council on 28 September 2018. Available at: https://digitallibrary.un.org/record/1650694/files/A_HRC_RES_39_12-EN.pdf.

United Nations Committee on Economic, Social and Cultural Rights. 2002. *General Comment No. 15: The Right to Water (Arts. 11 and 12 of the Covenant)*, E/C.12/2002/11.

Van Koppen, B., Hellum, A., Mehta, L., Derman, B. and Schreiner, B. 2017. Rights-based freshwater governance for the twenty-first century: Beyond an exclusionary focus on domestic water uses. In E. Karar, ed. *Freshwater Governance for the 21st Century*, pp. 129–143. New York: Springer.

Van Koppen, B., Smits, S., Rumbaitis Del Rio, C. and Thomas, J. 2014. *Scaling up Multiple Use Water Services: Accountability in the Water Sector*. London: Practical Action, IWMI/WLE – International Water and Sanitation Centre IRC – Rockefeller Foundation.

Varghese, D. 2017. *Investor–State Dispute Settlement: Millstone around Right to Water*. Minneapolis, MN: IATP.

WHO. 2003. The right to water. *Health and Human Rights Publication Series*, no. 3. Geneva: WHO.

Wicht, C. 2011. The world social forum in Dakar, 2011. Available at: http://la.indymedia.org/news/2011/03/245266.html.

Windfuhr, M. 2013. *Water for Food: A Human Rights Obligation*. Berlin: German Institute for Human Rights.

Winkler, I.T. 2017. Water for food: A human rights perspective. In M. Langford and A.F. S. Russell, eds. *The Human Right to Water: Theory, Practice and Prospects*. Cambridge, UK: Cambridge University Press.

World Forum of Fisher Peoples (WFFP) and World Forum of Fish Harvesters and Fish Workers (WFF). 2013. *Call for Governments to Stop Supporting the Global Partnership for Oceans (GPO) and Rights-Based Fishing (RBF) Reforms*. [Online] Available at: www.rtfn-watch.org/uploads/media/WFFP-WFF-Call-on-Governments_GPO_200313_01.pdf.

Ziganshina, D. 2008. Rethinking the concept of the human right to water. *Santa Clara Journal of International Law*, 6: 113–128.

INDEX

acceptability 153
access 6, 28–33, 192; conflicts 128; defining and measuring 10; dynamics of scarcity 24–25; equity 153–154; exclusion from 32; food security 12n2, 17, 18–19, 26, 41; GFFA Communique 68; hydrological complexity 23; India 69; inequitable 113; informal markets 136; irrigation 101; to land 134; local organizations 71; Palestine 129; right to food 165, 178–179, 186, 187, 189; right to water 178, 183, 184–185; socio-economic factors 65, 153; as socio-political construct 31–33; Sustainable Development Goals 173, 174; water governance 123, 124, 129–132, 152; water security 16–17, 22, 26; water storage continuum 45
accountability 9–10, 33, 123, 168, 177, 178
accounting 8
adaptive management 71
adaptive multi-paddock grazing (AMP) 93
adequacy 153
administrative boundaries 70; *see also* boundaries
Africa: agriculture 1; animal-source foods 51; barriers to access 29; Chinese financing of infrastructure 167; climate change 80, 82; Coca-Cola 146; dams 143; data-poor environments 7; drinking water and sanitation 38; droughts 42; food insecurity 19; food waste 52; hydrological complexity 23; irrigation 26, 27, 76, 77, 105; land grabs 148; open defecation 40; pastoralism 79, 108–109; permit systems 138, 139; population 22; Post Harvest Losses 51–52; rainfed agricultural systems 75; rural population growth 21; water markets 136; women and gender discrimination 76, 131–132
African Americans 129–130
agency 153, 178, 188
agriculture 1–2, 190; AQUASTAT database 8; China 152; climate change 80–83; demands from 3, 22, 45; dietary changes 49; economic value of water 137; energy competition 46, 47; foreign investments 171; GFFA Communique 173; groundwater extraction 47; improving water productivity 89–96, 192; irrigated systems 76–78, 82, 89, 100–107; land grabs 148; Mekong River Commission 169; national policies 150; pastoral systems 78–79, 82–83, 107–112; pollution from 33–34, 35, 55n3; poverty reduction 20; rainfed systems 27, 36–37, 75–76, 81–82, 89, 96–100; right to food 184–185, 187; social movements 168; Sustainable Development Goals 173; trade 21; urban systems 79–80; vulnerable groups 187; water governance 125, 127; water management 65–132; water pricing 147; water quality 18; women 131–132; *see also* food production; livestock
agroecology 71–75, 80–83, 96, 102, 113, 140, 192

Index

Albania 8
algal blooms 75
allocation 17, 193; conflicts 128; gender discrimination 131; global discourse on 191; inequitable 113; water governance 123, 124, 125–127, 150, 153, 194
Allouche, J. 140
Amazon region 43–44
anaemia 20
Anand, P.B. 181
Angola 8
animal feed 49–51, 55n3, 74–75, 92–93, 107–108, 112; *see also* livestock
Ansar, A. 143
aquaculture 93–94, 106–107
AQUASTAT database 8
aquifers 21, 45, 97, 144; brackish water 104; irrigation 101, 105–106; rainwater harvesting 99
Argentina 49, 144, 172
Aronson, J. 109
Asia: animal-source foods 51; climate change 82; drinking water and sanitation 39; food insecurity 19; food waste 52; hydrological complexity 23; irrigation 26, 76, 105, 106; meat consumption 50; open defecation 40; rainfed agricultural systems 75; salinization 77; water markets 136; water resources 4, 22; women 76; *see also* Central Asia; East Asia; South Asia; Southeast Asia
Australia: drinking water and sanitation 39; hydrological complexity 23; market-based allocation 126–127; right to water 180; water governance 135, 136; water rights 134
availability: climate change 43; fluctuations 149; food security 12n2, 17, 18–19, 26–28, 41; hydrological complexity 23; rainfed agricultural systems 75; right to water 178; Sustainable Development Goals 173; variations in 4; water governance 152; water security 16–17, 22, 26

Bangladesh 22, 136, 151
Barling, D. 153
Barrett, C.B. 51–52
basins 5, 7, 69–70, 89, 91, 124, 142
Bell, A.R. 136
benefit sharing 70
beverages 145, 146–147
biodiversity: agroecology 72, 74; concentrated animal feeding operations 75; ecosystem services 109; pastoral systems 79; rainwater harvesting 112; water governance 123
biofuels 46, 47, 68, 149, 150
biomass 66, 85
Bjornlund, H. 135
blue water 21, 148; biofuel 47; climate change 82; economic water productivity 91; water footprints 93
Bolivia 1, 189
Botswana 108
bottled water 145, 168
boundaries 70, 124, 142, 149, 186; *see also* transboundary issues
brackish water 66, 103–104
Brazil 42, 43–44, 49
Brooks, D. 189
Bues, A. 149
Burchi, S. 139
Burkina Faso 36–37, 99, 132

C4 crops 90
California 107
CAM crops 90
Cambodia 80, 169
Canada 180
canals 101, 104
capabilities 177–178, 181–182
carbon dioxide (CO_2) 27, 43, 80–82
Caribbean 27, 39
caste system 32, 131, 153
catchments 142
Central America 42
Central Asia: animal-source foods 51; drinking water and sanitation 39; groundwater irrigation 106; salinization 77
centralization 124
CGIAR Comprehensive Assessment of Water Management in Agriculture (CA) 13n5, 92, 105
CGIAR Dryland Systems 107
Chad 108
Cherlet, J. 137
children 1, 4, 34–35, 40–41, 51
Chile 134, 135
China: dams 143; dietary changes 49–50; food security 152; hydrological complexity 23; infrastructure financing 167; irrigation 26, 76, 105, 106; water rights 134
circular economy 73
civil society 168, 171, 188
class 16, 32, 65, 129–130

climate change 3, 4; adaptation and mitigation 45, 192–193; agricultural water demand 27; agroecology 72; biofuels 47; CGIAR initiatives 167; competition for water 125–126; FSN stability 41, 42; impact on agroecosystems 80–83; improving water productivity 89; India 69; irrigation 27, 97; livestock production 50; Paris Climate Agreement 68; policies 5; rainwater harvesting 99–100, 110, 112; Southern Africa 48–49; United Nations Framework Convention 177; water availability 43; water management 66
co-management 113
Coca-Cola 145, 146–147, 167
collective action 71, 73, 126
Colombia 149, 181
Committee on World Food Security (CFS) 170
commodification 3, 154, 180
Common Property Resources (CPR) 133
the commons 123, 168
community-based management 99
competition 4–5, 125–126, 152
concentrated animal feeding operations (CAFOs) 50, 74–75, 92, 93
conflicts 5, 31, 128–129; decentralization 141; international law 186; land acquisitions 194; between rights 186–187; upstream-downstream 110–111; water allocation 126; water grabbing 151; water user associations 103
conjunctive use systems 100
conservation: agroecology 73; basin management 70; collective 112; dams 143
Consultative Group for International Agricultural Research (CGIAR) 6, 107, 166, 167
consumption patterns 8, 28, 49–51, 113, 194
contamination 50, 80, 151, 185; see also pollution
Convention on Biological Diversity (CBD) 5, 72, 176
Convention on the Elimination of All Forms of Discrimination against Women (CEDAW) 176, 184, 188
Convention on the Law of Non-Navigational Uses of International Watercourses 169, 185
Convention on the Rights of the Child 184
Convention to Combat Desertification 176

corporatization 53–54, 144–148, 154
costs: dams 143; human rights standards 186; irrigation 103; labour 96; rainwater harvesting 110, 112
crop architecture 66
crop breeding 85–87, 90
crop failure 41–42
Cui, X. 49
cultural norms 6, 32, 88, 103
culture: agroecology 73; indigenous people 179; right to water 184; water allocation 126; water governance 129

dams 25, 108, 142–144, 155n3, 168; see also hydropower
data 7–8, 9
De Schutter, O. 149
decentralization 73, 124, 141–142, 176
decision making 125, 151, 193; global level 165, 166; participation 124, 127; politics of allocation 194
deforestation 44
demand for water 4, 22, 27, 28; agriculture 45; groundwater irrigation 106; growth in 65; managing 88; policies 25; urbanization 40; water management 66
Democratic Republic of the Congo (DRC) 24
demographic changes 3
depletion 84, 90, 92
desalination 104, 105, 151
desertification 109, 176
Developmental Water Management (DWM) 140
diets: balanced 113; changing 6, 28, 49, 54, 192; diversification 34; water content 36–37
disabled people 132
disaster planning 70
discrimination 9, 32, 130–132, 134
disease 1, 3, 18, 25; access to water 31; global burden of 34–35; irrigation 27, 29; see also health
diversification 66–67, 97, 113, 140
diversity 73, 74
Domènech, L. 29
domestic use 2, 4, 10, 141, 181, 184, 188–189, 191, 194
Dominican Republic 131
drainage water 83, 87, 91, 101–102, 103–104; see also wastewater
drinking water 35, 39, 192; Flint 130; international law 186; lack of access to 3; right to 2, 172, 177, 183–184, 195;

SDGs 38; Sustainable Development Goals 173; UN agencies 167
drip systems 87–88, 102
droughts 41–42, 43–44; Australia 135; California 107; climate change 81, 82, 83; drought tolerant crop varieties 87; need for research and development 113; pastoral systems 78; Southern Africa 48; urbanization 40
drylands 51, 78–79, 81, 107–109, 110, 112
Dublin Principles 137, 145–146, 167, 183
dust storms 79, 108

East Asia 26, 39, 105
ecological sanitation (eco-san) 74
economic growth 25–26, 89, 143, 152
economic productivity 90, 91–94
economic value 53, 124, 137, 145–146, 183, 191
economic water scarcity 24
Ecosystem Approach Principles 176
ecosystem services 107, 108, 109
ecosystems 2, 3, 192; agricultural 75–80; agroecology 73; degradation of 108; integrity 18; marginal quality water 104; protection of 186; right to water 183, 195
Ecuador 150, 189
efficiency *see* water efficiency
Egypt 83, 87, 101–102, 104
El Salvador 144, 171–172
elderly people 132
electricity 25, 27, 28, 68; *see also* energy
emergent contaminants 34, 35
employment 76, 80, 91; *see also* livelihoods
empowerment 29, 33, 77, 103, 173, 177
energy 3, 46–49, 194; basin management 70; demand for water 28; global policies 67; irrigation 102, 106; policies 5; water-energy-food nexus 140–141; water governance 123; *see also* hydropower
The Energy and Resources Institute (TERI) 146
environmental degradation 78–79, 83, 92, 107–109, 110, 142
environmental justice 6
Environmental Protection Agency (EPA) 70
equality 33, 177, 189
equity 9, 33, 177, 193; access 153–154; China 152; dams 143; decision making 127; informal markets 136; irrigation 78, 101, 106; Mekong River Commission 169; rainfed agriculture 100

Ethiopia 10, 36–37, 42, 108, 144, 149
ETO Consortium 190, 196n15
Europe: drinking water and sanitation 39; droughts 42; food waste 52; hydrological complexity 23; irrigation 76; rainfed agriculture 75
European Commission 5
eutrophication 33, 50, 74–75
evaporation 85–86, 87–88, 90, 102, 107, 110
evapotranspiration 16–17, 21, 45; biofuels 47; climate change 80–81; crop yields 85; irrigation 101; monitoring 66
exports 21, 68, 69, 85, 97–98
extra-territorial obligations 190–191, 196n16

Falkenmark, Malin 24
famine 6
Fargher, W. 135
fertilizers 18, 33–34; agroecological approaches 74; human excreta 74; irrigation 29; management 35; rainfed systems 96; wastewater 48
fisheries 45, 94, 106–107, 143, 175–176, 195n5
Flint 129–130, 180
flooding 5, 41, 43; Australia 135; climate change 81, 82, 83; flash floods 113; urbanization 40
food: contamination of 80; demand 6, 89, 96; energy use 46; losses and waste 51–53; street food vendors 35, 129; variability in supply 45; water-energy-food nexus 140–141; water footprints 84; *see also* food production; food security; food security and nutrition; right to food
Food and Agriculture Organization (FAO): agroecology 72–73; AQUASTAT database 8; food insecurity 21; food security 28; food waste 52; livestock production 51; methodological problems 9; right to food 187, 188–189; street food vendors 35; voluntary guidelines 175–176, 188–189
food availability decline (FAD) 6, 31–32
food insecurity 19, 20, 21, 23
Food Insecurity Experience Scale (FIES) 21
food preparation 25, 35, 47, 128, 141, 192
food processing 6, 18, 26, 89, 192
food production 5, 25, 28, 192; conflicts 128; food sovereignty movement 154; international law 186; multi-purpose

206 Index

infrastructure 141; private sector 154; right to water 184, 189, 191; Sustainable Development Goals 173; virtual water 84; water footprints 84; water re-allocation 126; *see also* agriculture
food security 1; dams 143; definition of 12n2; fisheries 106, 107; gender discrimination 131; governance 153; improving water productivity 89; informal water uses 139; international agreements 170–173; national policies 151–152; Sustainable Development Goals 173; transboundary governance 169; urban agriculture 79–80; virtual water 193; voluntary guidelines 175; water productivity 84; water scarcity 91–92
food security and nutrition (FSN) 2, 6, 11–12, 16–64, 65, 192; challenges 3–5; consumption and production patterns 49–51; corporatization 53–54; energy competition 46–49, 194; global governance 166–168; human rights approach 177–178, 189, 195; increase in water scarcity 113; losses and waste 51–53; marginalized groups 193; methodological problems 7; national policies 150, 151; pillars of 25–26; research and development 194; stability 41–45; tradable permits 134–135; transboundary issues 168–170; utilization 35–41; water governance 123–125, 153–154; water management 67; water pricing 103; water quality 33–35
food sovereignty movement 154, 188
food systems 54n1, 85
foreign investment 5, 171, 191
forests 28, 44, 51, 96, 123, 175, 192
Fox, Vicente 147
fracking 46–47, 148

G8 Land Transparency Initiative (G8LTI) 170
Gasteyer, S. 129
gender 6, 16, 193; access to food 65; access to water 29, 134, 192; dynamics of scarcity 25; fisheries 106; inequalities 3, 4, 10, 20–21, 32; irrigation 30–31, 76–77; national policies 152; power relations 144; Sustainable Development Goals 173, 174; water allocation 126; water governance 131–132, 153; water management 113; *see also* women

General Comment No.12 178, 179, 186
General Comment No.15 (GC 15) 165, 183–185, 186, 195
Gerbens-Leenes, P.W. 93
Ghana 132, 139, 149
Gibney, M. 190
glacial meltwater 82
Global Environmental Facility 166
Global Forum for Food and Agriculture (GFFA) 2, 68, 173
Global Harvest Initiative 5
global South: cultural norms 32; formal and informal practices 133; groundwater extraction 47; Integrated Water Resources Management 137; irrigation 76, 88, 102, 104; land and water grabbing 149; population growth 4; Post Harvest Losses 52; poultry 93; private sector involvement 145–146; trade relations 153; urbanization 40; water pricing 147; water productivity 84; water quality 34; women 10, 100
Global Water Partnership (GWP) 137, 166, 167
globalization 190
Gobi Desert 79, 108
governance 3, 5, 6, 12, 123–164, 194; access to water 129–132; agroecology 73; corporatization 54; dams 142–144; global 165, 166–168; India 69; international agreements 170–173; land and water grabbing 148–150; land rights 134; local 71; national policies 150–152; permit systems 134–136; politics of allocation 125–127; private sector and corporate involvement 144–148; reform processes 136–142; transboundary 168–170; voluntary guidelines 175; water rights 132–133
government allocation 126
grain imports 68
grain prices 66, 67
grazing management 109
green water 2, 8, 21, 96–100, 148; biofuel 47; climate change 82; economic water productivity 91; water footprints 84, 93; *see also* rainfall
Grey, D. 42
grey water 66, 93
groundwater 144, 148; Bangladesh 151; basins 69; climate change 43, 80–81; Coca-Cola 146; informal markets 136; irrigation 25, 26–27, 28, 47, 87, 97, 101–102, 105–106; overextraction 92,

106, 134; rainwater harvesting 99; saltwater intrusion 78; UN Water 166–167
Group of Eight (G8) 170
Group of Twenty (G-20) 2
Gulf Countries 67, 105

Halden, R. 55n3
Hall, R.P. 165–166, 181, 183, 185
Harris, F. 36
Headey, D. 41
health 2, 3; economic water productivity 91; food contamination 80; pollution 25; right to water 165, 184; urban agriculture 79; *see also* disease
Hellum, A. 165–166, 180, 189
High Level Panel of Experts on Food Security (HLPE) 30, 52, 54n1, 148, 189, 191, 195
Hilhost, T. 80
HIV/AIDS 183
Hodgson, S. 138
Hoekstra, A.Y. 84, 92
Houdret, A. 149
Human Development Report 2–3, 10, 25, 32, 144
human excreta 74
Human Right to Safe Drinking Water and Sanitation (HRSDWS) 177, 180, 184, 194, 195, 196n6
human rights 11, 12, 33, 154, 165, 177–195; Bolivia 1; international instruments 174–177; investment tribunals 172; lack of political will 3; private sector regulation 145; STEPS pathways approach 6; violations 2, 190, 196n16; water governance 124; water grabbing 53; *see also* right to food; right to water; rights
Hungary 167
hunger 6, 20, 31–32, 41–42, 173
hydrofracking 46–47, 148
hydrological complexity 23
hydrological cycle 16–17, 18
hydropower 46, 47–49, 142–144, 150, 167

identity 126, 129
imports 68, 85, 97–98, 152, 193
India: caste system 131; Coca-Cola 145, 146–147; dams 25, 143–144; diets 36; food contamination 80; gender 30; groundwater irrigation 26, 28, 106; Indus Waters Treaty 170; lower caste women 32; meat consumption 50; saltwater intrusion 78; tradable permits 136; water allocation 127; water scarcity 68–69
indigenous knowledge 111
indigenous people 1, 190; access to water 186; Amazon region 44; climate change 42; displacement of 193; ICESCR 185; land and water grabbing 149; livestock production 51; right to food 179; structural violence 33; UN Declaration 175; water governance 135
Indus Basin Irrigation System 147
Indus Waters Treaty (IWT) 170
industry 1, 4, 25–26, 32, 190; economic value of water 137; percentage of water use 2; water for production 10; water governance 127
inequality 4, 32–33, 192, 193; China 152; defining and measuring 10; gender 3, 4, 10, 20–21, 32; Sustainable Development Goals 9; water scarcity 6
informal settlements 1, 40
infrastructure: access to water 17; conflict situations 128; displacement 193; drinking water and sanitation 40; hydrological complexity 23; Integrated Water Resources Management 137–138; irrigation 44, 101; lack of 22, 24; multi-purpose 141, 180; storage 45; UN Water 166–167; water allocation 126; water governance 123, 126
institutions 133
insurance 66–67
Integrated Water Resources Management (IWRM) 7, 137–140, 141, 166, 194
interdisciplinary approaches 71–72
Intergovernmental Panel on Climate Change (IPCC) 27, 42, 81
international agreements 170–173, 190
International Centre for Settlement of Investment Disputes (ICSID) 171–172
International Conference on Water and the Environment (ICWE) 136–137
International Covenant on Economic, Social, and Cultural Rights (ICESCR) 174, 178, 184–185, 189, 196n16
International Finance Corporation (IFC) 167
International Law Association (ILA) 169
International Union for the Conservation of Nature (IUCN) 166, 167
International Water Association (IWA) 167
International Water Management Institute (IWMI) 167

investment: extra-territorial obligations 190–191; hydrological complexity 23; international agreements 171–173, 190; irrigation 77, 88, 97, 101, 113; rainfed agriculture 100; rural areas 148; sanitation and drinking water 31; *see also* foreign investment
Investor-State Dispute Settlement (ISDS) 171
Iraq 77
irrigation 1, 2, 76–78; access 28–31; AQUASTAT database 8; China 152; climate change 82; customary rules 139; deficit 90, 92, 94, 95–96, 99; demand for water 4; droughts 42; drylands 107; global food production 26; groundwater 25, 26–27, 28, 47, 87, 97, 101–102, 105–106; improving water productivity 90, 92, 94–96, 100–103, 192; India 25; informal markets 136; infrastructure 44; marginal quality water 103–105; modernization 87–88, 100, 101, 102, 113; supplemental 90, 96–100; Tanzania 150; urban agriculture 79, 80; water efficiency 83–84, 87; water for production 10; water governance 125; water management 65–66; water quality 18, 34, 35
Israel 23, 128–129, 149, 167

Jamaica 144
Japan 23, 108
Jawahar, P. 34
Joint Monitoring Program (JMP) 38, 167
Jordan 88, 92, 104, 111–112, 128, 151–152

Kemerink, J.S. 142
Kenya 79, 99, 108, 139, 181, 189
knowledge 7–8, 11; agroecology 73; food sovereignty movement 154; indigenous 111; water management 74
Koran 1

land: access to 134; corporatization 53–54; foreign investment 191; land degradation 51, 78–79, 81, 83, 107–109, 110; land grabbing 53, 133, 148–150, 171, 187, 188, 192; land productivity 6, 94–95, 102, 113; rights 168, 189, 193; voluntary guidelines on governance of tenure 175; water governance 141; women's ownership 76; *see also* tenure
landscape management 71
Lang, T. 153

Laos 169
Latin America: animal-source foods 51; drinking water and sanitation 39; hydrological complexity 23; irrigation 27, 76, 105; rainfed agricultural systems 75; *see also* South America
Learning and Practice Alliances 100
least developed countries 39
Lefore, N. 29
legal pluralism 133, 138
Lein, H. 151
Lesotho 48
licensing 134, 138
livelihoods 2, 153; economic water productivity 91; irrigation 76; legal pluralism 133; right to water 184, 186, 188, 190, 195; water governance 125; water re-allocation 126
livestock 78–79, 107–112; access to water 28–29; agroecological approaches 74–75; anti-microbial use 34; climate change 82–83; droughts 41; feed consumption 92–93; impact of dams 143; improving water productivity 90, 92; pollution 55n3; rights 186; trends in production 49–51; *see also* pastoralism
local needs 154
local organizations 70–71
local ownership 113
London 79–80

Maastricht Principles on Extraterritorial Obligations in the Area of Economic, Social and Cultural Rights 190
Maharashtra 127, 136
malaria 25, 27, 29
Malawi 48, 132, 139
Mali 108
Malmquist, L. 36–37
malnutrition 20, 53, 81
marginal quality water 103–105
marginalized groups 4, 54, 130–131, 149, 152; access to water 2, 3, 17, 31; governance of the commons 123; livestock production 51; neglect of 193; rights 189; structural violence 3, 33; water for agriculture 187; water governance 124; water reform processes 194
markets 44–45, 96, 103, 124, 126–127, 136; *see also* permit systems
Mauritania 108
McKeon, N. 153, 154
measurement issues 83–85, 86

meat consumption 49–50, 152; *see also* livestock
Mehta, L. 25, 33, 181
Meinzen-Dick, R.S. 136
Mekong River 143, 169
Mekonnen, M.M. 92
Merrey, D.J. 139
Mexico 42, 147, 170
micro-irrigation 74
Middle East: animal-source foods 51; desalination 104; dust storms 79, 108; ecosystem degradation 108; grain imports 68; groundwater irrigation 26, 105; human rights approach 189; hydrological complexity 23; pastoral systems 78–79; rainfed agricultural systems 75; water resources 4, 22; water technologies 66
Millennium Development Goals (MDGs) 5, 9, 10, 38–40, 173, 174
mining 1, 3, 28, 70, 148, 168, 190
Mitra, A. 10, 30
Molle, F. 139–140
Mongolia 79, 108
Morocco 149
Movik, S. 136
Mozambique 132, 138
Muchena, F. 80
mulching 74, 87–88, 102
multi-scalar approach 113, 193
multiple use of water services (MUS) 133, 180–181

Narmada project 143–144
neo-Malthusian perspective 5–6
Nestlé 167
networks 71
New Delhi Statement 136–137, 154n2
New Zealand 39
Nicaragua 144
Nile Basin Initiative 169
non-discrimination 33, 177, 178, 179, 185, 188, 189
non-governmental organizations (NGOs) 143, 146, 167, 188
North Africa: drinking water and sanitation 39; food waste 52; grain imports 68; groundwater irrigation 105; human rights approach 189; hydrological complexity 23; rainfed agricultural systems 75; water resources 4, 22; water scarcity 92; water technologies 66
North America: drinking water and sanitation 39; droughts 42; hydrological complexity 23; irrigation 76; rainfed agricultural systems 75
nutrient cycle 35
nutrient recycling 92
nutrition 1, 2, 20; climate change impact 43; guidelines 50; right to water 165; Sustainable Development Goals 173; WASH 40–41; *see also* food security and nutrition

obesity 20, 153
Oceania 38, 40
open defecation 39, 40
Organization for Economic Cooperation and Development (OECD) 5
Ostrom, E. 133
overgrazing 51, 78–79, 109, 112
ownership 103, 113, 141

Pacific region 26
Pacific Rim 171–172
Pakistan 47, 106, 136, 139, 170
Palestine 128–129, 149
Palloni, G. 41
Paris Climate Agreement (2015) 68
participation 33, 124, 127, 137, 142, 143, 177, 178
pastoralism 51, 78–79, 82–83, 107–112, 133; *see also* livestock
Pepsi 167
peri-urban agriculture 80, 103, 104
permit systems 124, 134–136, 138–139, 151
pesticides 18, 25, 27, 29, 55n3, 74
Phillips, D.J.H. 49
policies 3, 11, 150–152, 192; export-oriented 69; global 67; improving water productivity 94, 96, 113; pastoralism 108–109; rainwater harvesting 111; trade 21; virtual water 68, 85; water governance 123, 124–125; water scarcity 25
politics: of allocation 125–127; food discourses 188, 191; global governance 166; water footprints 8
pollution 4, 5, 33–35, 54, 55n3, 91; Coca-Cola 146; data on 7; diseases from 25; foreign investments 171; increase in 3; irrigation 27, 29; livestock production 49–50, 74–75; marginal quality water 104; mining 168; Sustainable Development Goals 173; urban agriculture 80; urbanization 40; water depletion 84; water quality 18; water treatment 47

polycentric governance 123
polycentric networks 71
population growth 4, 5, 143, 152; climate change 81; demand for water 22; dietary changes 49; India 69
Post Harvest Losses (PHL) 51–53
poverty: access to water 17, 22; capabilities 181–182; China 152; Developmental Water Management 140; extreme 132; food insecurity 20; groundwater irrigation 106; human rights approaches 33, 177; improving water productivity 89, 92, 107; rural 148; South Africa 182–183; Sustainable Development Goals 173; United States 129–130; urban slums 186–187; water-energy-food nexus 140; women 32, 144
power relations 71, 153, 192; access 33; gender 10, 32, 144; global governance 166; irrigation 31; water allocation 126; water-energy-food nexus 141; water governance 124, 128, 129, 142, 153; water management 113; water scarcity 25
prices 28, 193; grain 66, 67; privatization 145; water re-allocation 126
pricing 88, 147, 183; irrigation 103, 106; Maharashtra 127; water management 66
prior appropriation 134
private sector 144–148, 150, 154, 168, 190, 193
privatization 144–145, 168, 180, 182
productivity *see* water productivity
property rights 6, 126, 127, 129

quality 31, 33–35; concentrated animal feeding operations 74–75; hydrological complexity 23; marginal quality water 103–105; Mekong River Commission 169; right to water 178; transboundary issues 70; waste discharge 151; water governance 129, 152–153; water security 16–18, 26

race 16, 32, 65, 129–130, 153
rainfall 4, 16–17, 21; climate change 80, 81–83, 125–126; drylands 107; land degradation 109; rainfed agricultural systems 27, 36–37, 75–76, 81–82, 89, 96–100; variability 42, 43, 75; *see also* green water
rainwater harvesting (RWH) 99–100, 110–112; *see also* water harvesting
Ramsar Convention on Wetlands 5, 177

Rao, N. 10, 30
recycling 66, 73, 83–84, 87, 101–102, 104
reform processes 136–142, 194
regional cooperation 169–170
Renault, D. 36
research and development 113, 194
resilience: agroecology 73; rainwater harvesting 99, 110, 111, 112; restoration of degraded systems 109
restoration of degraded systems 109–110
revegetation 110
rice 69, 78, 102, 169
right to food (RTF) 3, 10, 165–166, 177, 178–179, 194–195; agroecological approach 73; Bolivia 1, 189; conflicts between rights 186–187; Ecuador 189; General Comment No.15 184, 185, 186; grain prices 66; ICSID cases 172; private sector regulation 145, 193; STEPS pathways approach 6; threats to the 190–191; voluntary guidelines 171, 175, 179, 188–189
right to water (RTW) 3, 10, 165–166, 177–178, 179, 180–192, 194–195; Bolivia 1, 189; Ecuador 189; General Comment No.15 165, 183–185, 186, 195; ICSID cases 172; private sector regulation 145, 193; STEPS pathways approach 6; threats to the 190–191; UN endorsement 2, 31, 196n6; United States 130
rights 134, 174, 193; competing 186–187; customary 125, 126, 129, 139, 151, 153; fluid nature of 132–133; groundwater irrigation 106; indigenous people 179; land and water grabbing 149; local organizations 71; Palestine 129; peasants' land rights 168; permit systems 138–139; pricing 103; water governance 123, 127, 129; women 131–132; *see also* human rights
Ringler, C. 34
Rio Declaration on Environment and Development (1992) 168–169
riparian rights 134
risk 44, 53–54, 66, 76, 96, 110
Rockström, J. 96
Rosegrant, M.W. 52
Rossini, P. 135
runoff 43, 82, 83, 87, 91; blue water 21; pollution 18, 25; rainwater harvesting 99–100, 110; recycling 101–102; supplemental irrigation 99
Russia 23

sack gardening 79
Sadoff, C.W. 23, 42
salinization 77–78, 83, 90, 92, 101, 104, 128
sanitation 1, 10, 18, 35, 38–41, 192; ecological 74; lack of 2, 3; right to 2, 3, 31, 165, 172, 183–184, 191, 193, 196n6; Sustainable Development Goals 9, 67–68, 173; UN agencies 167; water security 17; women 37–38; *see also* wastewater; water supply, sanitation and hygiene
São Paulo 43–44
Sardar Sarovar Dam 143–144
Scaling up Agroecology Initiative 72–73
scarcity 4–5, 17, 22, 54, 68–69, 91–92; dynamics of 24–25; economic water productivity 91; food sovereignty 188; improving water productivity 89, 94–95; increase in 113; inequality in access 6; marginal quality water 103; Sustainable Development Goals 9; trade 21; virtual water 84, 85; water allocation 126; water markets 44–45
Schwab, K. 55n3
Seckler, D. 101
self-determination 179
self-sufficiency 67, 89
Sen, Amartya 6, 31–32, 177–178, 181–182
Senegal 181
sewage effluent 103–105; *see also* wastewater
Sharma, B.R. 69
Sheahan, M. 51–52
shortages 6, 65, 113, 128
silo driven discourses 7
slums 1, 9, 186–187
small island developing states 39
social justice 6, 12, 154, 165, 189, 193
social learning 71
social movements 143, 168
social relations 3, 113, 126, 129
socio-cultural practices 124
socio-economic factors 17, 29, 65, 153, 192
socio-political dimensions 24–25, 31–33
soil: agroecological approaches 75; contamination 50; pastoral systems 79; System of Rice Intensification 102–103; water management 74
soil erosion 18, 92, 99, 108, 113; climate change 81, 82, 83; rainwater harvesting 110, 112
soil management 96, 97, 99
solar pumps 28, 30, 47, 106

solidarity economy 73
South Africa: access to water 32; Developmental Water Management 140; drinking water and sanitation 40; hydrological complexity 23; hydropower 48; legal pluralism 138; markets 136; permit systems 139; right to water 182–183, 189; water rights 134; water user associations 142
South America 19; *see also* Latin America
South Asia: animal-source foods 51; drinking water and sanitation 39; food waste 52; hydrological complexity 23; irrigation 26, 27, 100, 105; open defecation 40; water resources 4, 22
Southeast Asia: climate change 82; drinking water and sanitation 39; food waste 52; groundwater irrigation 105; hydrological complexity 23; peri-urban agriculture 80
Southern African Power Pool (SAPP) 48–49
Special Rapporteurs 178, 187–188, 189, 192, 195
stability: food security 12n2, 17, 18–19, 26, 41–45; hydrological complexity 23; water security 16–17, 18, 26
STEPS pathways approach 6
stigma 130–131
storage 66, 113; continuum of options 45, 144; improving water productivity 90; rainwater harvesting 99, 100, 110; soils 75; supplemental irrigation 99
street food vendors 35, 129
structural violence 3, 33
Suárez, S.M. 171
subsidies 26, 28, 88, 103, 112, 147
subsistence 89, 141, 182, 193; conflict situations 128; indigenous people 51, 175; right to food 178–179; right to water 183, 185, 186, 190, 191, 195; water for production 10
substantive freedoms 177–178, 181
suitability mapping 100
supplemental irrigation (SI) 90, 96–100
supply-side approaches 5, 106, 136
sustainability 9, 186; agroecological approaches 113; pastoralism 109; rainfed agriculture 100; right to food 179; water management 193
Sustainable Development Goals (SDGs) 2, 5, 9–10, 19, 38, 67–68, 137, 166, 173–174
Swaziland 48
Switzerland 189

synergies 73
Syria 95, 97–99
System of Rice Intensification (SRI) 78, 102–103

Tanzania 1, 36–37, 132, 150–151
tariffs 148
Tasgeth, M. 151
taxes 148
technology 44, 66, 92; agroecological approaches 74; hydropower 48; improving water productivity 92; irrigation 30; women's access to 100
temperature rises 81, 82
tenure 124, 133, 152; gender discrimination 131–132, 134; right to food 189; voluntary guidelines 175; water governance 141
terraces 74
Thailand 169
Theesfeld, I. 149
'threshold of irreversibility' 109
tradable permits 134–136
trade 5, 66–67, 69; demand for water 28; food security 21; improving water productivity 89; international agreements 171–173; power relations 153; virtual water 6, 84–85, 193; water governance 123
transboundary issues 5, 70, 89, 168–170
transfers 148
transparency 33, 168, 177
transpiration 85, 87, 90
treated sewage water (TSW) 103–105
Turkey 143

Uganda 108, 139, 144
Uluguru mountains 1
UN Convention on Shared Watercourses 177
UN Water 166–167, 187–188
UN Women 174
uncertainty 4, 27, 66, 71, 133
United Kingdom (UK) 173
United Nations (UN): agroecology 72; Convention on the Law of Non-Navigational Uses of International Watercourses 169, 185; global governance 166; human rights instruments 174; marginal quality water 104; Millennium Development Goals 5, 9, 10, 38–40, 173, 174; right to water 2, 31, 165, 180, 195, 196n6; Sustainable Development Goals 2, 5, 9–10, 19, 38, 67–68, 137, 166, 173–174; treated sewage effluent 105; 'Water Decade' 136
United Nations Committee on Economic, Social and Cultural Rights (UNCESCR) 183, 184–185
United Nations Committee on Food Security 72
United Nations Convention on the Rights of Persons with Disabilities (UNCRPD) 132
United Nations Convention to Combat Desertification (UNCCD) 5
United Nations Declaration on the Rights of Indigenous Peoples (UNDRIP) 175
United Nations Declaration on the Rights of Peasants and other People Working in Rural Areas 175, 186, 188
United Nations Development Program (UNDP) 5–6, 32, 144, 167
United Nations Economic Commission for Europe (UNECE) 176
United Nations Educational, Scientific and Cultural Organization (UNESCO) 167
United Nations Environment Programme (UNEP) 24, 167
United Nations Framework Convention on Climate Change (UNFCCC) 5, 177
United Nations Human Rights Council (UNHRC) 31, 165, 183, 189, 195
United Nations International Children's Emergency Fund (UNICEF) 38, 167
United States (US): California drought 107; Flint 129–130; fracking 46; irrigation 26, 76; livestock production 49, 50; market-based allocation 126–127; meat consumption 50; Mexico-US International Boundary and Water Commission 170; obesity 20; pollution 55n3; right to water 180; water rights 134
Universal Declaration of Human Rights (UDHR) 174, 178, 180, 196n16
urban agriculture 79–80, 104
urbanization 4, 21, 28, 40, 187; basin management 70; China 49; demand for food 89; demand for water 22
user-based allocation 126
utilization 12n2, 16–17, 18–19, 26, 35–41

values 11, 73, 74, 137
Van Koppen, B. 138, 165–166, 180, 183–184, 188
Vandenhole, W. 190
vegetation growth 110, 111–112

La Vía Campesina 168, 188
Vietnam 47–48, 80, 105, 169
virtual water 6, 67, 68, 83, 84–85, 86; food security 193; optimizing flows 89, 192; trade policies 69; water footprints 8
voluntary guidelines 170–171, 175–176, 179, 188–189
Voluntary Guidelines on the Responsible Governance of Tenure of Land, Fisheries and Forests in the Context of National Food Security (VGGT) 170–171

Wallender, W.W. 36
wastage 51–53, 113, 192
wastewater 10, 34, 35, 151; fracking 46–47; irrigation 104–105; nutrients in 48; treatment of 66; urban agriculture 80; *see also* sanitation
water: corporatization 53–54; crisis 2–3, 32; dynamics of scarcity 24–25; energy competition 46–49, 194; governance 123–164; importance of 1–2, 192; international agreements 170–173; sharing 70; shortages 6, 65, 128; stability 41; Sustainable Development Goals 9, 67–68; treatment 66; wastage 52; water-energy-food nexus 140–141; water for life/water for production 10; *see also* groundwater; rainfall; right to water; water efficiency; water management; water productivity
water depletion 84, 90, 92
water efficiency 83–84, 86, 192; agroecological approach 73; China 152; improving yields 85–87; irrigation 100, 101–102, 103; pricing 147
water-energy-food (WEF) nexus 140–141
water footprints 8–9, 32, 83, 84, 86, 93
water grabbing 53, 148–150, 151, 171, 192, 194
water harvesting 74, 96, 97, 99–100, 110–112
water management 12, 65–132; agroecosystem level 71–75; basin level 69–70, 89; climate change 80–83; Comprehensive Assessment of Water Management in Agriculture 13n5; conventional strategies 85–88; corporate involvement 53; global level 67–69, 89; improving water productivity 89–96; Integrated Water Resources Management 7, 137–140, 141, 166, 194; irrigated agriculture 76–78, 82, 89, 100–107; local level 70–71, 89; measurement issues 83–85, 86; Mekong River Commission 169; national level 70, 89, 150–151; pastoral systems 78–79, 82–83, 107–112; rainfed systems 75–76, 81–82, 89, 96–100; sustainability 193; Sustainable Development Goals 173; technology 44; water rights 191
water markets *see* markets
water productivity 36–37, 83, 84, 86; fisheries 107; improving 6, 66, 89–96, 113, 192; irrigated agriculture 100–103; markets 44–45; rainwater harvesting 110
Water Resources Group 167
water security 12, 16–18, 21–23, 26, 54, 174
water stress index 24
Water Supply and Sanitation Collaborative Council 167
water supply, sanitation and hygiene (WASH) 17, 18, 29, 38–41, 74, 141
water user associations (WUAs) 101, 103, 127, 131, 142
watersheds 7, 69–70, 142
Welle, Katharina 10
Willett, W. 28
Williams, T.O. 139, 149
Windfuhr, M. 187
women 1, 3, 4, 10, 193; access to technology 100; access to water 2, 134, 184–185; agroecological approaches 74; anaemia 20; CEDAW 176; climate change impact 42; competing rights 186–187; disadvantage 71; Dublin Principles 137; empowerment 29; fisheries 106; food sovereignty 188; inequalities 20–21, 32; irrigation 29–31, 76–77; livestock production 51; national policies 152; power relations 144; rainfed agriculture 75, 100; sanitation 37–38; structural violence 3, 33; Sustainable Development Goals 9, 173, 174; Tanzania 1; water governance 129, 131–132; water user associations 103; *see also* gender
World Bank 143, 148, 166, 167, 170
World Commission on Dams (WCD) 5, 142–143, 155n3
World Committee on Food Security 195
World Economic Forum (WEF) 174

World Food Summit 12n2
World Health Organization (WHO) 31, 34–35, 38, 105, 167, 182
World Summit on Sustainable Development (WSSD) 173
World Trade Organization (WTO) 172–173
World Water Assessment Programme (WWAP) 2
World Water Council (WWC) 166, 167–168
World Water Forum 167–168
World Wide Fund for Nature 146, 166

Xie, H. 34

Yang, C. 49
yields 28, 66, 85–87; climate change impact 80–82; economic water productivity 91; improving water productivity 94–95, 96; rainfed agricultural systems 75; supplemental irrigation 97, 99; System of Rice Intensification 102
Young, M. 135

Zambia 48, 132
Zeng, R. 46
Ziganshina, D. 188
Zimbabwe 48, 108, 139, 189